INVISIBLE BOY

INVISIBLE BOY

a memoir of self-discovery

HARRISON MOONEY

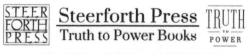

Steerforth Press

Truth to Power Books

LEBANON, NEW HAMPSHIRE

For information about permission to reproduce
selections from this book, write to:
Steerforth Press L.L.C., 31 Hanover Street, Suite 1,
Lebanon, New Hampshire 03766

In 2020, Steerforth Press launched Truth to Power Books: investigative journalism,
iconoclastic histories, and personal accounts that are nuanced, thoughtful, and reliable
— qualities at a premium in the Internet age — and that inform through storytelling,
not argument.

Cataloging-in-Publication Data is available from the Library of Congress

ISBN 978-1-58642-346-9 (Paperback)

Manufactured in the United States of America

1 3 5 7 9 10 8 6 4 2

For Silvia. Exousia! For Courage.

The acceptance of our present condition is the only form of extremism which discredits us before our children.

—LORRAINE HANSBERRY, LETTER TO A STUDENT, APRIL 27, 1962

CONTENTS

INVISIBLE BOY

AUTHOR'S NOTE

These are my recollections, encrypted by trauma, reinterpreted in my mind by a shifting self-image, rewritten again and again for the page. Some may remember these moments unfolding differently, I'm sure. But I am confident that my memories are mis-shapen, not mistaken. I have tried to be as accurate as possible, and yet as gracious with myself as I have learned to be with others.

This is a true story. Only the names have been changed. In addition to my long recall, this book is supported by rigorous research—newspaper archives, rare books, the Wayback Machine—as well as interviews with childhood friends, my mothers and my fathers, old acquaintances, eyewitnesses, relevant strangers, and nearly every person who appears within these pages. I am grateful to those who took the time to speak with me, to share their own impressions, to confirm my version of events. I would like to thank Ben and Ashley, particularly, for their input, and their willingness to confront and acknowledge the forces, seen and unseen, wreaking havoc on our lives.

I have done my best to treat the words of others journalistically, adhering to the sentences that echo in my head and corroborating them, where I could, with those who spoke or those who heard.

You can't transcribe from memory, however. In token of this, I have eschewed quotation marks throughout.

I acknowledge here that what is said is not the same as what is meant. It doesn't matter anyhow. Intent is not impact, and if we continue to prioritize the virtue of our thoughts above the violence of our actions, we will leave a trail of victims in our wake. Mine is a story of impact; I write for the millions impacted in similar ways.

PART I

THE IRRATIONAL

Here I am at home; I am made of the irrational.
I wade in the irrational. Irrational up to my neck.
—FRANTZ FANON, *Black Skin, White Masks*

I

==

CIRCUS

(or The Boy Who Wore a Very Loud Hat)

I don't know where I came from, but I remember craving something sweet.

So I stopped at the coffeeshop on my way home. I must have been about sixteen—I drove down in my black Toyota Echo—but I left there feeling eight or nine years old. I was standing in line for a donut, or six donut holes in a box, when an elderly white woman turned around, saw me behind her, and shouted out: LITTLE. BLACK. WAIF.

She said each word sharply, with beats in between, loud enough for everyone to notice. The room fell so silent I heard my tinnitus— the ringing that starts when the world goes away. One moment, I stood in a long line of people. The next, I was locked in a liminal space with a stranger whose hatred immobilized me. It felt like the power went out in the building, but I couldn't breathe, just as I couldn't see, and I found myself wondering: How do I move? So I knew that the power had only gone out from my body.

And then it was over. The elderly white woman's partner laid hands on her, lovingly, graciously, leading her back to the counter to order.

A dutchie, a cruller, and two double-doubles.

I looked around at the tables, hoping that the woman was shouting at somebody else, and I saw that it couldn't be anyone else, and the rest of the coffeeshop's customers already knew that. I felt every pair of eyes identify me, the weight of the white gaze descending, impressing upon me, imagining who might this little Black waif be, and where did he come from, and what did he do to provoke this poor woman? But interest in me faded quickly, and suddenly I disappeared, as though nothing had happened to anyone. No one saw anything.

The power of their denial teleported me outside. One minute I was there, and then I wasn't. I was simply whisked away, as if by magic.

When I got home without any donuts, my white family wouldn't believe me. I must have misheard or done something wrong, they insisted, and five sets of cynical eyes took me back to the scene of the crime. Let's go through it again. My mother, who micromanaged all that I imagined, suggested that, somehow, I'd shown disrespect. It felt like she wanted to blame me. I wanted to help her. But nothing I could think of would explain the old lady's explosion. I didn't jump the queue. I didn't fail to hold the door. The woman was in front of me. I didn't stand too close, I didn't dance or curse, I didn't try to snatch her purse.

She was probably demon-possessed, said my mother, who saw the devil everywhere. But even this failed to account for the outburst. What was it about me that so offended her evil spirit, and why would it suddenly erupt, right there in the coffeeshop, and why, if my mother's suspicions were true, would the Lord leave me so unprotected?

What was I wearing, I wonder now. I don't recall. I've lost sight of myself, over time. My day-to-day style that particular summer was Hawaiian print, mostly, so maybe the loudness offended the woman. But it could have been Sunday, and then I'd be dressed up for church.

Who could be bothered by church clothes? A demon-possessed sort of person, perhaps. Maybe my mother was right, and the incident wasn't about race at all.

• • •

I was adopted.

I began in Vancouver, British Columbia, the westernmost province of Canada, cut from my birth mother's womb in July 1985. She was fifteen or sixteen years old, in foster care then, just a wayward Black youth who engaged in premarital sex with the star of her high school soccer team. He was a white kid. His family was German. Keeping this biracial baby was out of the question, but so was abortion. The families were Christian. Surrender was all but imposed on the mother. She had little say in the matter. She took me to term and they took me away, born to no one, a ward of the Salvation Army's Grace Hospital.

Eleven days later, the paperwork cleared. A wealthy white couple arrived to collect me.

They didn't take me far. The city of Abbotsford is an hour's drive east into the Fraser Valley, named for the river that emerges there from the canyons, at sea level. The fertile region is rich with raspberries and religion and is derisively nicknamed the Bible Belt of British Columbia, on account of its many churches. In Abbotsford, the largest Fraser Valley community, there are nearly one hundred congregations—one for every thousand residents—and the nickname is a point of pride. If this is the Bible Belt, pastors would say, then Abbotsford must be the buckle.

The mostly white suburb, which borders on Washington State, is also the site of the only recorded lynching in Canadian history. The fourteen-year-old victim, a Stó:lō boy named Louie Sam, was hung from a tree by a mob of Americans dressed as his people, 101 years before my arrival and just down the road from my house, by the minigolf course.

But I didn't know that then. Abbotsford's history never came up. We were starting from scratch.

I was raised in a vacuum, brought up between bedsheets, educated at home from Grade 4 to Grade 12 through a Christian curriculum published in Florida. Some children thrive on independent study. For me, a Black adoptee, cut off from my community and trapped in an all-white cocoon, it meant finding my way with no context for my situation, no sense of shared struggle or circumstance, and no contact with those who could help me to see what I needed to see to make sense of the world.

In a roundabout way, my white family created me, for all creation stories begin with a separation. They gave me a new name. They gave me a language that limited how I envisioned myself. They told me that I was delivered, not into the arms of a woman who loved me, but out of the darkness. My creation was sinful: two sinners had sinned, that's how I was made, that's what I was, and sin makes God sick to his stomach. He can't even look at it. But somehow, He saw me, they said, and He gave me to them. I believed them, and so I was Saved. I became born again. Thereafter I came to imagine my Blackness as proof of my brush with the fires of hell.

What a relief to escape with the skin of my teeth.

• • •

Black in a white family, someone might scoff, oh, the horror. Did they tie you to a chair and make you eat unseasoned steak?

Actually, yes. I was five years old then, and I wasn't allowed to self-season.

Black people, my mother said, holding the salt, are predisposed to heart disease. You've had enough already. Eat your dinner.

The white rice and broccoli, boiled violently, I could endure. But the meat was too tough for my mouth. I chewed and chewed. I couldn't seem to break it down or swallow it. They told me that I had to. When I tried to leave the table, defiant as any preschooler, they bound me to the seat with yellow rope. I would not be excused until finishing every last bite. So I struggled and cried and I peed my pants, cleverly, thinking they'd have to untie me. They didn't. I sat in the mess that I made for myself, overworking my steak, and won my escape by throwing up at the table, with two or three pieces to go.

Upstairs in the bathtub, my mother made a joke at my expense. She washed my hands and said: Uh-oh! I scrubbed too hard and the colour came off!

I looked at my white palms, confused, and I started to sob.

Oh, Harry, you fall for that every time, she said. Everyone has white palms. She scoured my right arm with the warm, soapy wash-cloth and showed me that nothing had changed. You see? You're still Black, so stop crying.

My adoptive mother grew up on an Iowa farm. You could call her a slice of America's heartland—a concentrated dose would be more accurate. She was deeply patriotic and politically conservative. She told me that the Democrats were godless and corrupt, and that the Reverend Martin Luther King had cheated on his wife.

He called himself a pastor, she would say. He was a hypocrite.

My mother was a serious Christian, radically Saved, and the Godliest woman I knew in my life. She spoke with the Lord every day, and He told her all kinds of things. Sometimes He ratted me out.

Once, she caught me stealing from the candy cupboard out in the garage. My father had left it unlocked, so I grabbed what I could, and I tried to get past her. She busted me right away.

Empty your pockets, she said, in the kitchen.

How did you know? I asked, shamefully, putting my Chupa Chups down on the table.

7

God whispered into my ear, she explained. Now pull down your pants.

Then she spanked me with a rubber spatula.

My mother could be loving. But most of the time, she seemed angry with me. I was a loud and indefatigable little boy, hopelessly disruptive and endlessly distractible. I was always in trouble. Sometimes I knew I was in a good home. Sometimes it felt like being stranded in a hostile country. Seeing myself through my mother's eyes made me afraid, and when I began to mimic her gaze in her mirror, as all children do, I shuddered at the bad son looking back. I saw so much sin, and God hates sin.

But I was told He loved me.

On Thursdays, I went to Wee College, a kind of Christian daycare boot camp in the basement of a church, where the preschoolers learned Bible songs and stories, did Bible crafts, and read our Bibles quietly before and after naptime. We marched around the Sunday school room, imagining that we were Christian soldiers, onward, and pretending that our Bibles were our weapons.

Music time made me the happiest. The best song, by far, went like this:

Yes, Jesus loves me
Yes, Jesus loves me
Yes, Jesus loves me
The Bible tells me so

Here was the love I was after. The answers were all in the Sword of the Spirit, and all the best stories besides. I wanted to tell my own story one day. Maybe it would make the next edition of the Bible.

I wanted my story to be a love story, so I clung to the one I was told. My romance of origins started with God looking down on me, lost in my birth mother's womb. Moved by affection, he intervened, saving my life for some heavenly purpose, as yet undetermined.

I wanted to meet with Him. I wanted to be seen by eyes in love with me again. It seemed to me that if God could whisper in my mother's ear, then certainly he could engage with me. God is Love, that's what they said, and I wanted to believe them more than anything. So I spent twenty years or so looking for Him, and I never felt loved for a second.

• • •

When I was seven, my mother took me across the Fraser River to the big tent revival in Mission.

Believers saw many miraculous things at these meetings.

At a revival in Marysville, Washington, my mother told me, a man with a face like a Picasso had asked for healing, and the revivalists watched in awe as his cleft palate dissolved, his teeth straightened, and his nose, which had hung low and asymmetrical since birth, drifted back to where it belonged like a little lost continent. At a recent revival just outside Toronto, my mother had heard, believers emerged from the Spirit-filled tent flecked with gold dust. They were finding it in their hair and on their clothes even days afterward. Someone thought to test it: 24 karats. The best gold. And just yesterday, on the Mission revival's first night, a woman conversed with an angel. She was sitting in the parking lot, she said, debating whether to turn around and head home, when an angel appeared in the back seat of her car and encouraged her: *Go in, and be with your people.* The woman obeyed, and that night, she was touched, and she spoke in tongues for the very first time.

This was why I had come. I didn't need my face rearranged, and at seven years old I had little use for gold, but I wanted to see an angel, and preferably one that would assure me I was in the right place too. Sometimes I wondered if I had been brought here by mistake—that these people were not my people. But that couldn't be true. God didn't make mistakes.

My older brother, Ben, was adopted as well, but my parents could have lied to him about it, if they wanted. He looked just like them and my two younger brothers, the ones who were theirs, biologically.

My difference demanded a clear explanation. I liked to joke that the family had spun a massive baby wheel like on *Press Your Luck*, fingers crossed for big bucks, big bucks, no whammies, no whammies, and had landed on me—a whammy from another mammy. We all thought that was very funny, but they insisted they did not see colour, and anyhow the truth was far more uplifting: the whole episode, from my maculate conception to my miraculous adoption, was all part of God's plan for my life.

It certainly sounded like Him. At church and at school, I encountered no one like me, except in the Bible, whose heroes often boasted strikingly similar origin stories—men chosen by God before they were even born and separated from their mothers at a young age to be prepared for some miraculous mission. There I was in the story of Joseph, sold to merchants and taken from his family as a boy, only to reappear years later as a prince of Egypt, perfectly positioned to save the Israelites from starvation. I saw myself in the story of Moses, born to a slave girl and sent down the Nile River to be claimed instead by pharaoh's daughter, God's inside man when the time came to deliver His people out of Egypt. There I was again in the story of Samuel, the prophet's apprentice whose mother prayed for a child and was given one, provided she surrendered her anointed son to the temple after he was weaned.

Even Samson, the legendary judge, was a highly relatable figure. His mother was barren until God gave her a very special child with a very special calling whose hair was a total mystery to everyone and impossible to manage.

Needless to say, no one knew what to do with my hair either.

These men's mothers were merely vessels, destined to be forgotten until their wombs were repurposed for the glory of the Lord.

I saw myself in these heroes, in their displacement, in their call to forsake their genetic families just as Jesus had called his disciples to go, instead, with God. Certainly I had questions about where I came from, about what happened to this woman, my birth mother, before and after she brought me into the world. I knew she was born in West Africa, in Ghana, and came to Canada with her father when she was just a child. I knew that circumstances led her to the foster system and that, when I was born, she was living with an elderly Christian couple in Richmond, just a short drive west. I was told that she had remained nearby, though I didn't dare seek her out—it would only hurt my adoptive mother. Plus, as I understood it, to waste any time on a vessel like her, to look back rather than to the path before me, was to doubt God, and that was simply no way to meet Him. Only through faith would the veil of the natural world give way to the supernatural.

Logic was on my side. It just made sense. It seemed to me that if God had no plan for my life, he wouldn't have bothered to intervene on my behalf. He had drawn a woman across the Atlantic, away from her own family, who might have attempted to claim me otherwise, and into a God-fearing household. He had closed my mother's womb until she chose adoption, then guided her to the same church, and even the *very same church pew* as the God-fearing woman who worked to facilitate my adoption to a God-fearing family. He had orchestrated everything. It was classic God.

Here I was, then: ready, on my mark, awaiting further instructions. Was I his inside man, like Moses or Joseph? His warrior, like Samson? What did he want from me? I trusted that I would receive guidance at the revival.

The preacher spotted me the moment we entered the tent. He was onstage, shouting skyward into a microphone as he led the revivalists in passionate prayer, when, suddenly, he opened his eyes and looked directly into mine, like a hungry cat espies a little bird through a window. As I followed my mother along the perimeter of the riverside tent toward our seats, the Man of God stared at me like some intriguing thing and proclaimed these words: This is not a circus! Do you see any lion tamers here? Do you see any clowns? The Lion of Judah cannot be tamed, and God will not be mocked!

I had been to the circus once. The clowns were my favourite. On the way out, we purchased a pair of fluffy rainbow wigs, one for me and one for Ben, who had been kept home today for lying. They were still in the dress-up box.

The revival's similarity was clear to me—the big tent, the energetic, expectant crowd, the promise of signs and wonders that must be seen to be believed. But there was one major difference: at the circus, you saw the things that were promised. At the big tent revival, the best parts of the show were often invisible. The Man of God, a sort of holy ringmaster, heralded a similar spectacle—signs and wonders, marvels and miracles, undeniable evidence of the supernatural—but with a significant catch: these things must be believed to be seen.

The preacher rattled off several other things the big tent revival was not. It wasn't a carnival, which means *celebration of the flesh*, he said—it was an outpouring of the Spirit. Neither was it a theatre, because a theatre is a place of make-believe, and Shakespeare is dead, Molière is dead, and Tennessee Williams, a Sodomite, he reminded us, is dead as well.

But I am the Lord your God and I am not dead, the preacher bellowed. It is your church that is dead!

This line earned rapturous applause and several amens, and some people fainted.

That is why I have commanded this disciple to humble himself under my mighty hand, the preacher shouted over the din of the delirious crowd, referring to himself, to travel north from his own country and deliver this message to the people of Abbotsford, British Columbia: *I am bringing forth a revival in this land!* This tent has no room for jugglers! Or fire-eaters! Or acrobats! For this tent is filled with the Holy Spirit! I am restoring the living church, and I will reveal myself to you, if only you ask.

If that was true, I wondered what God was waiting for. I had been asking for my entire life; there had been no revelation. People said God was everywhere, but He never seemed to be where I was. Sometimes I felt as though He had turned his back on me completely, and I struggled to understand why, after all this trouble. I knew it couldn't be an issue of faith. If I truly didn't believe in God, I reasoned to myself, then why did I feel so utterly abandoned?

My mother cut through a row of worshippers to reach a pair of empty folding chairs near the back of the tent. I took the long way around, a lonelier path, though I did still have to squeeze past a man on his knees, wailing loudly, and tiptoe around Tilda Eubanks, a woman from church, who was whimpering, flailing, face down in the grass. By the time I reached my seat, my mother was already deep in prayer with both eyes closed and her arms outstretched. I stood silently at her side and scanned the sanctuary for the supernatural.

The preacher was a small, unimposing man. He wore a black turtleneck tucked into tan corduroy pants and thick-rimmed tortoiseshell glasses. He looked like a huge dork. But he oozed power. He would place his palm on a worshipper's forehead and shout a nonsense word—*shazam!* perhaps—and they would fly backwards as though they'd been shot. At one point, he *shazammed* a whole row. Everybody fell down.

To further illustrate his power, the Man of God told us about a chance meeting with the rapper MC Hammer. The preacher was at a conference in Las Vegas and there was a big hip-hop concert the same night, so his hotel lobby was full of thugs and immodestly dressed women. As he boarded the elevator, the preacher asked God to let His light shine before these lost souls, so they may give glory to Him instead of foul-mouthed false idols, and just as he said *amen,* who should board the elevator but MC Hammer himself, the best rapper in the world, flanked by two monstrous bodyguards.

These were some big, big brothas, the preacher said, puffing out his chest as he gestured playfully in my direction. More intimidating than *this* young man, that's for sure.

Everybody looked at me and laughed, and I was humiliated but I laughed too, because that's what we were doing.

As the elevator ascended, the three men would not stop staring at him, but the preacher was not afraid, because God was with him—and he knew it.

And that's when MC Hammer turned to him and said: My man! The spirit of the Lord is *all over you*!

The rapper lowered his head, showing subservience, and asked the preacher to pray for him and his bodyguards right there in the elevator, and all three men received a blessing from the Lord that day, hallelujah, can I get an amen.

At this, the place erupted in a frenzy of praise and worship. The same spirit that MC Hammer could feel in that elevator was all in the air like a gas leak, and the revivalists appeared delirious and drunk, giggling and groaning, screaming and shouting in tongues, falling all over themselves. The air was cacophonous with cries of joy and weird, low moans.

The Lord was making everyone feel very good.

I'd never seen energy like this. There were women skipping and twirling, waving flags and scarves. Then they would faint into the arms of an usher, who would immediately cover them with jackets or shawls so that no one could see their underpants. There were people crying for no reason. There were men leaping higher into the air than I'd ever seen—ten, twenty feet up, it seemed to a boy with little sense of where the sky began.

We went to church every week, but even the most spirited Sundays at Abbotsford Pentecostal Assembly seemed utterly uninspired compared to the big tent revival. There were no surprises. God never did anything out of the ordinary. Most services followed a predictable pattern. First, we drank coffee and mingled and gossiped and complimented one another's outfits. When enough members of the worship band arrived, they played a fast song to get people's attention, then two or three more once everybody found their seats. This part of the service was my favourite. You could sing as loud as you wanted and nobody got mad. You could clap or even play the tambourine if no one else was using it. Sometimes people would dance. Then there was a slow song, and the dancing would become swaying, and some people would raise their hands and others would get on their knees, and everyone would close their eyes. Then came the special song, a ballad that moved everybody, and the church would descend into free worship, singing the chorus over and over and over until the words melted away, and soon the whole room was singing their own words, or maybe they were praying, and the most affected people were weeping and wailing.

Then the preacher's wife would close the worship service with a prayer and tell us about upcoming church events. There was a Bible study on Wednesday for single mothers. There was a bake sale, and all the proceeds were going to our sister church in Uganda. There was a loonie potluck next Sunday to subsidize the cost of vacation Bible school so everyone could register their child this summer, and everyone should, because the church had invested in a special curriculum that focused on sexual purity and was vital to our youth in these wanton, wicked times.

Then came the tithe. On some occasions, generally before she took the tithe but sometimes after, prompting a do-over, the preacher's wife might receive word from the Lord that somebody was being tempted to hold onto their money like Ananias and Sapphira, a couple of charlatans from the book of Acts who tried to lie about how much they made on the sale of their house. Ananias goes to the temple and offers what he claims is the customary 10 per cent of the proceeds, but the apostle Peter says: You have not lied to men but to God. Ananias drops dead. When Sapphira comes to pull the same stunt, she dies too, because God has no patience for liars at church. The tithe was serious business.

If you were lucky, one of the elders might select you to fetch and carry the offering bag, which was the fanciest pouch in the world—red velveteen with brass fittings and long hardwood handles on either side. You brought it to the altar empty, and after the preacher's wife asked God to double-bless anyone who gave generously and obediently, you followed the bag up the aisles, catching it at the end of every pew and sending it along the next one. Some people put pocket change in the bag. Some people put big bills in the bag. Others wrote big cheques, and you had to give them special envelopes so they could claim the donation on their taxes. One time, a man gave the Lord his gold Rolex. By the end, the pouch was teeming with treasure, so you took it to the treasurer—usually also the preacher's wife, doing double-duty.

And then the Man of God would take the stage. He would typically begin by releasing the children to Sunday school for Bible stories, songs and skits, puppet shows, arts and crafts, games, and sometimes even snacks. But some Sundays, the preacher just forgot about us and Sunday school was quietly cancelled. Nobody dared correct an anointed Man of God. Other Sundays, the preacher kept us on purpose, his message too important to dismiss the children, so instead you had to try your best to sit still and pay attention. Troublesome kids could be scolded or sent away. One fidgety young boy was publicly rebuked *in the name of Jesus*, just as the preacher might have cast out a little demon, and that's what I was acting like, my deeply embarrassed mother told me in the foyer after the service.

You knew the sermon was almost over when the keyboard player returned to his seat to give the preacher's wind-up an inspirational score. Then there was an altar call, where he would prayerfully invite the Holy Spirit to tell you if the message was meant for you, and if it was, you were to come to the front for prayers and blessings and healings and miracles and all the other good God stuff. Sometimes only a few people responded. Sometimes there was nobody left in their seats. Either way, the preacher and his team of elders and ushers would pray for these people, and on a good day, some would be slain in the Spirit. There were rarely any miracles, even though people were clamouring for them, but no one much minded an anticlimax. By then everybody was hungry, so we all went to Mama Panda's for the Sunday buffet.

There was no big brunch at the big tent revival, and no Sunday school either. It was a Wednesday night. But there had already been one miracle. The kneeling wailer presented himself to the preacher, who stopped the worship band mid-song to share the man's testimony. He was a former professional hockey player whose career ended on a dirty hit that left him with a serious concussion and several broken bones. The man said he could no longer endure brightly lit rooms, so he had balked when the Lord led him to attend the revival, and what's more, his right shoulder had never fully healed—it clicked and popped painfully when he tried to raise his right arm.

But God healed me, the man said, staring directly into the light, and now listen!

The preacher held a microphone to the man's elbow. He raised his right arm several times. Nothing clicked.

It wasn't a major facelift, but the Man of God reacted like it was, sprinting back and forth across the stage, screaming *hallelujah* over and over. The revivalists followed his lead. When the preacher *shaz-ammed* the hockey player and he collapsed into the arms of an usher, who laid him down gently, the band started up again and the place became a holy mess. The worshippers darted about the sanctuary, leapfrogging chairs and one another until the music overcame them and the holy mess became a holy hoedown. A conga line formed as the drummer played a military beat, and I joined the worshippers as they looped up the aisle, out into the parking lot and back, shimmying and singing the whole way:

The army of the Lord
The army of the Lord
The army of the Lord is marching on

As I returned to my seat, I felt a Bunyanesque hand touch down on my shoulder. I spun around expecting to finally meet my guardian angel. Instead, it was the hockey player.

Hoo boy, he sighed, his eyes disappearing into a squint as he crouched at my hip. The anointing is all over you, brotha.

I should have been encouraged by his words. They validated what I wanted most to believe about myself; they echoed what many others had said to me in the past. But they also echoed the preacher's MC Hammer anecdote, which I had not enjoyed. As the hockey player ended our encounter with an awkward attempt at a Black kind of handshake, I grew uneasy. Searching the tent for signs and wonders, I saw only others seeing me, and as the revival wore on, I wrestled with a grim suspicion that the source of all this attention was not some conspicuous aura or intangible quality, but something much easier to see.

This anxiety was not new, and it was as difficult to disregard as my mere existence in a place like Abbotsford, where one was likelier to see God than a creature like me. Some people had no clue how to react. Some people stared. Other folks nodded righteously, as though I meant to make a polarizing statement, coming in like this, and they were on my side about it. You'd think I was wearing a very loud hat.

I daydreamed away the sermon and snapped to attention just as five children were led to the stage. There was a murmuring at the opposite end of the tent whence they came, and the usher who marched them single file to the altar like five little ducklings was whispering into the Man of God's ear. He nodded knowingly, then turned to share his news with the assembly.

Church, he said, these children, in their faith, have met with God. Right here in this tent, they've seen an angel.

I let out an audible groan as the lucky quintet received a standing ovation. While I was caught up in my thoughts, the other kids had remained alert, and they were rewarded with the very vision I had come to witness. I had missed my chance to see and be seen, and worse, my inattentiveness had cost me the chance make my mother proud that she had brought me. As she clapped feverishly for the better children, who were now being interviewed by the preacher, I was overcome with jealousy and shame, and as she joined the revivalists in extending her arms to the altar, I could only cross mine sullenly, hoping to suppress the heaving desperation to be exalted in the eyes of my mother.

The preacher asked the first child: What did you see?

The boy said: I saw . . . an angel.

What did it look like?

It was tall. It had yellow hair and a white dress and wings.

That's an angel! the preacher said, at which the congregation applauded and launched into another round of amens.

The preacher moved on to the next child: And you, little girl, what did you see?

An angel.

What did it look like?

It was bigger than people. It had yellow hair and wings.

Could you see its face?

No. It was too bright.

Where did you see it?

Over there, the little girl said, pointing to a corner near the ceiling. Every eye followed her finger.

Praise God, the preacher said. And you three? Where was the angel when you saw it?

The trio pointed to the same corner of the tent, corroborating the testimony of the first two, and the congregation broke into spontaneous worship.

Great is Thy faithfulness
Great is Thy faithfulness
Morning by morning new mercies I see
All I have needed Thy hand hath provided
Great is Thy faithfulness, Lord, unto me

But I didn't sing. Instead, I scanned the ceiling for the angel, looking into and between the lights, investigating every corner of the big tent. I stared intently at the spot where the angel supposedly had been. Was it still there? Maybe if I looked hard enough, it would make one final appearance. I squinted and strained to unveil the invisible. I wanted to see an angel more than anything.

And then I saw an angel.

It was just a flicker, like a frame from a different movie spliced into the reel—there and gone in the blink of an eye. But in that millisecond of darkness, for I had blinked, or perhaps even fallen briefly asleep, I beheld something so bright that its shape was unmistakable even behind my eyelids. It was the shape of a man in a robe, but it was high above me, where nobody could be, higher even than the giant floodlights erected along the perimeter of the tent. And it was in motion. I opened my half-shut eyes and saw nothing, so I threw myself into another good, long blink, and there it was again, floating and flashing away like the cobwebs and clouds one might see after staring too long at the sun—traces of the divine, like the gold-dusted revivalists of just outside Toronto. Though my worldly eyes had seen nothing, something had cast an angelic shadow on my retina, and as the evanescent vision escaped, its shape expanded, resembling in no uncertain terms a pair of wings unfolding.

An angel, probably.

I would have preferred a more direct encounter, perhaps with some physical evidence left at the scene—a flaming sword, maybe, or even a signed photograph. I thought of the prophet Elijah, who challenged the prophets of Baal to a contest on Mount Carmel, calling on God to burn up his offering while they made fools of themselves asking a false god to do the same. The Lord responded with a showy, all-consuming fire from heaven. Very straightforward. My hope was for something like that. But this felt as though the all-consuming fire had indeed fallen from heaven, only to miss the altar by six or seven feet—a Godly demonstration so imprecise as to raise more questions than it answered.

Although maybe that was the point. I had come to the big tent seeking evidence of things unseen, but *faith* is the evidence of things unseen, the preacher was saying at that very moment, faith like a child. A more overt revelation would have been more convincing, yes, but it would do little for my faith.

I was meant, after all, to convince myself.

It wasn't easy. I knew what I saw, but I didn't really know, and there was a real concern that I didn't see anything. It could have been a trick of the light or an optical illusion. It could have been a power surge. And then there was also the possibility that I really did fall asleep for a second. We had been singing and dancing for hours, and it was hot in the tent, and I was up way past my bedtime. But it seemed equally likely, and perhaps more so given the setting, that these rationalizations were sneaky little lies whispered by the devil and his demons, who go where the angels go, seeking to undo and undermine their work at every turn. They would be eager to sow doubt in my heart, and here they were, I thought, trying to convince me that the very thing I had come for—a direct encounter with God—was something unremarkable, explainable: hallucinatory visions; flash blindness; a micro nap. Anything to lead me away from the very simple truth: I saw what I thought that I saw.

Mom, I said, tugging on my mother's skirt. I saw an angel.

She threw up her hand and she shouted: My son saw it too!

The preacher saw me for the third time and smiled. Bring him up here.

The usher summoned us from our seats. He led us to the risers, up the metal steps, and set us apart from the others, on the far side of the stage.

The preacher wasted no time slaying my mother. *Shazam!* He shouted with a wave, never breaking his stride, and she fell, like a flower petal, as an usher laid her gently on the floor, beneath a blanket. I could hear her speaking softly in tongues as the preacher zeroed in on me, alone.

Church, he said, now even this beautiful, Black child has witnessed the angel's appearance.

He seemed more amused than enthused, and the revivalists responded with a smattering of perfunctory applause, as for an animal that had pulled off a neat trick. In that moment, I felt isolated and on display, like a captive chimp, and I wanted nothing more than to escape this invisible circus, these awful, zoo eyes, letting my damnable hat fall away as I clambered, screeching, into the trees.

But a domesticated creature can never go home. He no longer knows the way. You will find him on the edge of the wilderness, begging men for his dinner.

The preacher's powerful hand was above me now, and I shuddered at what he might divine from a single touch. Would he sense my anxiety? Could he even understand it, or would he simply mistake it for a liar's apprehension and strike me down like hapless Ananias and Sapphira? My doubt returned, now yoked to a dread that I had been summoned onstage just to be dragged out by the ankles for deception. I started to fear for my life.

Church, I had the pleasure of meeting this boy's mother yesterday, he said, and she told me about her son, who she adopted, at God's urging, from an African teen. You see, there are many ways to spread the gospel.

The congregation laughed, and again I was humiliated. But it was a minor concern, for I would be dead soon.

In the Bible, the preacher continued, God often reveals himself to the least of us. The resurrected Christ first appeared to Mary Magdalene, a prostitute, and now the angel of the Lord has revealed himself to this young man, taken from his mother's breast, from the milk of the world, and given the pure milk of *the word*, that he may be edified. Child, are you ready to taste and see that the Lord is good?

Yes, I said, braced for my death, and growing more at ease with the idea.

But the preacher did not kill me. Instead, he bowed his head.

Heavenly Father, let this child continue to see you, he said. Keep him from wickedness. Keep him from sin, from the enemy's strongholds, the ghetto, the corner, the club. Keep him from gangs, and sexual immorality, and vulgar music, and the mentality of bondage. This boy has been plucked from the withering branch, from the darkness, and brought into light, to abide in the house of the Lord. By this, the Saviour says, my Father is glorified, that you bear much fruit.

Child, he said, are you ready to bear fruit?

Yes, I said.

Tonight, you have seen the truth, he continued. You are anointed. Do not backslide, and do not turn away from Him, even as you encounter prejudice and hatred from non-believers, from the wicked, because you are a bondservant of Christ. God in heaven, let this child's light shine so brightly that the world sees no colour, no race, but only you.

He placed his hands on my temples and my knees began to wobble.

He said: The Gospel of John tells us that if the world hates you, know that it hated Me first. If you were of the world, the world would love its own. Yet because you are not of the world, *but I chose you out of the world*, therefore the world hates you.

I felt the elders approaching from my blind side, ready to lay me down beside my mother, and I started crying for no reason.

Child, he said, are you ready to be hated by the world?

2

SUPERBOOK

(or The Boy as He Floated Away)

The big tent revival ruined us for regular church. We came away desperate for more of the strong stuff, more revival, more, but it wasn't available where we were going. After one night in the fullness of the presence of God, or three nights, in my mother's case, we were struck by the absence of presence at Abbotsford Pentecostal Assembly.

It wasn't just us. Released from the big tent, a legion of radicals marched back to Abbotsford, ravenous, raving, only to find disillusionment and disapproval. That Sunday, at churches all over the city, over-the-top demonstrations of Spirit-filled praise were met with the same response: We don't really do that here. The radicals soon found that their big tent energy was considered creepy, even disturbing, in a more traditional church setting. They spoke in tongues and jumped for joy and ran around the room, and they were asked to rein it in or take it elsewhere.

Even at APA, there was little appetite for this sort of behaviour. The progressive Pentecostal megachurch built its reputation, not to mention its sizable congregation and its building—the giant pink structure that spanned several north Abbotsford blocks—on a more modern, spirited service. It was one of Abbotsford's first houses of worship to go electric. Members had long been encouraged to *feel* the music, scandalizing the city's influential, anti-dancing, Mennonite community. But anything beyond a bit of swaying could be controversial. APA was rowdier than most, but not by much.

So when a zealous Tilda Eubanks began skipping up and down the aisles while waving a hand-sewn Crusader flag, she was kindly encouraged to knock it off.

The same thing happened to me. Inspired by the frolicsome woman, and still coming down from my angel sighting, I decided to bust a few moves. Dancing and singing, my eyes closed, I felt downright buoyant. But then an old lady slapped me on the side of my neck. I spun around, startled. She offered a cynical *siss*. I looked to my mother, confounded, embarrassed. She glared at me reproachfully and pointed me back to the pew.

As I sat and sulked, an usher detected a teachable moment. He leaned in and said: Dance for the Lord, not yourself.

I didn't really understand the difference. I decided not to dance at all.

The rest of the radicals were not so easily demoralized. When the free worship came, they broke into a cacophony of tongues that outlasted even the praise band, who tried to put a stop to things by putting away their equipment.

The caterwauling continued until the pastor's wife cut through the clamour, standing up to quote from First Corinthians. If anyone speaks in a tongue, let there be two or at the most three, each in turn, and let one interpret, she declared. The Apostle Paul made it abundantly clear: to speak in tongues without translation was not what the Lord had in mind. It was strictly self-serving. It edified no one. At worst, it was just showing off.

Then Nora Neeson rose in defiance, delivering a word from the

Lord in her prayer language. The elderly Irishwoman generally commanded a great deal of respect, but not on this Sunday. She was shouted down before she could finish her prophecy.

I'd never heard anyone booing at church before.

At its core, this was a theological disagreement. On the Day of Pentecost, the Holy Spirit arrives without warning, and the apostles, the book of Acts tells us, begin to speak with other tongues. The fundamentalists believed that these tongues were not intended to be dissonant nonsense, but actual, recognizable languages that foreigners would likely understand. The radicals, however, believed their tongues were nonsensical perhaps, but not nonsense. They weren't meant for foreigners either: each was an exclusive, heavenly language that signified a personal relationship with God, like an inside joke or a secret handshake.

When the service let out, in the foyer, my parents and APA's radicals claimed persecution. We were living out loud, and we would not be silenced. We would not hide our light beneath bushels, or censor our passion for Christ, and we did not appreciate being repressed. Neither did the fundamentalists appreciate Mrs. Gazette's retaliatory jab, echoed by both Nora Neeson and my mother, that we might seem a little silly, but at least we weren't a bunch of sanctimonious devil-worshippers.

The Man of God tried to mend fences. He suggested a small Bible study—a care cell.

The radical faction began meeting Saturday nights at my family's house, and this splinter group did their best to recreate the raucous and uncompromising big tent atmosphere, right there in our living room. But it was an exile. We had been sent away like a bunch of Ishmaels. Resentment was inevitable. In no time at all, care cell devolved into a gathering of malcontents, convinced that the revival had been stifled by a megachurch ashamed of its own gospel, more interested in maintaining influence than in meeting with God.

They baptized themselves in righteous anger. Their tongues became sharp, became forked, and the fury of Saturday nights became frightening to me. On my way to the kitchen, to see if the lemon drop cookies I made were a hit with our guests, I saw women laid out on the floor like dead bodies, men standing up on the couch, shouting over them, and others at war with invisible entities, screaming at wallpaper, windows, and whatnot. I watched from a distance, too anxious to enter the room and take part in the madness. It followed me anyhow. From my bedroom, just above their heads, I heard it all, and I felt it too, rumbling beneath me, disturbing my sleep. It shook the whole house like an earthquake—the big one. Sometimes it seemed like the evil rebuked back to hell floated upstairs and into me. My dreams every weekend were nightmares.

But we kept showing up at APA every Sunday, right until the morning Nora Neeson broke the tension with another disagreeable prophecy.

Thus saith the Lord, she began in Irish English, the time has come to get a new horse.

She pronounced *Michelob* over the church, and a wave of sharply drawn breaths rippled all throughout the sanctuary. She was cursing the whole congregation. Michelob was a brand of beer, my parents explained as we left for the last time, but Nora Neeson had intended to say *Ichabod*, which means *the glory of God is no longer here*. APA was a dead church. My mother agreed. It was time to move on.

The next Sunday, we stayed home and watched *Superbook* videos.

• • •

Superbook, known in Japan as *Personal Computer Travel Detective Team*, was a Bible-based anime series. The program was produced by the Christian Broadcasting Network, an evangelism company founded by Dr. Pat Robertson. This Man of God was very influential in our home. My mother was reading his latest book—*The Turning Tide: The Fall of Liberalism and the Rise of Common Sense*—and his show, *The 700 Club*, aired every single day, upstairs and downstairs.

Created in collaboration with the Japanese studio that made *Speed Racer* and *Samurai Pizza Cats*, *Superbook* was aimed at the children of Asia, who were raised in a godless place, dominated, Dr. Robertson said, by false religions like Buddhism and Shintoism. The theme song set the stage: Chris and Joy were horsing around in the attic when they accidentally knocked a magic Bible onto a computer keyboard, thus *computerizing* the word of God, as well as their dog, Ruffles, who was sucked into the text. As the kids and a wind-up robot named Gizmo chase a Yorkie-poo around the Old Testament, they meet anointed heroes like Moses and Joseph and Samuel, learning Biblical lessons in every encounter.

The show was a hit. On *The 700 Club*, the hosts claimed *Superbook* was so successful that, after it aired, the Bible became Japan's best-selling book.

It didn't air in Canada, however. In Abbotsford, *Superbook* videos were available exclusively at the House of James, the Christian book and music store, where the series was offered as a sorely needed, Christian alternative to secular Japanese cartoons like *Dragon Ball* and *Dragon Quest*. The growing popularity of anime was a genuine concern in Abbotsford in 1994, especially among the revivalists at the care cell, who had barely managed to fend off the New Age propaganda of Captain Planet and the Care Bears, and now came these new cartoons from Japan, which peddled the same dangerous, Eastern ideas like magic, mysticism, and supernatural powers.

Just how brazen was the enemy becoming? *Dragon Ball* and *Dragon Quest* were both about summoning dragons that would grant eternal life, an obvious allusion to the great dragon called the devil and Satan who deceives the whole world, according to the book of Revelation.

Suffice it to say, many Christians were not comfortable with this because eternal life is a gift from God alone. There was little doubt among the radicals that these Japanese imports were the latest satanic deception. The children were told to avoid New Age nonsense from Asia. Spirit-led mothers like Mrs. Gazette championed *Superbook*, urging God-fearing families to choose CBN's Bible-based, Japanese-style programming rather than allowing the real Japanese programming to mislead or bedevil the next generation.

People think it's harmless, but demons can easily attach themselves to even the most basic artifacts of pagan cultures, she told us, scanning the living room art for examples, like these Fijian elephant statues, or this Oriental tapestry, or even the Samurai Pizza Cats.

Mrs. Gazette had identical twins who were my age. Luke and Light were forbidden from consuming any secular TV shows, or listening to secular music. Mostly they read religious horror novels about small towns overrun by demonic activity, and Christians caught up in a battle for souls. They loaned me *This Present Darkness* by Frank Peretti, where a down-on-his-luck pastor discovers a local New Age group is working with demons to take the town over. Too close to the truth, the pastor is falsely arrested for rape, but he gets out eventually, vowing to fight unseen forces forever.

It didn't all make sense to me, but I got through it, proud to have finished my first book for grown-ups. My secret? You only engage with the words that you know. In the end, it turns out that you didn't miss anything.

My mother purchased all thirteen volumes of *Superbook*. I watched them again and again every Sunday. Ruffles really gets around the first half of the Bible, and it's no place for a Yorkie-poo. The dog is mercifully apprehended in the final episode, escaping Bible times as things are getting really dicey. The children, their dog, and the robot get out as Jerusalem falls to invaders from Babylon.

Mrs. Gazette's passion for spiritual warfare had begun at the

Marysville revival, where she was delivered from a demon causing migraines. The searing headaches came almost daily, and they were often debilitating. In her worst episodes, the woman swore that she could see and even hear the pain that she experienced.

No one could explain what was behind the chronic pain. Doctors were stumped. Scans returned nothing.

But when there's no natural explanation, she liked to say, there's a supernatural explanation. After reading a *Christianity Today* article about the miracles in Marysville, Mrs. Gazette crossed the border for the first time since Woodstock and drove two hours south, in search of healing.

She wasn't the only one. Hundreds of Canadians headed down to the First Assembly of God Church, where the charismatic, midweek services had become a phenomenon. Every Wednesday and Thursday night, the Man of God gathered a hundred of his most ardent young followers for what he called *warfare prayer*—a deafening babble of tongues and battle cries that served as a warm-up for the main event. When the atmosphere was right, the pastor and his youthful army spilled into the sanctuary, lost in a delirium so infectious that the *Seattle Times* called the church the only place where you didn't have to do any drugs to get high.

Mrs. Gazette arrived on the same night as the Prophet Mary Greenland, a Woman of God who was building her own private army. The Holy Spirit had called Mary Greenland out of Alaska to the Pacific Northwest, a region brimming with witchcraft and New Age influence. She was in search of Prayer Warriors who could purify the land on both sides of the border, for God was not bound by our maps, and prepare the way for the coming Great Revival.

The prophet was welcomed as a visiting dignitary. She was invited to scout from the stage of First Assembly, and that's where she first beheld Mrs. Gazette. The Woman of God came down from the altar call and said to her: Daughter of Christ, there is an evil spirit

31

sitting on your shoulders. He's a little demon, no larger than a baby baboon, and he hates that you're in God's house and he does not want to let you go. Tonight, the Lord wants to release you.

Mrs. Gazette was stunned. Just moments earlier, she'd felt a migraine coming on, and speak of the devil, why, here it is now.

There, Mary Greenland said, touching her forehead. It's begun to squeeze you by the temples. Do you feel that?

Yes, said Mrs. Gazette. She was wincing, embattled. She struggled to stand.

The prophet asked: How long have you suffered from migraines?

As long as I can remember.

Did your mother get migraines too?

Right up to the day she died.

And suddenly Mary Greenland's lapel mic was on. This woman has a generational spirit, she announced, as though she'd found gold in the hills.

The prophet explained: possession may be nine-tenths of the law, but it's only one-tenth of demonic activity. Demonic oppression is much more common. The enemy works tirelessly to keep us in bondage, and one of his tactics is psychological torment: chronic headaches, nightmares, poverty, agoraphobia—any affliction that could cause you to stumble, or worse, to blame God for your troubles. If the devil can harden your heart to the Lord, there is no need to demonize you—you're already captive. This is why the apostle Paul warns believers to put on the full armour of God, that you may be able to withstand the wiles of the devil. The Helmet of Salvation alone isn't near enough. You need the Breastplate of Righteousness, the Shield of Faith, and the Sword of the Spirit, so you can cut off these unwanted attachments before they're passed down, before your soul ties act as a bridge to pass demonic *trash* to the next generation.

We can inherit the curses of our parents, even our grandparents, without even knowing, the prophet said. It's why we suffer the same afflictions; it's why we repeat their mistakes. *It's the same demon.* You may have done nothing at all to invite this attachment. But if your mother was vulnerable to demonic oppression, the demon could feel entitled to possess you as well.

Then the Woman of God commanded the generational spirit to leave Mrs. Gazette by the authority of Jesus Christ.

Delivered, Mrs. Gazette remained in Marysville for several days, training alongside Tilda Eubanks and my mother to launch the first Canadian chapter of the Prayer Warriors. Mary Greenland taught the women many rituals, and they returned an elite unit, to my mind, deputized by the Alaskan prophet to wage a holy war in their unholy country.

At the border, the Canada Customs agent asked if the trio had anything to declare.

That the Lord reigns in Abbotsford, British Columbia, Mrs. Gazette said, emboldened by faith.

When she got home, Mrs. Gazette deputized both of her sons. Her spiritual gift was intercessory prayer—according to the Prophet Mary Greenland, she could cast the devil out of an egg—but Luke and Light had the gift of spiritual vision, and they were delighted to find out about it. Before long, they were seeing demons everywhere: at the mall and the pharmacy, hanging from lampposts and maple trees, inside and perched atop cars passing by.

The enemy knew it was being seen, and the Gazettes' powers made them targets. The boys soon spotted several spirits skulking around their own house. Light was chased by a demon on his way home from the corner store to buy milk. A quick-thinking Luke trapped a demon in the guest room mirror by anointing the dresser with olive oil. One night, at midnight, two witches drove a station wagon through the bushes and into their backyard, they said, and the hags burned a pentagram into their lawn. Mrs. Gazette prayed the symbol away, and the grass and the bushes grew back, quite miraculously, before I could see for myself.

The Gazettes were mostly concerned for the neighbourhood, especially the nearby elementary school. At care cell, the Prayer Warriors agreed that Valley Christian School was too strategically important for the enemy to be creeping around outside. The devil was no doubt eager to attach himself to the children of the Lord before they could grow in their gifts and rebuke him.

Not today, Satan.

Early one morning before the bell, the Prayer Warriors walked the perimeter, rebuking every demon in the name of Jesus Christ. Then they claimed the area for God by tearing pages from the Bible and burying them along the property line. When the ritual was through, my mother led me inside to my classroom, where my teachers and my classmates saw me as a thing possessed.

• • •

Valley Christian School was founded in 1983, after the Mennonite Educational Institute became overrun by Sikhs. As far as I knew, they were still under siege over there. MEI was widely regarded as Abbotsford's best school, for it was the richest, and the cost of tuition reflected (and likely explained) its elite education. The private K–12 offered steep discounts for Mennonite Brethren members, but those attending other churches were ineligible for these savings. Many were priced out, and spots they believed were rightfully theirs instead went to the wealthy Sikh families clustered in Abbotsford's west end, the brown side of town, who were not at all troubled by the Christian curriculum and happily paid the full price for enrolling their children.

The halls of MEI soon filled with turbans. It was a scandal, so far as I understood what was a scandal, and what was explained to me. The religious headwear defied the institute's strict uniform requirements, for one thing, and God's commandment to reject idolatry and false religion besides. But MEI rejected calls to impose a turban

ban and expel those—of all races and religions—who defied it. Who could say no to a boatload of money?

Others appealed to no rulebook at all. They simply felt it was an affront for a Christian school to prioritize Sikhs over Christians just because they could afford the tuition. But MEI argued that accepting these students was simply a form of evangelism that, as it happened, would allow for an expansion of its promising athletics program, thanks to the influx of capital.

Feeling persecuted by the institute's unwillingness to purge its Sikh students, a group of disgruntled families pronounced Ichabod on MEI and set out to form a school committed to putting God's children first. Valley Christian School began with thirty-five students. Two years later, Sikh terrorists blew up a plane and enrolment at VCS spiked. By the time the upstart elementary relocated from Principal Solomon's barn to the labyrinthian basement of Central Heights Church, the student population was approaching 150.

But they had never seen a boy like me.

For its first seven years, VCS was an all-white school. This did not seem to have occurred to anyone until my first day of kindergarten, when I arrived, making it no longer so. They promised that it didn't really matter. Several teachers and parents volunteered that they were colour blind, and this was a real relief, but I could tell that I remained to them a surprising thing, weird and not necessarily good, like a cat elected mayor, and I often wondered what they saw in place of melanated skin.

A problem child, mostly. Conflict with classmates and teachers was constant—my mere presence was adversity—and I was soon labelled a difficult student. I had trouble fitting in, the community agreed, and a bad attitude at the best of times. Some suspected that I suffered from attention deficit disorder—(and I do, raging ADHD in fact, though I call it *the brilliance*)—but my mother wouldn't hear it. She refused to discuss medication.

Ritalin makes kids depressed, she explained.

Spankings for every offence would suffice.

The after-school beatings did little to change my behaviour. Pity my second-grade teacher. The perfectly named Miss Kruger took a one-year sabbatical after she had me, and this was my fault, mostly, I would be told. The woman seemed to find my voice uniquely shrill, and once mused aloud that it might have something to do with the shape of my skull. I was unconvinced. Was it not a bony circle like everyone else's?

I possessed as well, she often complained to my mother, the preternatural ability to hinder my classmates while learning and thriving myself. This was far from ideal in a Grade 2/3 split. The children in Miss Kruger's charge were mostly third graders, but she had also been entrusted with four advanced readers from the grade beneath, and she rued this arrangement all year, because I was among them.

By then, I was reading young adult novels, and the second-grade work was unchallenging. I finished, and strained to sit idle, impatience erupting, while Miss Kruger taught the older kids. The teacher tried to slow me down with confounding, third-grade worksheets that I'd never seen. It didn't work. I could not be contained.

Miss Kruger maintained order with a basic three-strikes system. The first time you got into trouble, you wrote your name down in her reprimand book. Strike two meant a star beside your name. Strike three was a checkmark and a parent-teacher phone call and, at my house after school, another spanking.

The teacher was not above showing mercy after a third strike—just not in my case. Many parents were sensitive to their children being singled out in this way, and Miss Kruger bent over backwards to avoid placing calls that would get her berated. But this barrier no longer existed for me, not after so much practice, so there was little hesitation about calling my mother to rail against her rotten little son.

One day I hid the paddle, and my mother was forced to spank me with an open palm. It didn't even hurt. But it was a mistake to let her know that she was weak. After that, she began to outsource the punishment to my adoptive father, a pilot, who often spent days or weeks overseas. His hands, like his transatlantic flights, landed with considerable force. As soon as he walked in the door, in his pilot's hat and Canadian Airlines uniform, a crisp white short-sleeved button-up with the three-striped epaulettes of a first officer, tucked into a pair of navy blue pants, my mother would tell him how many spankings I deserved, and he would wallop my backside before he changed clothes. It was an imperfect system: detached from my discomfort, my mother could be overly punitive and, detached in general, my father rarely questioned the severity of what she made him do.

Miss Kruger, meanwhile, grew to despise me. She came to believe that I considered myself smarter or better than her other students, and perhaps even her—arrogant, she said in my report card, adding that all of my classmates agreed.

He's always squinting at me, she complained on parent-teacher day. It's disrespectful.

So my mother said I should stop squinting. But I couldn't see the blackboard if I didn't. Eventually, Miss Kruger wondered if I might need glasses. An eye test confirmed it. I saw the big E, but the rest was a blur, so they fit me for super-thick lenses.

Driving home, I noticed another big letter: the K, for the Kmart at Sevenoaks mall.

You've never seen the K before? My mother was astounded.

Miss Kruger was blown away as well. I showed up the next morning looking like a little Arthur Ashe in massive gold glasses. She tried not to laugh, and the other kids followed her lead, but nobody tried hard enough.

No matter. They were mean to me before. My glasses were just new material. And what an improvement! Turned out I'd never seen anything clearly, and these things were taking so much heat, they felt like a shield from the usual jokes about Blackness. Four-eyes was an awesome nickname, the best they'd ever given me, and these glasses were far and away the best thing I'd been given. My glasses made me see the world again, like starting over, and they only made me faster and better at school. I was crushing the 2/3 split now.

But Miss Kruger fought back. She had to put me in my place. One afternoon, a boys-against-girls flash card battle was won by the girls, even after I was first to the right answer. Miss Kruger ignored me, and one of the girls said my answer again. Our opponents rejoiced as I protested, loudly.

That's what I just said! I shouted.

Learn to lose, the teacher snarled.

This outburst legitimized the resentment of several boys I regularly beat at sports. They too believed I had trouble accepting defeat, on account of my penchant for winning. Most of the boys kept their distance, except for my sole friend, the new kid, who had to start somewhere. But one of the boys was determined to fight me. He challenged me daily.

Teacher was right. You're a loser, said Eric, when I told him I wouldn't fight, not now, and not by the flagpole at three. Go cry to the teacher, you Black loser.

Black was the insult back then, but the sting was long gone; it was common, and not that creative. I shrugged, standing next to the new kid, who made me feel stronger.

I'm rubber, you're glue, I responded, which meant that Eric's insults bounced off of me and stuck to him instead.

Guess that makes *you* a Black loser, said the new kid.

You're not rubber, you're tar, Eric said. Tar-baby, tar-baby.

So I ran to tell the recess monitor, Miss Donkers, who cried when the children made fun of her name. She gave him a warning. He left me alone for the rest of the day.

But the next day at recess, I kicked the game-winning goal, and Eric, the goalie, charged out from his net. He punched me so hard in the mouth that I swallowed two baby teeth.

Wiping my tears, I looked up to discover the bully was getting a hug from Miss Donkers. He spun around, pointing to me as I made my way over. The recess monitor nodded, draping her arms down before him. She gave his chest a little rub and waited to confront me.

Eric says he lost his temper because you were being arrogant, said Miss Donkers. No one likes a poor winner.

Then it was time to account for myself when I could not account for my teeth, and I was utterly baffled that anyone could find a little boy bleeding and assume the assault was deserved.

So I said: It's because I'm *Black*.

I hadn't intended to say anything. I was merely trying to draw attention to the hole in my face.

Miss Donkers reacted as though I had alleged a grand conspiracy. She put her hands on her hips and bobbled her head, utterly nonplussed, like it was frivolous and disqualifying to have even suggested such a thing. Then she backed away from Eric as if she hadn't taken sides, and she began to scoff, like dogs react to sudden gusts of wind.

Good riddance to *that* nonsense, she finally said, clapping her palms like two chalkboard erasers. The accusation thoroughly explored, she forged ahead, urging the both of us to apologize and repent for our equal roles in the quarrel: the bully, for punching a gap through my teeth, and me, for my attitude, not to mention that completely unfair accusation—no one at VCS cared I was Black.

I was to go first, and I did as I was told—it was that, or I would have to spend the rest of recess inside. But it didn't feel right, and it didn't seem true. There was a brown boy in the grade beneath me now, from a Sikh family that had been Saved. In a cruel coincidence, we were both named Harry. The first-grader's mother arrived to pick him up one afternoon, and his baby sister briefly toddled through the pick-up area.

Look mom! shouted a little boy. Another Harry!

The naive comment earned hearty laughter from parents and teachers alike, but it gave me pause. I realized that some kids thought Harry was what I was, not who I was, and I wondered how it was possible to be both colour blind and, somehow, still fuzzy about my humanity.

Driving home, my mother sided with the recess monitor: I *was* arrogant. I had a very bad attitude. It came up time and time again at school.

It's because I'm Black, I said again, in search of validation.

Don't give me that nonsense, she said. See? You think everyone else is the problem. That's arrogance right there. It's you, Harry. You are the problem. Get over yourself.

I hung my head in shame, pressing my tongue into the fleshy gap where my teeth used to be and contemplating how I could possibly think any less of myself. What was there to be arrogant about? At school and at home, the takeaway was clear: I was a bad banana, through and through. Whence this overconfidence?

A joke made the rounds at school. My bully was the first to tell it to me.

What did God say when he made you? Eric asked, and when I said I didn't know, he answered: Oops! Burned another one.

You're a jerk! I shouted.

That was my first strike. Harry, come write down your name, said Miss Kruger.

I tried to explain—it is vital to whatever self-worth I have left that I continue to believe I am chosen, anointed, *necessary*, and that whatever otherness I may feel is part of God's perfect plan for my life and not some accident, error, or joke—but my language was limited, and I wound up repeating myself.

He's a jerk, I said.

Strike two, Miss Kruger responded.

Later, another student told me the same joke. What did God say when he made Harry—oops, I mean, you.

I said nothing, having learned from past mistakes. Instead, I calmly and quietly broke the boy's pencil in half. The teacher saw me snap. She called strike three.

Outraged, I refused to have any more to do with her rigged reprimand book, and when she summoned me to her desk, I merely traced the star with a purple pencil crayon, absolving myself.

I was instantly suspended. Miss Kruger called my mother. Come and get your son, she said.

But my mother refused. She argued that a suspension was no punishment at all. I would only sit at home, watching TV, having fun, and I wouldn't learn anything.

You keep him, she said.

They settled on an in-school suspension.

The next morning, I was plucked from the split classroom and sent away to a small storage closet in an empty, eerie nook of the Central Heights basement. There I found a stack of third- and fourth-grade textbooks and worksheets, meant to keep me busy.

Truthfully, I didn't mind the closet. There was no one to talk to but neither was there anyone to tell me I was misbehaving. No one was upset with me. No one seemed unsure of what to do with me. No one worked to protect the others from me. It was a safe space.

Miss Kruger didn't miss me either. Every morning I assumed my time in solitary confinement was through, only to learn I had not yet demonstrated the humility required to rejoin my classmates. I imagine they all found my absence refreshing. Day after day, I returned to the closet to learn independently. Things could be worse.

When I finished the worksheets, I wandered off to the school library. VCS had just one young adult collection: the Trailblazer

41

Books, a series of short Christian novels in which children encounter the great missionaries of history. In *Trial by Poison*, the scariest one, which I read several times, the mother of a young West African girl is imprisoned by savages, and condemned to eat a deadly poison bean. So the little one turns to the Presbyterian teacher Mary Slessor, a wise and compassionate Scottish woman who is famed for adopting six African children. Only the white missionary can save the girl's mother. The African people are monsters—superstitious fools who embrace ignorance as a cover for their cruelty. They have no regard for human life; they are charlatans, cannibals, witches, slavers, and baby-killers.

But this was the case for the African characters in every book I'd ever read, with the exception of Curious George.

All of these books had it backwards, but I didn't know that then. I only knew what I was told and shown while I was reading, so I was frightened by the extremity and inhumanity of my heritage, and relieved to have been kept from such an awful, godless place.

Better alone in Abbotsford than surrounded by Africans in Africa, I thought.

But it was a mistake to enjoy my seclusion.

The faculty began to wonder why I was so happy, alone in my nook, and moreover, why my own mother had permitted them to leave me there. Not long after bringing me back, Miss Kruger asked: Harry, how often are you punished at home?

Every time my mother speaks with you, I explained. The spankings are daily. The spankings are bottomless.

My hope was that Miss Kruger would see how her system caused me nothing but abuse, and why my banishment became a welcome week away from everyone.

Instead, it prompted an investigation. The VCS faculty imagined the worst: that they were bound to punish me daily out of love, because my mother was punishing me daily from malice. The parents' council volunteered to look into the matter, as the Christian school had no formal system for probing suspected abuse.

The scrutiny was very distressing to my mother, who felt unfairly targeted as an American.

Canadians looked down on Americans, she explained, which was why everyone assumed the worst about her now. They prejudged her the moment she walked into that school to register me for kindergarten. One person said it was wrong to adopt me at all, because she was white. And they think Americans are the bad guys? How could it be wrong to love your son?

I had not considered the pressure that I put on my mother just by existing, and I struggled with shame over making her life so distressing. In my interview, I swore that I was only ever spanked, and that these punishments were painful, but deserved.

Corporal punishment was a wedge issue in Abbotsford. Children's rights advocates had been loudly insisting that spanking a child was the same thing as hitting a child, what with how spanks are the same thing as hits. In 1973, the Ministry of Education banned the strap in BC public schools. But private schools like VCS resisted the new rules for years, holding fast to the old rule from Proverbs, which instructs: *He who spares his rod hates his son, but he who loves him disciplines him promptly.* Principal Solomon still practised corporal punishment on occasion, and the school had briefly considered it for me. There was concern, however, that it might get out and hurt their accreditation case. But spankings were more than okay in the home. I was not being abused. I was being disciplined according to the Bible. My mother was acquitted, with apologies.

Still she blamed me for the whole ordeal. When she hung up the phone, she congratulated me on very nearly talking my way into the foster system, just like my birth mother. I was ashamed, and I went away thinking that I might be cursed. It was as though I was being inexorably drawn to repeat some Black woman's mistakes, swimming against an invisible current. I tried to stay out of trouble, and it found me. I tried to fit in, but something was off, and there appeared to be no natural explanation.

At year's end, Miss Kruger called my mother with good news: I was not invited back to her class in the fall. After marking all my busywork, the teacher realized that I had inadvertently graduated from the third grade as well as the second. I could skip to Grade 4, if I wanted. This was great news to my mother and me. She proudly accepted on both our behalf, and at the graduation ceremony, I appeared twice, like a cell in mitosis, at the top of both classes, suggesting that someone was raising me right after all.

If ever I was arrogant, it was the night I collected two diplomas, and my mother was exalted.

The feeling was short-lived, however. After the ceremony, Miss Kruger pulled my mother aside to offer a dire warning about my future: I would be a year ahead of my classmates, perhaps, but socially I was years behind. No amount of scholastic achievement would teach me to fit in, or cure my bad attitude. Her abiding hope in advancing me to the fourth grade was that I would be intimidated by the older boys and finally learn some humility.

It seemed, to me, a uniquely dispiriting kind of goodbye, and I spent the break afraid of going back to school.

But I never returned.

That summer, the schism that shook APA made its way to Central Heights Church. The new radicals argued that the non-denominational megachurch, founded decades earlier by ex-Mennonites wary of labels, should adopt a more radical theology. More dancing. More tongues. No translations. But they were rebuffed and several folks, including the church bass player and the man who ran the sound booth and his wife, who ran the overhead projector, left for the pink megachurch up the road.

The biggest losses were at the elementary school downstairs, which suddenly found itself without a principal and several teachers. It was a troubling setback. The school barely had enough personnel to handle the first five grades, so any outgoing staff, Principal Solomon especially, was a problem.

Neither had the school secured a permanent building or government certification—the student body was technically just two hundred children homeschooling together in a basement. That made the transition to proper homeschooling a relatively easy one for VCS families, and parents often threatened to remove their kids if they were not appeased.

These threats increased when the school announced the new acting principal, Everly Kuhorn. The woman was perfectly qualified—she was pursuing a master of education degree from the University of British Columbia, in Vancouver—but this was not a community wowed by degrees from liberal schools in cities by the sea. How could someone steeped in secular education serve families that did not support the practice? Rumours abounded that the new principal was a humanist, a postmodernist, a Unitarian at best, doubtless influenced by worldly teachings in direct defiance of 1 John, which warns believers thusly: *If anyone loves the world, the love of the Father is not in him.*

Sure enough, the acting principal tried to replace several textbooks.

For years, VCS had been married to the Abeka Homeschool Curriculum, written and distributed by Southern Baptists based in Florida. Abeka taught Biblical values and was built upon a solid, Christian worldview. But that wasn't enough for Mrs. Kuhorn. She argued that Canadian children were not well-served learning American history—and a one-sided version at that. Her argument sounded suspiciously liberal and supported my mother's contention that Canadians are bigoted against Americans.

When Mrs. Kuhorn went on to suggest a Canadian history textbook that touched briefly on Indigenous issues, an explicit attempt to replace Christian teaching with lies of the world, the knives came

45

out. The acting principal was diagnosed with a Jezebel spirit, a particularly nasty demon that latches onto women who are ambitious and difficult, or maybe it makes them that way. It's unclear.

The Bible hates Jezebel more than anyone. Few deaths are covered as gleefully as that of the idol-worshipping queen of Israel, who is defenestrated and eaten by dogs, in the end. But even that couldn't destroy the demonic attachment. The spirit of Jezebel remained active, sowing division and disunity in the body of Christ, and several VCS families, including my own, wanted no part in any of that.

So we left, and we never looked back.

• • •

My new Grade 4 class was delivered by Canpar Express, the Canadian courier service. The full Abeka homeschool kit was a massive shipment, with textbooks, workbooks, quizzes, exams, and answer keys for every subject, along with dozens of VHS tapes, each containing a week's worth of classes, recorded live from real classrooms at the Pensacola Christian Academy.

It was a seamless transition. Attending class remotely was not unlike attending VCS, but invisibly, which was preferable by then anyhow. Both schools opened class with prayer, much of the curriculum was the same, and if there were other Black students enrolled there, then they were invisible too.

But there were some striking differences. The Academy's footage appeared to be from another era, judging by the way everyone was dressed, and it was unmistakably from another country, precisely as American as Christian. At the beginning of each class, students recited two pledges of allegiance: one to the flag of the United States, and another to the Christian one, a mostly white flag with a little red cross in a royal blue square in the corner.

And they never forgot to pray for the president.

It's a little weird, since we're Canadian, I said once, but my mother reminded me that I was technically just as American as I was Black, which was half, because of her.

Here, she was wrong. My Abeka curriculum made it quite clear, and I showed her the passage to prove it: *Mankind can be divided into several large groups called* races. *The people of each race differ from those of other races in the color of their skin, in the size and shape of their head, in the kind and color of their hair, and in many other physical features.*

The same could not be said for Americans. I was only American inasmuch as I was being raised as one.

Whatever. American education is better, she said. Canadians act all high and mighty, but their textbooks are full of liberal crap. I tried to read a Canadian book on adoption. Do you know what it said? That adopted kids get sad around their birthdays, every year. They said it reminds them of something they've lost. But that's ridiculous. You love your birthday, don't you?

Of course, I said. I get so many presents. That's ridiculous.

See? Canadians don't know what they're talking about.

Within a few weeks, I was so settled into my virtual school environment that I could name several students who sat by the camcorder serving as a stand-in for me. Tyson had big metal braces. Beside him was Aaron, whose shirt was untucked in the back. These kids were my neighbours, in some sense. I liked to imagine that they were my friends. I even developed a crush on a girl. Brooke wore a bright-pink beret. She said one day during a presentation that her hobbies were shopping and boys, which piqued my interest, because I was a boy, and I'd been smitten ever since.

But it was no use. She didn't even know that I existed.

Sometimes I wondered if anyone did anymore. Being invisible had been a refreshing change of pace at first, but as time wore on, the isolation wore me down completely. We stayed home most days, with no church and no school. My best friends might have been actors for all I knew.

So I was delighted when the Gazettes came to live with us while they hid from child protective services.

The twins had been at each other's throats during a road trip, Mrs. Gazette explained, and they had directly defied her demands to quit horsing around. Somehow, her son stabbed his double with a multi-tool, and that was the last straw. So she did what any good, Christian mother would do: she flicked on her hazards, pulled the car over onto the shoulder, and spanked them right there on the side of the freeway.

Some busybody saw her. The passerby took down the vehicle's licence and reported Mrs. Gazette to the proper authorities. The family returned home to a message from a social worker asking to come by the house for a wellness check. The Gazettes were convinced that the liberal, Canadian government was eager to persecute them for living Biblically, so they fled, and for roughly six months they lay low at our house, with their car hidden in the garage.

Mrs. Gazette believed the devil had orchestrated the fiasco on the freeway, and she was hardly the only Prayer Warrior being tormented. One night at care cell, the enemy attacked Tilda Eubanks.

The unmarried woman had once been a witch. Since reformed, she remained vulnerable due to her sinful, occult past. Apparently, Tilda Eubanks had once pledged her life to Satan, performing rituals, casting curses, and burying sacred objects in the woods behind her home to consecrate the land for wicked purposes.

But then she got Saved and renounced all that. Now, she was a sanctified Prayer Warrior who danced, waved flags, and made strange whooping sounds during prayer. So when she suddenly went silent and still in the middle of our living room one Saturday night, the group assumed a demon, lying dormant, had awakened to possess her. Soon, the deliverance of Tilda Eubanks was the only show in the house.

The battle dragged on for hours, long after midnight, with the revivalists encircling the erstwhile witch and laying hands, in shifts. Sometimes it seemed as though they were winning, and the woman would stand upright, breathing softly through her mouth. Sometimes, when it seemed as if they were losing, like when my mother took a break, Tilda Eubanks would hunch and huff and grunt.

Then it happened: all of a sudden, the woman let out a hideous, high-pitched squeal, like a teakettle at full boil, as though she had exhaled the evil spirit like a lungful of smoke, and she collapsed so heavily that the family cat fled to high ground. The animal leapt from its bed of fake grass in the antique mahogany cradle at the base of the stairs, sprinting up and away to its hiding place under my bed.

I was horrified.

When I replayed this moment in my head, the cat was recast as the migraine baboon from Mrs. Gazette's night in Marysville, and every night for weeks, I had bad dreams. In my recurring nightmares, I was chased by a witch in my backyard. I would wake up outside, turn around and she'd be there, staring through murderous eyes, inescapable, three times my size. Some nights I could run, but I couldn't get back in the house. The witch had done something. Other times, my legs were made of sand, and she would stand above my body, shouting incantations, doing spells to me.

One night, I dreamt that I almost got back inside safely. That was the night that I first saw the Scary Man. I located myself at the front door, on the wrong side, locked out after everyone else was asleep. Terrified, as usual, I crept around the house to the garage. It was open, and I made it past the van to the top of the landing by the button that brought down the door. Still no sign of the night witch. I looked back to be sure she wasn't after me.

The Scary Man was sprinting up the driveway. He wanted to come inside, and he was moving so quickly, his body was behind him, somehow, and his legs were—where?—beside me, all together now. He was wearing a black ski mask, black turtleneck, and black gloves, and he reached for me, both hands outstretched. I stared into his eyeholes to plead with the man underneath, beholding not eyes, but the absence of eyes, and that's when I woke up, mid-gasp.

The Scary Man lived in the house after that. One night, I felt him beside me. Another night, I saw him in the hallway, on the ceiling. I woke up once to see him sprint into my bedroom, in pieces again, and before I could make any sense of him spatially, he turned into bats and flew into my mouth, and I woke up, for real, with strep throat. I told my mother how I got it—the Scary Man came back—and she asked me how often I saw him and said that he might be a demon.

The next time you see him, she said, you rebuke him. Don't be afraid. If you call on the name of the Lord, he'll protect you. The most powerful Man of God ever, Smith Wigglesworth, once woke up to find the devil sitting on his bed, Satan himself, just to scare him. Do you know what he said? Oh, it's just you. And he rolled over and went back to sleep. So if you see a demon, just remind him that your God is bigger.

I didn't want to have to rebuke any demons. But only a week or so later, I woke up in the hallway and saw him coming up the stairs. The Scary Man was hopping, but he didn't make a sound. And then he lunged at me, still silently. I threw up both my hands and screamed: I rebuke you in Jesus's name!

It worked. He yelped and ran past me, right into the Big Room at the end of the hall, where we kept the Nintendo, and he dove behind the sectional, unnaturally fluid. I wouldn't see the Scary Man again for many years.

But warding off this one evil spirit did not make me feel any safer, and neither did waking up. I'd already seen an angel, and I shuddered at what else could appear to me in the dark, now that I knew about what else was out there. By then, I was bound to a reality in which anything, literally any object, could be a vehicle for demons. The whole house was haunted; there were stimuli everywhere. And everything threatened to come to life, suddenly, menacing me out of nowhere.

I learned how to move through the hallway without opening my eyes for any reason. I memorized the number of steps to the bathroom. I knew that the creak meant that I was too close to the stairs. I couldn't see clearly without my glasses anyway. Why even risk seeing anything? So every night, I took them off like taking out my eyes, and I stayed that way until the sun came up.

The enemy was after me, and as these dreams persisted, so did my sense that each one was the work of the devil. There were demons camped outside of my old school. There were demons in my home. There were demons in pursuit, all day and all night. Was it me they were actually after? Or perhaps I was afflicted already. Nightmares were often the work of soul ties, after all, and I was the child of an African woman, a pagan from a pagan place where the enemy could attach itself to anything.

I didn't want to see a demon. I didn't want to know what the enemy looked like. If I saw an evil spirit, I would imagine the enemy everywhere, and that was the same thing as seeing the enemy everywhere.

• • •

The demon waited until I was unprotected, for the enemy has no shame whatsoever. It attacked me, an eight-year-old child, while my mother was gone for the weekend to grow in her gifts.

She was summoned to a Bible boot camp in Alaska—a free event for the Prayer Warriors. Mrs. Gazette was invited to the free conference too, but she couldn't afford the flight out, so she watched over all of the boys in the meantime.

The night my mother was due to return, I came down with a terrible headache. Feeling light-headed, I lay on the couch and waited for the pain to subside. For a short while, Mrs. Gazette simply monitored me, asking if I was still in pain. But then she began to pray and told me to lift my hands to heaven. There was an urgency to her voice, so I did as I was told.

I closed my eyes.

When I awoke sometime later, my mother was there, along with Tilda Eubanks, Mrs. Gazette, and Luke and Light. They were looking at me like I'd just come out of surgery.

All hell had broken loose while I was sleeping. The twins had seen a demon on the back of the sectional. The group agreed: my headache was the devil; Prayer Warriors assemble. When my mother called to say that she'd landed, Mrs. Gazette told her they were locked in a battle to free me from some kind of soul tie. So my mother rushed back to join the fight and, freshly edified from the free conference, roundly boxed that little demon's ears and cast him out.

The Prayer Warriors were relieved, but my heart sank. *I* had a demon? Where did I get it? From my biological mother? From hers?

I asked the room: What did I do?

Maybe nothing, my mother explained. But we don't know what's in your history. There's a lot of devil worship and child sacrifice in Ghana, and that's where your birth mother comes from, and if her family was still living there in the seventies, then they're the ones that sold the slaves. That kind of wickedness echoes across generations.

It's not a coincidence that Ghana sounds just like Gehenna, said Mrs. Gazette. That's another word for hell the Bible uses.

You could have shamans, cannibals, or witch doctors *in your DNA*, my mother told me. Just about anything could try to lay claim to you. But you're a child of God now, so the enemy no longer has the right.

I understood in that moment that the soul ties to my past, the invisible cords that stretched from my new home to Africa, were the root of all evil, and these were my roots. Here was the reason behind my bad attitude. This was the source of my struggle to fit in. I was a child of God and godlessness, all at once. But no man can serve two masters, I reminded myself, just as no child can have two mothers. The problem was within me, and it would linger there until I found a way to disconnect.

That night I had a new nightmare, vivid enough to be confused for waking life. A crowd of black-hooded villains encircled my bed, faceless and formless, closer every time I blinked my eyes. I startled awake and they were gone, but it was as though these figures had taken all love away with them. In the darkness, I experienced a solitude so awful that I wondered if my family had been raptured. My heart ached for someone to recognize me.

The Rapture hadn't happened, though. I raced downstairs, fearful of everything, sick, and my mother was sitting alone at the table watching *The Tonight Show* and reading the *Vancouver Sun*.

Sobbing, I told her all about the hooded figures.

She said they were demons. Perhaps the soul tie had only been frayed, but not severed, and whatever soul ties I may have imported like a vector-borne disease were doing their best to reclaim the standing they held previously. They were trying to get back in. She leapt into action, retrieving the vial of olive oil from the kitchen cupboard. I followed behind as she made her way from room to room, anointing every foreign artifact in the house: The Fijian elephant statues. The Oriental tapestry. Me.

Then she took me into her lap and began to pray, and there, swaying softly on the kitchen floor, my mother waged warfare against the spirits attempting to claim me as their own.

He's not yours, she said to the enemy. He's mine, he's mine, he's mine. And I gave in to her completely, swaddled in the arms of a powerful Prayer Warrior that I was blessed to call mine in return. I gave her my full weight and out of the blue came a vision.

I was on a wooden raft, drifting apart from some grim coast, as a group of monstrous, hateful savages shouted and cursed, shaking spears. They summoned me back, but they hated me. They wanted me dead or enslaved, maybe eaten. They threw sticks and stones at my vessel. But every object tossed fell short and sank into the ocean. Nothing could reach the boy as he floated away, and as the grim coast faded into the horizon, becoming a line in the sand, and wave after wave of warm water washed over me, swaying me softly out to sea, there was peace in my heart.

And I thought: Good riddance to *that* nonsense.

3

GATEWAY

(or The Boy Whose Crown Was Worthless)

I had to be my brother's slave. It was just for the day.

We were playing together outside, Ben and I, in the sweltering heat. He was twelve. I was nine. It was probably August, just after my birthday. We'd been out there for hours, jumping on the trampoline—the rubber, rectangular kind. The circular, mesh ones were safer, the experts insisted, but that made them less fun, we felt.

First, we played Crack the Egg. You curl into a ball and try to stay that way while someone jumps around you. Ben could not be cracked, but he could bounce me from the middle to the springs. I had to lose the game to keep from getting hurt. Then we played Do As I Do, and did difficult flips. When the heat became oppressive, we brought out the hose, and we sprayed one another, and used it to fill up the trampoline, letting it bulge until it touched the grass, and made a pool. We were muddy and sweaty and soaked, and the front lawn was flooded.

I had to use the bathroom, but I didn't want to go inside the house.

It was hotter in there, somehow. You got sticky right away, and there was no path to the toilet but to cross my mother's vision in the kitchen, and that would be the coldest moment of my day. She was barely there that summer.

Just poop in the bushes, Ben said.

So I crouched down and did, and we laughed. Then he pounced on his leverage.

I'm gonna tell Mom you did that, he said.

Please don't, I responded, still squatting. I'm begging you, Ben. Don't tell Mom.

I *won't* tell Mom, my brother told me, smirking, *if* you be my slave.

Ben was inspired by a Jughead adventure. When the Gazettes moved out, just after Christmas, they left a stack of Christian *Archie* comics, with some normal ones mixed in, all from the forties and fifties. In *Sleepy Time Pal*, starring Jughead, Reggie sees a hypnotist on TV and learns how to hypnotize Archie's best friend. Jughead is tricked into being his slave.

Slavery didn't seem so bad. Jughead gets a burger in the end, the same as always. And at school, in my bedroom upstairs, I learned that many slaves were treated very well by many masters. Who would treat me kinder than Ben, my best friend? We were growing up together, two adopted sons, one white, one Black, like *The Fox and the Hound*, with secret games and handshakes, secret worlds—a secret language for ourselves. On long road trips, we would play Fogarty Fogarty Fee, an improvisational game we made up, a limitless rock/paper/scissors where you could be anything you could imagine, versus whatever your brother decided to be, and evolve, as necessary, to gain the upper hand with each attack.

The only thing you couldn't be was God. He broke the game.

Once I began as a barrel of monkeys. Over time, I became an intergalactic alliance, and Ben was defeated in space, which was common, since every game ended the same way: backed into a corner by a clever transformation, you shrivelled up into infinity, and your brother found a way to be infinity plus one, and you were finished.

Better slavery than a spanking, I said.

We shook on it, and right away, he kicked his flip-flops off, and they went flying from the yard into the street.

Retrieve my footwear, slave, he said.

So, I went out to get his shoes, and then he made me put them right back on his feet before he kicked them off again, and when I brought them back, I found him on the trampoline.

Slaves stand in the mud, he said. Stay there, and sing a song about how great I am.

I did as I was told. Ben is great, I sang, he's oh-so great, and I'm a silly boy. I wish that I was half as great as Ben.

He said: Again! But louder this time. And hop on one foot, in a circle.

Things could be worse, I had thought. But they got worse. Later, when we came inside for lunch, he double-crossed me.

Remember, Ben announced in a loud voice beside the fridge, you're still my slave.

And this caught my mother's attention. Closing her Bible, she stood up from the table to interrogate us further. What do you mean, Ben?

My brother insisted he couldn't disclose what had happened outside. It's a secret, he said. But my mother would not let it go. She threatened to ban us from Super Nintendo, and that's what we planned to play next.

He confessed.

My mother was aghast.

That is completely inappropriate and downright revolting, she said. You don't do that, you're not a bushman, and I was punished. The punishment handed down by my mother was that I had to honour the shameful agreement and serve as my big brother's slave for the rest of the day.

I was crushed.

I had not considered that my mother might reward my brother's betrayal, or institutionalize his supremacy over me. It was unthinkable, and the optics were brutal. A Black son enslaved by his white family members? It sounded so grim out of context. But I knew that my mother was colour blind, and in this moment, she seemed to engage with even less of me than that, like she was exhausted from being my mother.

That summer, my mother was especially short. She had committed to a season of fasting and prayer ahead of the Morris Cerullo Miracle Crusade, where she would sit as a Prayer Warrior delegate. The Prophet Mary Greenland, who gave her the gig, said she often prepared for these events with a forty-day fast in the manner of Jesus, Elijah, and Moses, the big three of the Bible.

But my mother set a more modest goal. For thirty days, she lived on broth and water.

The ordeal was building her up spiritually, no doubt, but she was suffering physically. It showed on her face and the veins that emerged as her skin became wan and translucent. She wore the weary countenance of a marathoner, minus the mileage. Mostly, she sat at the kitchen table with her eyes half-closed, reading the word, meditating on God, or half-open, watching soaps and CBN and Sally Jessy Raphael.

Maybe when I'm finished, she would tell us, I'll fit into the swimsuits that I used to wear in Fiji.

It didn't seem worth it to me. It's not like we went to the beach, or the pool, or anywhere swimsuits were sported. Ben and I had a term for my mother's refusal to let us do anything: the Fun Limiter. It was in full effect that summer. My mother wasn't up for much, so everyone was grounded.

I wanted to feed her. I wanted my father to come home from flying and beg her to eat, or anyone else to come over and see her, just wasting away, skin and bones. But she was starved for community, too, set apart from the parents at school and the people at church, without friends. She was torturing herself, and someone had to intervene, but what could we do? We were nobody. We were silly little boys who pooped outside and wrecked the yard, and she was the boss.

Of course, she continued to feed us, McDonald's and Burger King mostly, but some nights she got a bit weird, and she'd cook some extravagant thing, out of nowhere and way out of character. For my birthday, she pulled out an old family recipe: Sticky Brown Sugar Fried Chicken, the yellowing index card read, and it took her all day, and it tasted like nothing I've ever had since, and she watched us all eat it, just smiling, deliriously happy.

That was my birthday, though. My special day. But now I had debased myself. She barely had the strength to stand for long enough to handle it.

So she washed her hands of me.

That was the worst part: the choice to look past me—to keep things the way that they would be without her. While pooping, I'd thought I could run to her later, if Ben turned out to be a real tyrant. But now I knew better, and so did my brother. His power over me was terrifying. I followed him upstairs, as he commanded, with my head hung low, and made a little trampoline of tears inside my glasses.

Fortunately, Ben knew as little about being a slaver as I did about being a slave. He bossed me around here and there—get me a Coke, do a jig, be my footstool—but mostly we played Super Nintendo in the Big Room, in front of the fan. It was too hot for much else. But Ben did not forget his role as master. When I was winning, he would order me to lose, or he'd give me a command that could not wait, and win while I was underfoot, or dancing, or downstairs. It was underhanded, but if I resisted or complained, he threatened to tell our mother, and who could say what happened after that.

So I obeyed him. I did not like being a slave, and I was glad for the day to be over, for I knew that I would be free in the next one.

At bedtime, my mother warned me against telling anyone what happened, and then I was never quite free. I was bound to keep quiet. People will blow it all out of proportion, she said. Remember what the Gazettes went through? The enemy is dead set on destroying Christian households, so don't go running your mouth around town.

The move to suppress made me reassess what had really happened. Replaying the day in the dark, I discovered the great shame between us, like a poop in the bushes. The stink of it would follow us forever, if I ever spoke about it, and my family would be judged, when it was my fault.

I was lucky to be homeschooled. The VCS parents would lose their whole minds if they heard about this. They would launch a new probe, and they'd blame my poor mother, alleging abuse where there was none, convinced that my race was the reason for my subjugation—not something I did, only something I was. Typical American, the parents would scoff, she couldn't go a decade without making her Black son play slave boy, how horrid. They'd call it unforgivable, and skin her for a minor blip in judgment. They might try to have me removed from the house.

But my mother was good. She was fasting, for Christ's sake, and she wasn't herself when she made me a slave, she was starving. The colour was gone from her eyes, two donuts now, glazed but not sweet, filled with nothing but deep disregard. She was normally better than that—you should taste what she made for my birthday— and I shouldn't have put her in such a position at such a bad time in her thirty-day fast.

That's how I think of it now, if I only think once, and who wants to think twice about being a slave? I'd rather not recall the hottest day of August 1994. Yet some things are hard to forget, and forgetting too hard leaves a scar in the psyche that tells the whole story.

• • •

The houses on Glenn Mountain were all built in the 1980s, a development spiralling upward as the decade wore on, and they grew statelier and more preposterous the higher you climbed. We lived halfway up the hill in a home that seemed fancy, at first: a neoclassical four-bedroom residence inspired by the White House, right down to its tetrastyle portico. But it was folksy by the time you reached the mountain top. The houses near the summit were sprawling compounds, custom-built by celebrity architects, structures embedded in cliffsides, half-hidden, built to spill, defying gravity. Some of them had helipads. Some were just strange. One was an ode to the Tasmanian Devil; the Looney Tunes character's face was all over. There were statues of Taz in the fountain out front, and etchings in the river rock facade.

Other homes were tucked behind patches of forest surviving the upward expansion. They were practically houses of parliament, camouflaged by cedar-shingle siding, so you wouldn't even know that they were there unless you did. They were mostly inaccessible—the road ended before you could reach them—and inexplicable up close, defying what I knew about geometry. This one's the shape of a biplane, I guess? This one's a dodecahedron. But where is the garage? Where are the doors? And why would you live in a home that repels visitors? Some mornings, just after sunrise, I would make the hike and stand a ways off from the upper estates, imagining how to get in.

It was good to get out of the house bright and early. Mornings at home could be stressful. First to rise, always, I crept through the house, stepping over the creakiest floorboards, tiptoeing downstairs. I tried to stay quiet, to go undetected, but I was too restless, too prone to disturbance. Even in what I believed to be perfect silence, it seemed as if I emitted ultrasonic squeals, like a tomato plant in distress, and I would learn of my loudness when my furious mother emerged from the darkness like a ghost, bleary-eyed and lemon-faced, to confiscate my noisy toys and burst my balloons with her hands.

Shut. Up. She would shout this in a whisper, if she said anything at all before rampaging back to bed.

God, how I hated to wake her. Better to wander the mountain in search of adventure.

Bored half to death, left to learn at my own pace, I sprinted through the American fourth grade to a summer vacation that felt endless as soon it started. The care cell was on hiatus until the fall—the revivalists were cottaging—and so was life at home, because my father was their pilot and my mother had no energy. We went nowhere and no one came by. It was a treat to speak to anyone at all.

From my bedroom window, I could see all the way west across the Fraser Valley to the field of skyscrapers in the distance, and upstairs I felt like a rich kid. But it was the land that was rich, and we were poor caretakers. When my father was home, he would trim the trees and the bushes, and the light would return to the overgrown property. But while he was flying in the weeks between, the maples crowded the sky like a heavenly army, and the front hedges grew too high to see across, and jagged. They filled up with bees, and the fence became electric, and out in the yard with my brothers, I felt like a prisoner.

There were four of us: Ben and I, adopted separately, three years apart, when my parents believed they could never conceive, and Mike and Tom, the miracles, another three and six years after that. But my mother strained to treat us as identical, performing equality everywhere. Ben and I were not eligible for dual citizenship, so she did not pursue American passports for her biological children. Ben and I could not be breastfed, naturally, so nobody was breastfed. Mike and Tom were given formula, on principle. My mother bought four of everything, and every night before bed she laid out four cereal bowls, with four Flintstones chewable tablets resting on four spoons inside. For a spell, we fought over Bamm-Bamm and Dino, but over time I learned to take a Wilma for the team. And when an outfit came in four sizes, or better, four colours, she dressed us as four of a kind.

We were two pairs, of course. Ben was my analogue. Mike and Tom were something else. We recognized this from the patience they were given, which was immeasurable, and the way that my mother seemed to protect them, fiercely, from us. She rose up at once at the first sign of trouble. She never seemed too far away to be still on their side. They were hers in a way we were not. They were stars, and she orbited them. We were satellite children, I thought to myself, for these observations hung between Ben and me, noticed but never acknowledged aloud, and we certainly never talked about being adopted.

What was there to talk about? At home, we had everything: videotapes and video games, two hampers of stuffed animals right under my bed, a big box of guns—dart guns, water guns, spud guns, cap guns, Nerf guns—and four televisions. Ben and I had it too good to complain, that's what our mother would say, and there was nothing to be gained from a shared otherness but the sense that she loved us a little bit less.

Besides, she was always denying it.

Our stories were totally different, too. Ben was conceived in a church closet—Dutch Reformed, at a youth group lock-in, my mother explained. Co-ed sleepovers are a recipe for disaster. The families were deeply embarrassed by the out-of-wedlock pregnancy. They wanted nothing to do with your brother, and they're Dutch, so there's no changing *their* minds. He doesn't exist to them. But *your* birth mother called the agency to ask about you a few years ago. It would probably make Ben feel just awful to know that, so don't go bragging about it. If I were you, I wouldn't bring it up.

No other information was provided. I didn't inquire. To show respect for Ben, who could be very sensitive and would be hurt by the truth, I stood with him in secret solidarity, and stayed away from what we had in common.

There was too much at stake for me anyhow. I wasn't alone in the infinite summer. My big brother was with me; I loved him for that. Ben was my closest companion, my moon, my plus one.

But he was still my big brother. He had all the power. If anything made him feel small, he would make me feel smaller. He lashed out. He hit me. He split my head open by slamming a door in my face once; he gave me this scar. As much as I loved him, I knew not to trust him completely, not after that day in the bushes. You had to watch out for Ben, and I wanted someone to watch out for me.

I needed a friend.

• • •

That fall, my parents installed a new landline for Prayer Warrior business, and it was the hotline that rang with glad tidings of great joy: revival was calling at last. The church we had held out for was ready. All this time, the Lord had been preparing a place for us, and it was not unreasonable to assume that this radical new fellowship of charismatic Christians would ignite the Great Awakening that went before the End Times and established the Kingdom of God here on Earth.

It sounded like a heck of a church.

The perfect Man of God was on his way from San Diego: Pastor Don Crock had recently resigned from the Morris Cerullo World Evangelism organization.

My mother and I had just attended the Morris Cerullo Crusade—his double blessing was still in the glovebox—and it was exciting to know that the Man of God chosen to lead us was trained at his ministry school.

But even beyond that, a new church meant new friends, and maybe a Black friend for me, though I'd settle for anyone.

The revival was bound for Aberdeen Elementary, an historic school in the rural community of Bradner, a one-road town that would eventually amalgamate with Abbotsford, becoming its lower west side. The founders must have known about the boundary's expansion: the church was christened Westside Pentecostal.

On Sunday, we boarded the red minivan, a Ford Aerostar, taking the freeway out west. We took the last Abbotsford exit, then followed the small Fraser Highway, still westbound, for ages.

I had to imagine that downtown Vancouver was coming up quick. But civilization retreated instead. We seemed to be moving through ungoverned territory. The people who lived in Bradner were stuck in the past, and the Aerostar began to feel a little like a time machine. Climbing the last big hill, we joined a long line of vehicles held up by a horse and buggy, taking its sweet time. We followed the old Anabaptist the rest of the way.

The rider went right, down Bradner Road, then off-road, into a field of daffodils. The rest of us went left, in search of parking.

The front lot at the school was already full, so they sent us around to the abandoned cadet armoury. Just as well. It gave us boys the perfect chance to size up the pea gravel playground out back: there were two separate swing sets and a big metal slide, and the jungle gym—a mountainous dome made of rusted-out steel—was so clearly outdated and dangerous that we knew at a glance it was one of the good ones.

There was a line to get into the gymnasium. Idling in the entry-way, I imagined that I was a student, returning to Aberdeen after the summer. Before me, a bulletin board wore a dollar-store banner: WELCOME BACK! It was surrounded by construction paper hearts. But there was little else to work with. Nobody Black had attended here, twenty-odd years of class photos made that perfectly clear, and the double doors behind me, which opened to the rest of the building, were wrapped in heavy-duty chain, and padlocked.

The usher, a truly enormous man, called himself Pastor Mark. He held the door open for us.

A joyful noise poured out from the gym like there was a parade trapped inside, and as the usher directed us into the sanctuary, I remembered that a parade trapped inside is called a circus—this place was a circus. There were people waving flags and dancing with ribbons, and a dozen tambourines going all at once. There were leapers and kneelers, fainters, clappers and criers for no reason, and some people were sliding around in their socks.

Scanning the crowd, I saw children all over. Westside had some huge families—one seemed to number around forty, a colony with upward of twenty children, hair cut and combed the same way, and clothing that seemed to have come from a massive shared closet. To me, they looked a lot like Ben. There were none who looked like me, same as it ever was, though I told myself that I was not the only, but the first.

There was little time for disappointment anyhow amid such festivity. The tambourines set a delirious tempo and the praise band could hardly keep pace. The music became ramshackle, and the collective energy built to a manic high, and then a chorus came, and the outpouring of the Holy Spirit began.

Westside Pentecostal went wild.

The Great Revival was underway—in this asylum of ecstatic belief it was a fact, and the believers revelled in their rightness most of all. It was a similar feeling, I imagined, to having died and gone to heaven: the feeling of waking up, one fine day, up where we belong, of freedom not only from sin but from the lingering sense of displacement they say is a symptom. The feeling of homecoming. In lieu of other Black people, I was willing to settle for this particular ecstasy, since it was going around, but I was not sure that I felt it, which meant that I didn't.

An old woman rose to deliver a word from the Lord in her prayer language. She trembled as she spoke, as though surprised to be so fluent, and when she finished, she let out a weary sigh. And then she waited. A middle-aged man seated halfway across the room stood up to say the same thing, but in English.

Thus saith the Lord: There's gonna be a revival.

They sat down at the same time, and my mother leaned over, explaining that the man was the old woman's son, and the only one able to translate her prophecies. This was his spiritual gift.

It was a truly advantageous superpower, in my opinion, having never known that anyone could have it. I wanted to handle my mother's translations.

All children eleven and under were sent off to Sunday school. Forty kids or more marched out, through different double doors, to a multi-purpose room—a diorama, staged exactly like the service that dismissed us. The woman at the whiteboard introduced herself as Officer Frost, then remembered where she was and changed her name, for us, to Mrs. Frost.

Officer Frost was a pale, masculine woman, shaped like an egg and dressed in a white skirt and an off-white top, like an egg. She worked as an evangelist at Matsqui Institution, the prison just down the road, as well as a guard there, and now she had a third job as our Sunday school teacher.

God had called Officer Frost to prison ministry for His divine purpose, which was saving the lost. It broke His heart when someone died without knowing Him and their soul went to hell, said Officer Frost. That is why He gave us the great commission, commanding us to go out into the world and harvest lost souls, as many as we can, to save them from themselves and from the isolation, misery, and torment waiting for them if they don't repent of sin. Because it's not that hell is hot, it's that you're totally alone. You think you've felt alone before? Just wait until God turns his back on you at the Day of Atonement and forgets that you ever existed.

I did not realize that God could forget I exist and I was frightened, so I asked a cheeky question: How can hell be lonely when there are demons everywhere?

Officer Frost said: Because you can see your family, but they can't see you.

I had not known about this part of hell. I shuddered to think, and I shuddered again as she read us the relevant passage from Luke, chapter 16, the parable of the rich man and Lazarus.

Both men die. The rich man goes to Hades. Lazarus, a beggar who lay hungry at the rich man's feet, is sent to heaven (Jesus calls it Abraham's Bosom). But the rich man can see Lazarus from Hades and he's thirsty. He begs Father Abraham to send the beggar down to him with water. The request is denied. So the rich man begs Father Abraham to send Lazarus to visit his living brothers, to beg them to repent, or else they'll wind up in this suffocating, loveless prison too. But Father Abraham responds that they have already been warned by Moses and the prophets.

Officer Frost was one such prophet. In 1981, when she first read this passage, she knew that the parable was a call to preach the gospel in prisons. At that time, the Matsqui Institution behind her house was transitioning from a drug treatment facility to a medium-security federal prison with 446 inmates at capacity, so she applied for a job. And when she explained to the warden that she was a born-again Christian, called by God to prison ministry, she got the job, for the warden was a born-again Christian as well.

Over the next decade, Officer Frost personally led over two hundred felons to the Lord. But she was not looking for a reward. Her reward was in heaven, for the Bible says: On the day of the Rapture the righteous will be given crowns to cast at the feet of Jesus, crowns with a jewel for each soul Saved. Some people would have plain ones, like the worthless, paper crowns that come in Christmas crackers. Others, like our Sunday school teacher, would have crowns bejewelled by God himself, reflecting His light like stained glass.

I had not known about this either, and I could think of nothing more humiliating than to be marked for eternity as the boy who arrived at the gates of St. Peter with nothing to show for himself but himself. So I was glad when someone asked Officer Frost to explain how she Saved all those souls.

The first thing I do is take their shoes for their own safety, she said with a laugh, and the second thing I do is to tell them that Jesus Christ loves them. I say: The only true freedom you will ever find is in the Lord. He'll set you free of everything that's been holding you back, and he'll deliver you from your past. He'll show you a love that you've never been shown, and he'll take all your struggles away.

Then Officer Frost would invite the inmates to recite the Sinner's Prayer. Just five consecutive sentences later, their souls would be Saved for eternity.

I asked: Do they get to go then?

And the Sunday school teacher responded: Excuse me?

Do they get to go free after they're Saved?

And she said: Of course not. They're in prison for a reason.

But at least they'll be free after death, I told myself, so it was good that these people were imprisoned with someone like Officer Frost.

Then Officer Frost turned our questions around, asking: How many souls have *you* Saved? Come to the front. Say your name, favourite colour, and how many people you led to the Lord.

This was the most frightening moment so far, for I hadn't Saved anybody—I'd hardly *seen* anybody—and I did not wish to confess this to the class.

Unfortunately, others were more eager. The colony kids responded at once, all at once, and suddenly half of the class was in line at the whiteboard, single file by size. The score of Van Asseldonk children were mostly named James, we would learn, and somehow they all were accomplished evangelists: twenty souls Saved, thirty souls Saved, truly unreal numbers.

They might have been lying. But the Van Asseldonks were a formidable confederacy, upholding one another's claims, so the rest of us had no choice but to assume their reality.

I regretted that I hadn't come with twenty other Harrys. I wished that Ben were with me—he was sitting on zero souls, just like me, as far as I knew—but he was twelve, too old for Sunday school. Dizzied with dread, by myself, I sunk down in my chair as the classroom lost all hue and saturation.

As the crowd began to thin, I saw a second holdout, just across the aisle, another boy who wasn't white. His skin was light brown, and his hair was pitch-black. His shoulders were slumped and his head hung so low that you could see the part in his bowl cut.

This child, I heard somebody whisper, was Native.

I mostly knew Natives from TV, where they were the natural enemy of cowboys. They came in waves, like generations, and they were a force to be reckoned with. In real life, however, you never encountered more than one at a time, and it always seemed like something terrible had happened to them.

Well I was here to make friends, and I did not want to be associated with this morose, little boy any more than I already would be, or worse, to be lined up behind him. So I stood up before him. When my turn came, however, the boy was still glued to his seat, and I was the end of the line. I had not considered that one or even two could skip the queue, and now it was too late to turn around. I served myself up to be publicly shamed, and the only way forward was through.

My name is Harry. My favourite colour used to be pink, but now it's gold, like my glasses, and I have never Saved a single soul, I said, ashamed, and left my body, and I joined the others, judging, shaming, staring at the boy whose crown was worthless.

I blamed the other brown boy at first. He was supposed to follow me, bearing the brunt of the judgment when I shrugged it off.

Instead, we were judged separately, humiliated separately. I was in last place and the Native boy was off the board completely.

During singalong, I saw that he was opting out of everything. I saw, as well, that no one seemed to care, and I began to feel responsible for helping him assimilate. If he needed a friend, so did I. We could help one another. I made a plan to speak to him at craft time.

But I didn't make it to craft time. I spoke out of turn and they sent me away.

Officer Frost was discussing the Tower of Babel from Genesis chapter II. After the flood, there was only one language. Mankind became one nation under God, and not for long, if the humans could help it: they were building a tower to heaven. But the Lord didn't go for that. He threw a wrench into the works by confounding their languages, halting construction, and the builders abandoned the project to form separate nations.

Why would God do that? I asked, interrupting the teacher. It's mean.

Before I could add that you can't get to heaven that way, or my father, the pilot, would stop there for fuel, I was banished to the foyer, a trapezoid enclosed by doors, and scolded by the helper who went with me. Mrs. Van Asseldonk explained that it was not cruel of God to erase humanity's common language, and it was blasphemous to say otherwise.

So I apologized.

Don't apologize to me, she said, apologize to God.

So I apologized to God.

The lesson of the Tower of Babel is that people should focus on God's plan for our lives, not each other, Mrs. Van Asseldonk said, and you should spend some time reflecting on that.

Then she took me by the hand, beyond the bathrooms, to the tantalizing door opposite the sanctuary, which led to the rest of the school. This one was padlocked as well. She headed next for the gymnasium, but that's where my mother was, so I went boneless. Mrs. Van Asseldonk wasn't taking me outside or into a bathroom, so I did not resist when she tried the only other door: a storage room between the toilets, with extra toilet paper and two columns of stackable chairs—one yellow, one blue. She couldn't find the light switch, so she propped the door wide open with a wedge of wood above the upper bracket, and she left me standing there. As soon as she was gone, I scaled a stack and from my seat on high, I pulled the stopper out and let the door slam.

For forty-five minutes, I sat in the dark, singing songs to myself. When the foyer got noisy, I followed the other kids back to the gym, still determined to befriend the boy from earlier.

But I walked into a spiderweb of fingers.

Aren't you adorable, said a woman with a handful of my hair. I wish I had these curls. I have to pay for mine.

Help yourself, I said, half-joking. People never asked permission but I didn't mind a touch from time to time, so I shrugged and let the scalp massage continue.

A second woman joined us, and she bought my compliance with butterscotch candy—a Werther's Original. I thanked her, untwisting the wrapper, and that's when she snatched at my hair. It's so spongy, she said, and she asked if I'd ever heard of Buckwheat from Our Gang.

Although the Little Rascals movie was in theatres that summer, I'd known about the character before, which impressed her.

You've seen it? That's precious, she said. Who's your mother?

I pointed her out.

Why, that's wonderful, both of the women agreed, and they rested their palms on my head and began speaking over me.

Did you know that Aberdeen Elementary is over one hundred years old? It opened in 1890, after the gold rush, when there were more whites than Natives all of a sudden, so we needed a school up here. The Natives went to St. Mary's Mission. They were always running off, and you would find them on the bridge and take them back. But that place closed ten years ago and now you've gotta bring them to church yourself!

None of this made sense to me. But here's what they were on about:

St. Mary's was the residential school across the Fraser, and the reason that the town was known as Mission. The mission was cultural genocide. In 1894, an amendment to Canada's *Indian Act* made attendance at these spaces compulsory for First Nations children. Roughly 150,000 Indigenous kids were forced to leave their families. They were transferred to the care of nuns and rectors, to be raised exclusively on Christian values, and deprived of the identities, communities, and languages that kept them from becoming good Canadians.

When the school is on the reserve, explained the country's first prime minister, the child lives with his parents, who are savages. He is surrounded by savages. He is simply a savage who can read and write.

A former rector of St. Mary's once explained that residential schools were meant to train the Indians and half-breeds to lead an industrious and Christian life. But this is only sugar-coating violence. The true purpose, according to a quote whose attribution changes constantly, for no one wants to wear it, was to kill the Indian in the child, addressing the so-called Indian Problem without getting any more blood on the hands of the settlers.

But killing is never not bloody. Residential schools were awful places, born of hatred, full of horror. There were kid-touchers everywhere. Pedophilia was all but institutionalized. Murderers too, for murder was a matter of opinion in these places. Whole generations were dumped into holes in the ground, acknowledged as mass graves a century later. Thousands perished in these hellhouses, branded as hallowed halls, and thousands upon thousands more were destroyed on the inside and sentenced to die, sometime later, from wounds left untreated.

The project was formally ended around 1950, but progress is never that swift or undeviating. St. Mary's closed in 1985, the year that I was born, and I was caught up in the aftermath: private adoptions that served the same sinister purpose. The Sixties Scoop era saw some twenty thousand Indigenous children delivered to God-fearing homes before policy changes diminished the practice, and white couples coveting children began to look elsewhere. By the eighties, the Baby Scoop era was said to be over. In fact, it was off to the races. Indigenous kids became yesterday's news, and adoptions of Black babies skyrocketed.

But I didn't know that then.

The women stopped groping me, finally, and the crowd had thinned enough for me to know the other brown boy wasn't there. I hung my head and went outside to play with Ben and Mike and Tom. That's when I spotted my target, at long last, scaling the jungle gym, all by himself. I dashed across the playground and met him at the top.

Hello, I said, I'm Harry.

He dropped into the cage without a word.

And so I did the same, and I landed in a Spider-Man pose. Miniature pebbles spilled into my socks, but the rocks in my shoes were a small price to pay. The free fall impressed him because we were children.

I'm James, he responded.

And we became friends.

James's parents were not in attendance. He came with his uncle, the Bunyanesque Pastor Mark. Westside had four ushers; each was enormous. I remember them even now as giants, ten feet tall at least, with baseball mitts for hands and pumpkins for heads. I couldn't imagine going home with one. They frightened me. But James stayed at his uncle's house on Saturdays and came to church with Pastor Mark on Sunday mornings.

The boy was not Saved, however, and he wasn't sure he wanted to be Saved.

This was exciting. No wonder I felt so attracted to him. The Spirit was shining a light on his soul. Here was my chance to put a jewel in my crown, to do something for the glory of God, and maybe even score a little glory for myself.

Then and there, I set my mind to making James a Christian.

At some point, it occurred to me that Pastor Mark was white. James was obviously not, so I reasoned that the boy must be half-Native, not full, which excited me too. I had never seen another kid who was half-anything, not even on TV, and I had some questions for him. I wondered if James ever felt like he didn't belong, if he felt like he didn't make sense. I wondered if James ever felt a suffocating pressure to disavow his heritage, to snuff out half of who he was, like being strangled unconscious, but not quite to death.

So I asked: Are you half-Native?

James said no. The question appeared to offend him.

I'm sorry, I said. Are you adopted?

The boy shook his head.

I got the sense that he was sensitive, like Ben, so I dropped the identity questions, and we didn't talk at all. We played. We scrambled all over the jungle gym pretending to be lizards until our guardians arrived to round us up. My father was with Pastor Mark. My mother was having a chat with the Werther's lady, who saw us and said: Why, aren't you two a natural pair!

• • •

James and I became inseparable on Sunday mornings. I asked if he could sit with us the week that Pastor Don arrived. My mother wasn't happy, but I promised to behave. She let it happen. So we sat down next to her, and when nobody took up the rest of the row, we slid over, to give ourselves space.

Attendance was dwindling by then. The interim Man of God, Pastor Van Asseldonk, wasn't a riveting speaker. His delivery was dry, and he went on too long. His three-week discussion on Genesis cost us a few dozen bodies, I guessed, but I had to imagine that Pastor Don's preaching would be a game-changer at Westside and bring them all back.

Everything was different for the Man of God's Canadian debut. The Crock family seized every role for themselves. The new worship leader was Pastor Don's oldest son, Jameson Crock, who was nineteen or twenty, impossibly handsome, with spiky blond hair, a gold earring, good posture, a fabulous tan, and a wonderful voice, above all. Jameson Crock played a synthesizer like Michael W. Smith, and he lent a rock star swagger to the praise band.

Mrs. Crock was taking over Sunday school, it was announced, and this was a certain improvement. Officer Frost was intense, and her patience with me was already exhausted. The woman agreed to stay on as a helper, but I was delighted to see her demoted.

Sunday school was cancelled for the day. The Man of God had brought a word for everyone that morning.

Pastor Don was enormous—a pot-bellied man. If he weren't the preacher, he'd have made a good usher. He wore an expensive suit and shiny shoes. His brown hair was frosted at the tips. He had a tan, just like his son. It was as if the Crocks had visited a tropical island on the way to Canada. But California was known for its sunshine.

The Crocks had been held up at immigration. Apparently, the customs agents thought it was unusual for a man to uproot his entire family, sell his house quickly and at a loss, and leave a well-paying ministry job in San Diego to plant a new church on the outskirts of Abbotsford.

It looked to them like he was fleeing the country.

But Pastor Don explained that it was not unusual to heed the call of God, or to obey the angels who nudged him awake, late one night, and commanded he go up to British Columbia.

I told them, gentlemen, don't worry, I'll be back, he said, and I won't be alone. I'll return with an unstoppable army of the Lord, singing glory-hosanna to God in the highest! You think your badges permit you to stand in the path of righteousness? When that day comes—and it *will* come, for it's been prophesied—you'll fall to your knees and worship the Father in heaven, who parted the Red Sea and the Jordan River, and offers you eternal life, even now, as you blaspheme his name in your disbelief! And then the one agent turned to the other and said: I haven't been to church since I was just a little boy. I've wandered away from the Lord. Now I'm living in sin with my girlfriend and our child, who was born out of wedlock. But I feel the Spirit all over this man. I believe him. I know that the Son of God died for my sins. Pastor Don, will you pray for me? And Church, I led that lost soul back to Jesus, right there in the little office at the Peace Arch border crossing, and I told him about the revival that's coming to Abbotsford, British Columbia, and he said, Pastor, I'll bring my whole family.

I looked around for a man dressed as a customs agent, but I did not see one. Still, it was an incredible testimony, and the place erupted with applause and amens.

Pastor Don switched gears. But I don't know about this name, he said. Westside . . . Westside? He leaned back and said it like a brotha from the 'hood, and people laughed, so he flashed a fake gang sign and said it again—*Westsiiii-eeeeed*—and the people laughed harder.

It was indeed a silly name for this church, especially in 1994. By then, even I knew the word was a rap word.

Pastor Don asked: Is this *that* kind of church? Because I'm looking around, and I really don't think so.

He had me in stitches, but then our eyes met and I froze.

There you are, my man, he said. I see you hiding over there. God's got big plans for you, brotha. Who brought you to the House of the Lord this morning?

He's my son! my mother shouted, proud to claim me, in that moment.

How old?

He just turned nine.

Hallelujah, Pastor Don responded, chuckling. Get 'em while they're young, that's what the word says. Train up a child in the way he should go, and when he is old, he will not depart from it.

Amen, several people responded, including myself, and I sat up straight, eager to show I was well-trained already.

Westside, Pastor Don said again, with a smirk. Forgive me, but I think it makes the wrong impression, people. This is not a hideout for thugs. This is the house of the Lord!

More amens.

Man looks at the outward appearance, Pastor Don said. But the Lord looks at the heart. God doesn't see colour! Not even gang colours. He only sees lost souls, crying out for living water in the wilderness!

Pastor Don was really cooking now.

And I'm not saying we don't need a little flavour in the House of the Lord, he said with a swagger. We have to reach out to these people. Remember: *To those outside the law I became as one outside the law. To the weak I became weak. I have become all things to all people, that by all means I might save some.* We don't just need ushers and tambourine players. We need singers and dancers and rappers, and we need a choir! If you build it, they will come, and when they come, they're not just coming to church—they're entering a *gateway to heaven*. Forget about Westside. Thus saith the Lord: I have given you a new name! Like Saul became Paul and Simon became Peter, my disciple, you shall now be known as Gateway Christian Centre!

The congregation formerly known as Westside erupted as Mrs. Crock fired up the overhead projector, revealing our new name and logo.

Right around then, I discovered a big bag of Werther's Originals in my mother's purse. I showed it to James and we opened it, over-excited, and spilled the whole bag on the floor. We laughed to ourselves and collected the ones we could reach, making two little piles, and soon we were playfully bickering over which one of us had the most butterscotch candy.

My mother pinched me and I snapped to attention, but James swiped my Werther's when I wasn't looking. I swatted his arm away, smirking, and once I was certain my mother had moved on, I reached across, casually, grabbing as much as I could. He punched my outer thigh; I slapped his wrist. The sound was a little too loud, so we giggled and sat up straight, hoping that nobody noticed.

People think God is up here, at the altar, said Pastor Don. But that's not true. That's just where I am. God is everywhere, and the Bible says his blessings descend, equally, on everyone. This means they fall from the centre. So where is the presence of God strongest? Right there, in the middle of everything.

And every eye landed on James and me, horsing around in the fullness of God's divine presence.

Mrs. Van Asseldonk was indignant. She left her seat and crossed the aisle to sit between us, silently.

Unbelievable, my mother whispered. And right in the presence of God.

James wanted nothing to do with me after that. When the heat died down, I tried to reconnect with him. I tapped his knee. He wouldn't so much as acknowledge the touch; the boy was as distant and sullen as when we first met. We didn't speak again that day. Pastor Don dismissed us and I rushed outside to find my friend, but James was in his uncle's car, and Pastor Mark was pulling out.

He was in trouble. I could tell. I blamed myself.

My mother did too. Driving home, she was livid.

I knew I shouldn't let you sit with James, she said. The Lord told me not to, but I didn't listen. Now everyone at Gateway thinks I can't even control my son. We're getting McDonald's, but don't think for a second you deserve it.

• • •

All week, I assumed that the friendship was ruined, that James wouldn't sit with me ever again, and my hope of redeeming his soul was long gone. I was back to square one, stuck at zero.

On Saturday morning, however, he called, out of nowhere, inviting himself to sleep over. Delighted, I asked for permission, but my mother invoked the Fun Limiter, complaining that she hated being made to be the bad guy. So I begged her, and I promised to be extra good on Sunday. She reluctantly agreed.

Pastor Mark dropped off his nephew sometime after lunch.

James could hardly believe our house. To him, it was a mansion. He was in awe of the Super Nintendo, the cabinet of games and the four televisions, the toys and the stuffies, and the big box of guns, and the trampoline blew him away. There was so much to do, and he wanted to do everything. We played in the yard until dark, then we came in, had dinner, and played in the Big Room until bedtime. When everyone else went to sleep, James insisted we sneak back outside, so we tiptoed downstairs, and when the trampoline got cold, we crept back to the Big Room to watch *Superbook* and play *Super Mario World*. We pulled an all-nighter and rescued the princess at dawn.

We left for church early. Upon learning that he had a team of Prayer Warriors at his disposal, Pastor Don had promoted the trio to helpers and invited them to set the tone each Sunday with an hour of pregame prayer. They met at the back of the gym, skipping small talk completely and speaking in tongues from the jump.

With time on our hands, James and I went outside, and we sat on the swings, looking back on the playdate. We were both so exhausted, our memories failed us. We couldn't quite recall how we had spent the sleepless night. Our speech was disordered. We stopped making sense. We spoke to each other, unguarded, uncensored, and suddenly James hung his head, and his shoulders turned inward. He made himself small like he meant to disappear, and he told me about Pastor Mark, what the usher had done to him time and again in the bath, and explained why he'd called me, so eager to spend the night anywhere else but his uncle's apartment.

I didn't understand him. Pastor Mark had touched his private parts, he told me, but I wondered what that meant. I had no context for the claim. I only knew that James was so ashamed he wasn't swinging, so I slowed myself, and tried to meet his gaze.

In that moment, I saw the look of a boy who needed desperately to be Saved. This was my moment. I told him: God can take that from you, James. That's His promise. It will be like it never happened. Whatever you're feeling will just float away.

He stared at me, surprised, and I imagined it was good surprise, like maybe he was pleased by my response. I wonder now if what surprised him most was my conviction that salvation could erase a molestation. I was hopeless.

James put a toe in the pebbles and drew half a circle. He told me: I want to be Saved.

We recited the Sinner's Prayer, there on the playground, as we dangled from the swings like two unnatural pears. More than once, I had imagined that a halo might appear above his head upon accepting Jesus Christ into his heart. But this was just another flight of fancy. I saw only the part in his bowl cut.

My mother was still at the back of the gym when the service began, and I wanted to brag to her, but she was in some kind of trance. I spotted my brothers sitting with my father, but there was no seat saved for me, so I sat down in front of them, and as Jameson

Crock brought down the house, I praised God like I became Saved that day too.

When the worship was through, Mrs. Crock took the offering. The pot-bellied men brought the pouches up front, and Pastor Don asked God to bless the money, with his hand on Pastor Mark.

And that's when a man that I had never seen before exploded from his seat and charged the altar. He was a white man, with stubble and staticky hair and the look of a beggar who slept in the streets, and he was ranting madly, in what sounded, to me, like an occult language. He flailed like a marionette, with his hands in the air, and he flung himself at Pastor Mark. But the four giants caught him in mid-air and put him down hard, with a body-slam. He was no match for them. They dog-piled the man and quartered him, each usher taking a limb, and they carried him out to the parking lot, kicking and screaming.

Pastor Don went after them. His son fired up the band, playing louder than ever, just pounding away on the synth. It was never quite enough to drown out the commotion outside, but we really did try. The madman kept wailing, and worship was awkward, but spirited.

My mother said the man had a demon. She sensed it the moment he came in, and was glad to be stationed at the back of the church, where she could quietly do battle with the enemy. Unsure of what kind of evil spirit it was, she had prayed against several— the spirit of malice, then jealousy, alcoholism, whatever came into her mind. Finally, she named the spirit of murder, and the man spun around, she said, staring right at her, and that's about when he jumped up, all psycho, and tried to kill the Man of God before the Great Revival.

My father had a talk with me as well. He asked if Pastor Mark had ever been alone with me, and I said no. Then he said the man who attacked the ushers was James's father, and he was angry because of what Pastor Mark did to James. Some members of the congregation knew that Pastor Mark was a kid-toucher, but he had confessed and repented already. He truly believed the compulsion was gone, or at least, he had tried to believe, and he was the most disappointed of all by his actions.

So the demon-possessed man was Pastor Mark's brother?

My father said no.

This confused me. If Pastor Mark was white, and James's father was white, then James had white families on both sides. It seemed that an essential ingredient of the child had come from nowhere. Why did he look like a Native boy, then?

I don't know. My father shrugged.

But this sort of thing can happen, my mother cut in. Genetics are complicated. Sometimes there's a bit of something in the past, and it pops up—hello!—in your kid.

Pastor Mark will not be back at Gateway, said my father. If you see him, run away and call the cops.

Will James be back?

I doubt it, said my mother.

My body demanded a nap, so I went to my room, and I tried to make sense of the morning. It seemed unfair that a demon could possess you even if your rage was justified. And none of it seemed very fair to James. But there was no arguing with what I had seen, and it was not safe to acknowledge my feelings, that's how the demons get in, so I decided not to get too upset.

I tried to forget. But the memory only transformed, and it took on new elements later. One Sunday during night church, another boy I didn't know had tried to hang himself. It was just a cry for help, my mother told me. She was there. She said they found him in the multi-purpose room, dazed and confused, with an ugly laceration from the shoelace he used as a noose.

So I pictured what she was describing and it became something I saw. But I see only James when I think of the children at Gateway, and now, as I look to that day, I remember myself looking back. I stop singing over the madness outside. I turn around. That's when it happens, when I see my friend James for the last time, led out through the foyer. The boy's in a fog, and there's a little red ring around his neck, like his halo came in late and low, and shame overwhelms me as Officer Frost goes behind him, carrying his shoes.

4

HAM

(or The Boy Responsible for the Racket Coming In)

The time had come for me to speak in tongues. The gift eluded me, however, and it seemed as if only I was having trouble. As Gateway hit its stride, I fell behind, and out of favour with the Lord and his disciples. There was no way to recover. I tried to adjust my behaviour, to make myself better to make up the distance. But nothing I did could convince God to bless me or anyone else to believe I had value.

The ushers were still taking up the collection when Mrs. Crock made an announcement. Reading from the Gateway Christian Centre weekly bulletin, a one-page pamphlet folded into thirds and crammed with clip art, the pastor's wife explained that Sunday school had been rebranded, and that Children's Church, as it would now be called, was capped at ten and under.

Very few kids were affected, and no one that morning. But my eleventh birthday was only a few weeks away. Even when the woman at the altar tried to flatter me—isn't that exciting, Harry? You'll be the first to graduate!—I couldn't help but take these changes personally.

It was not the first time, after all, that a teacher had connived to promote me right out of her class.

Mrs. Crock had no patience for me. While her demeanour was friendlier than Officer Frost, it was only a mask, and the eyes that beheld me were deeply unfriendly. The pastor's wife was strict, and her anger was swift. The slightest provocation was grounds for dismissal, and every time I spoke or made a sound, she was provoked.

Outside, Harry, she would say in a singsongy cadence, the still, small voice of her mask, and you could hear the severity seething underneath.

It happened that Sunday.

Mrs. Crock, who was beautiful, was reading to the class from *Noah's Ark* by Peter Spier. The teacher was sitting in front of the whiteboard and wearing a blue pencil skirt. From my seat, if I slouched, I could see all the way to the place where her thighs came together—a dark, inverted pyramid that might have been a shadow, but it might have been her underpants, and I was aroused by the mere possibility.

High and long,
Thick and strong,
Wide and stark,
Was the ark.

Officer Frost manned the overhead projector, displaying the detailed illustrations that made *Noah's Ark* the best American picture book of 1978.

The story is pretty grim otherwise. God takes one look at humanity and decides that they all have to die, except Noah. The lone righteous man is commanded to build an ark of gopher wood, three hundred cubits long and thirty cubits high. He listens to the Lord, and later boards the vessel with his three sons, Shem, Ham, and Japheth, and their wives, and two of every living creature. Then it rains for forty days and forty nights, and after everyone is good and gone, the sun comes out, and Noah sees a rainbow.

It is, of course, best not to dwell on the mass death in this or any Old Testament story, especially in a children's adaptation, so the illustrator made an interesting editorial choice: when Noah shuts up the ark, it's a crowd of zoo animals, not people, drawn to drown in the waters outside. They're waving and cheering for Noah, in fact, for in one sense, he saved them—not *them*, necessarily, but two of their kind, and the animals all have a healthy perspective about that.

The image that intrigued me most, however, was the one with all the bunnies. Before the flood, two bunnies go into the ark. After the flood, there are more than a dozen, and this did not add up to me at nearly eleven and homeschooled, so I interrupted Mrs. Crock to ask: Why are there so many bunnies all of a sudden?

Rabbits mate like crazy, she said, prudishly. Some animals can't help it.

Does that mean sex? I asked. Several children snickered but the pastor's wife was not amused.

Outside, Harry.

I left the classroom unescorted, and not totally clear about what I did wrong. But whatever it was, I did not want my mother to know I had done it, so I stayed away from the gym. Instead, I slipped across the foyer to wait out the service from my usual seat in the storage room, and I continued to think about the bunnies.

I should have been thinking about the Lord, which was my next thought, and it aroused in me a chilly, all-over sensation that might have been the Baptism of the Holy Spirit, but turned out to be only shame, same as always.

Lately it was only ever shame. Shame over my trouble fitting in and my bad attitude, shame over acting out, standing out, getting thrown out and often forgotten about; shame over this incident or that, this impulse, that idiosyncrasy; shame at the shame I brought on my family, at the way I dishonoured and disobeyed them, defied their sameness and collective character, and defined them as the family saddled with such a shameful, shame-filled boy; and shame, shame, double-shame over the expanding universe of inadequacies that kept me, I could only assume, from being Baptized by the Holy Spirit.

That was my greatest shame of all.

Everyone else spoke in tongues. It was easy for them. Even kids had the gift. The youngest Van Asseldonk boy, who was six, maybe seven, was blessed with a powerful prayer language that never failed to energize the congregation. Give him a microphone and he'd break out in Double Dutch, shouting like a little auctioneer. It was a real sight to behold, and one of several attractive sights lost to Gateway when the family and all of its beautiful women abandoned the church unexpectedly.

Shame about the bunnies.

To its credit, all this shame passed the time quite efficiently. This was no sinking feeling. It was a big bang. A good spasm of self-condemnation went straight to my prefrontal cortex and, for a moment, I found myself suspended in space, paused mid-level like Super Mario at suppertime. It was a state of total disorder that could burn through half an hour, easy, before I regained consciousness enough to remember where I even was: an unlit utility closet, surrounded by boxes of cheap toilet paper and cleaning equipment.

When I snapped to attention there was an emptiness, and I thought it belonged to the building. Was church over already? I dropped from my perch and ran to the sanctuary, afraid that my mother was looking for me. I hit the crash bar heavily, and exploded through the double doors.

False alarm.

Pastor Don was still speaking—it looked like he had only just begun—so I had no choice but to act like the Boy Who Entered Gracefully and on Purpose, who was not the Boy Responsible for the Racket Coming In, and was in no way related to the Boy Who Only Left for Children's Church Ten Minutes Earlier. But the grown-ups saw right through me, with eyes like bayonets that tore at the seams of my disguise, so I imagined that I was invisible. I lowered my gaze and followed a green stripe on the floor to a vacant chair beneath the retractable basketball hoop, which was raised, out of order, and I tried to pay attention to the sermon.

The gym floor was covered in colourful pathways. They were sports courts—basketball in red, badminton in green—and when we put away the chairs, it all made sense. But with a church on top, the stripes were pure abstraction that could only serve one purpose, which was to lead you to an empty seat.

There were a lot of empty seats as Gateway neared its two-year anniversary. The Great Revival was still a ways off and coming, but people were leaving. It wasn't just about impatience, however. Some folks were put off by the rowdy services, the spiritual warfare, the electric guitars, the speaking in tongues without translators present. Some had been scandalized by the Pastor Mark incident, or the evening service suicide attempt. Others didn't care for Pastor Don, who was too polished and too loud, they said. One woman called him a smarmy American grifter.

My mother heard it all through the Prayer Hotline, which doubled as a grapevine for gossip.

The Gazettes were long gone. Mrs. Gazette's part in the Prayer Warriors was now played by a significantly shorter woman, Yvette Rempel. She had a faint Scottish accent.

Nearly every role at Gateway was recast by then. The giant ushers were replaced by smaller men; my father was an usher now, as well as the mastermind behind the bulletin's excessive use of clip art. Jameson Crock, the worship leader, was the only holdover from the band's early days. Even the church treasurer had been replaced. The original bookkeeper had left abruptly, and without an explanation.

When the new treasurer, a student in her twenties, got her first look at Gateway's books, she found they could not be balanced at all without the Van Asseldonk colony writing big cheques. Even more alarming was the money that had clearly been misplaced. She told her friends, and an entire generation ghosted Gateway.

That was fine, according to Pastor Don. More revival for us.

Gateway was not shrinking, the Man of God said before a half-empty gymnasium. It was being refined, like the army of Gideon at Mount Gilead, which numbered over thirty thousand before the Lord said unto Gideon: I don't need that many. You only need one mighty warrior, and baby, I'm it! If anyone is afraid, send them away. Two-thirds of the men went home, and the Lord said: Still too many! Take them to the water and only keep those who use their tongues, like a dog laps. Everyone who kneels at the riverbed, like so—Pastor Don mimed the cupping technique of a coward—send *them* away! And then there were three hundred, and the Lord said: Perfect. The Bible says that God woke Gideon up that very night. Arise, Gideon! Go down into the valley, for I have already delivered the Midianites into your hand. Hallelujah, *shamolo, shamolo.*

Pastor Don's prayer language was not *shamolo, shamolo.* It didn't sound like that, my mother's did, but you get the idea. The man had a habit of punctuating his sentences with a little bit of tongues to show excitement.

Well, Pastor Don said, dabbing his forehead with a handkerchief, the Lord woke *me* up last night. I said, Lord, why did you send me from California to fail? These people aren't ready for a Holy Ghost-filled church. They're leaving, Lord. And the Lord responded: Let them go!

Amen, someone said.

But it's not just that, Lord, Pastor Don continued. Some of the others are holding back. You pour out your spirit. My cup overfloweth. But these Canadians are so polite, they take such small portions, only as much as their little hands can hold. And the Lord said: Keep only those who are willing to use their tongues. *Send the rest away.*

I did not want to be sent away, not again.

At the altar call I made my way forward beside almost everyone, and it felt like a great privilege to be standing with the army of the Lord. But I was a poor Christian soldier without a prayer language. So I waited for Pastor Don to bless me with mine.

Son, the Man of God said when his polished black wingtips came toe to toe with my dusty Reebok pump-ups, would you like to be Baptized by the Holy Spirit?

It was the only thing I wanted. I said yes and I shut my eyes, just as Pastor Don's hot, humongous hands crash-landed in my hair, latching on like tentacles. This summoned the ushers, as catchers, if I should be slain. I felt their approach. I smelled my father's aftershave. They arrived speaking in tongues, and I became walled within a nonsensical echo chamber, encircled in a way that felt familiar and frightening, déjà vu of a nightmare I once had, or perhaps it was the Holy Spirit flowing through me, after all, and so my heart began to pound.

Nothing else happened.

But Pastor Don believed something was about to happen. That was his brand. Brotha, he said, are you ready to become a Man of God?

I said yes.

Amen, said Pastor Don. Then go right ahead.

I said nothing.

You're holding back, said Pastor Don. Don't you believe that God wants this for you?

I said, I do. But I can't just babble, can I?

It's not babbling, he said, with an air of false kindness. You may not understand it, but God does, and he is glorified by your faith, especially in moments of uncertainty.

Then Pastor Don told me a story about a man he knew, a travelling businessman who asked God for his prayer language and was given just one word: *exousia*. He asked for more but that was it, so in his faith, he said it over and over—*exousia, exousia*—even though he felt a little silly. One day, the businessman found himself at a Spirit-filled Greek Orthodox church, and when the people began to pray in tongues, he shouted the only word he had.

Exousia! Exousia!

After the service, a woman came up to him and asked if he spoke Greek. The man said no. Then the woman said: Well, you're speaking it. You're shouting power, power, power. And at that very moment, the man was rewarded for his faith and received the full Baptism of the Holy Spirit, and he fell to his knees and began to praise the Lord in fluent Greek.

Pastor Don asked: Do you believe that?

Yes, I said.

Then you can do it too, he said. Ask God for your prayer language and whatever comes into your mind, that's his response. So say it loud and proud.

But nothing came to mind except my mother's prayer language. I knew enough to mimic it. The language appeared to be built around a base word—*shamolo*, you'll recall—which was her *exousia* equivalent. Time and again, she would return to the word, like Monopoly players pass GO, saying *shamolo shamola, shattolio-lola, shattalah shebaka, shantala shamolo,* and in my distress I considered just copying her. But it would be a lie and a blasphemy, and dishonour my mother besides, so I did not dare. I could not imagine what would happen if people could tell, and by then it seemed likelier than not that I would be exposed, so I waited on the Lord to give me something I could work with.

Nothing else happened.

You just have to open your mouth and let Him speak, Pastor Don said. He was trying to prompt me.

Exousia, I mumbled, disappointing us both.

The Lord wants to bless you, the Man of God said. But you have to meet him halfway, and you have to guard your thought life. Any sin—even lust in your heart—could be holding you back. Keep your eyes on the prize.

I knew right away what he meant. I had tried to see Mrs. Crock's underpants. That was adultery. God must have told him.

Sensing my shame, Pastor Don gave my shoulder a comforting squeeze. But the man didn't know his own strength, and it hurt me. Knowing that I deserved far worse, I tried not to flinch, and I thanked him for trying.

Brotha, the Lord's got a special language for you, he said. I guess you've just got to keep faith.

Then he smiled with his mask and wandered away, to go pray for the woman in the wheelchair. The Holy Spirit must have been unhappy with her too. The Man of God commanded her to stand, but nothing happened.

• • •

What do you want for your birthday? My mother asked, that afternoon at the brunch buffet. Make me a list.

So I did, on a piece of pastel pink construction paper, and as soon as she woke up on Monday, I turned in a half-hearted wishlist, with only three entries. The number-one item was underlined, shouted, in capital letters, with three exclamation marks.

MY PRAYER LANGUAGE!!!

After that, way down the page, I wrote: books and CDs and a cross necklace, maybe?

Make me a real list, she said, as she crumpled it up.

I insisted the list was sincere. The only birthday gift I really wanted was the gift of tongues, and I needed my mother to know that about me. But she needed names, and she wouldn't engage with the list until I made it more specific. I sat down beside her, smoothed out the paper, and added some Christian musicians and authors.

I handed it back, with the number-one item unaltered, except that I circled it twice.

Unfortunately, the Baptism of the Holy Spirit wasn't for sale at the House of James, so I didn't get it for turning eleven.

The Christian book and music store had almost everything else on my wishlist, and when my mother was done showering me with gifts—her love language, according to a best-selling book—I had almost everything too. For my birthday that year, she gave me several new CDs, including *Wow* 1996, the Christian alternative to the secular hits compilation *Now* 1996. She gave me the new Adventures in Odyssey cassette collection, all four new titles from the Forbidden Doors series (the Christian alternative to the Goosebumps books, which were satanic and glorified the occult), my first-ever necklace (a sterling silver cross pendant on a chunky ball chain), and several new Christian music films on VHS to add to my impressive library, including Carman's *R.I.O.T.: The Movie* and *Change Your World Live!*, the Michael W. Smith concert video.

Not to be outdone, my father gifted me a used copy of *Preparing for Adolescence* by Dr. James Dobson, which he had taken out of Ben's room.

Read it first, he said. But that was never going to happen. Dr. Dobson was a nasally bore and his book didn't interest me. Out of respect for my father, I glanced at the cover, where a teenage boy appeared to be humping a street sign that read CAUTION: CHANGES AHEAD. I opted to watch the new Carman instead.

Carman was my favourite Christian singer, and his videos were epic confrontations with demonic forces. Evil took a beatdown every time. In "Satan, Bite the Dust," my favourite video, the singer plays an Old West sheriff. He kicks in the doors of a demon-infested saloon, on a hunt for the devil himself. Carman rebukes the spirit of alcoholism, one-punches the spirit of infirmity, and smashes the demon of false religion over the head with a sitar. Satan arrives as a man in black, dressed in a long black coat, black boots, a massive black hat, and he goes for his gun, but the Spirit won't let him unholster the weapon. He's finished. Carman reloads and delivers the titular line: *Satan, bite the dust.* Then he peppers the devil with heavenly bullets and rides away on a white stallion.

But the singer's latest offering was a departure. The devil wasn't in it. In *R.I.O.T.: The Movie*, a feature-length film, the singer plays a cop who leaves the city to escape the Latin gangs that murdered his wife, only to discover an infestation of Latin gangs in the suburbs, hiding in tunnels beneath the backyards. After a brief crisis of confidence, Carman remembers that God is on his side, and an invasion of ethnic gangbangers is no match for a Righteous Invasion of Truth. The officer puts all his trust in the Lord, who gives him the strength to defeat the ringleader, played by the Christian rapper T-Bone, in a knife fight. Thus the town is Saved, and several Latin gangsters too, upon seeing the power of God in action.

But it only made me feel inadequate. I was beginning to doubt that God would ever give me the strength to win a knife fight. He wouldn't even give me my prayer language. I pleaded for the Baptism of the Holy Spirit again that night before bed, but my prayer began and ended in English, which barely worked for prayer at all anymore, and the sting of silent rejection is the prevailing memory of my eleventh birthday.

I don't recall the sun shining for even a moment that summer. It seems unlikely. I can only assume I've mistakenly ascribed a gloom that was mine to the weather outside. But the days were dismal either way.

Even I knew it wasn't really about speaking in tongues. It was about belonging.

I didn't belong in Children's Church anymore, and by then it was hard to believe I belonged anywhere else either, especially Big Church, where the Lord continued to ignore me. Week after week, I presented myself at the altar call—looking for a reason, to borrow a phrase, probing through the night to find my place in this world—only to be rejected before the whole congregation.

Now was not the time to be the odd one out. If Gateway was being refined ahead of the Great Revival, I saw myself as the clear favourite to be burned away, the accidental Black kid, an obvious impurity, the problem child voted most likely to be forgotten in a storage room.

I could not afford to be more different. I had to speak in tongues. I simply had to.

Still, I knew it was this desperation that made me unworthy. I sought the Baptism of the Holy Spirit selfishly, that was the problem. It wasn't to glorify God. It was to glorify me. I just wanted to feel good about myself, and that wasn't the point of Christianity. It wasn't about belonging. It was about belonging to God, and crucifying the desires of the flesh, such as the desire to belong. These people were Christians, after all, and all of them were colour blind. If my Blackness was a sticking point, it's because I was stuck on it, not them, and it seemed to me that I couldn't move forward until I learned to silence the voice in my head that wouldn't stop bringing it up.

• • •

I was getting nowhere, but the church was on the move. The Spirit delivered three prophets to Gateway to give us our new marching orders.

The first was Philo Percy, a spindly man who stood perfectly upright, with a moustache wider than his narrow shoulders and hair like the quills of a short-beaked echidna. He was a powerful Man of God called to music and prophecy, Pastor Don said, in a grand introduction, and Jameson Crock stepped aside for the morning to let our guest lead us in worship. But Philo Percy was only gifted in prophecy. The man played guitar, but not well, and he sang with the timbre of a baritone and the range of a monotone—and this was our guest's own assessment.

The Lord had a different opinion, however.

To the Father, the Holy Spirit had told Philo Percy during one of their chats, his praise was a joyful noise, without all the affectation and melisma of today's music, and He was much more glorified by this than that, so never stop, it's part of your ministry now. And thus Philo Percy was called to be constantly humbled by God, like how the prophet Hosea was made to marry a prostitute.

But the rewards for obedience were great, Philo Percy said between songs, for it was this act of untuned humility that kept him attuned to the Holy Spirit and thus unlocked the prophecies of the Father. So it was important to bear with him, and support his ministry by purchasing his new CD, *Thine Is the Kingdom*, if you have any money left after the offering.

What an incredible privilege it must be to visit a community determined to embrace you, I thought, as I bought the new album.

The prophecy came to Philo Percy all of a sudden, midway through a chorus, and he took a step back from the mic to receive it. Then he nodded solemnly, raising both his hands to stop the music.

The Father has given me a verse for you, he said as we fell silent. It's from the book of Jeremiah, chapter 50, verse 25. Somebody please go ahead.

The first to his feet was the middle-aged man who could translate his mother's prayer language. He cleared his throat, and read the Percy prophecy aloud:

The Lord has opened His armoury,
And has brought out the weapons of His indignation;
For this is the work of the Lord God of hosts
In the land of the Chaldeans.

Now this was a complete jaw-dropper at Gateway Christian Centre—real look-under-your-chairs, game-show-type stuff—and a great murmur arose as the people realized how perfectly the prophecy applied to us. *The Lord has opened His armoury?* Why, there was an abandoned cadet armoury just next door! It had always been there, of course, because the Father knows what you need before you even ask, and now he was giving it to us, was the obvious takeaway, and all we had to do was go and buy it.

Miraculously, Gateway was in the market for a new building at the time. The defections and the debt had left the church unable to keep up with rent payments at Aberdeen Elementary, and the school district wanted us out. But with the prophecy from Philo Percy, the army of the Lord set their sights on the tumbledown structure across the field. It would mean incurring more debt, but not much more, because the abandoned armoury could be had for cheap, praise the Lord, and then we would have a place of our own, where we would be accountable to none but God himself.

The Prophet Mary Greenland was the next to arrive. She had to come down from Alaska, she told us, to see the seat of the Great Revival for herself. But she seemed surprised to find us in a school gymnasium, which was not the right place at all, she knew that in her spirit, just as the prophet Samuel knew to snub the seven sons of Jesse before anointing the shepherd boy, David.

Is this the only building you have? Because the vision that brought me is of an old chapel or training facility, she said. Is there anything like that around?

Again we rejoiced, for there totally was.

We were amazed and encouraged by the Prophet Mary Greenland's powerful visit, which included a formal welcome and anointing for the newest Prayer Warrior, Yvette Rempel, as well as yet another truly disturbing deliverance for original cast member Tilda Eubanks, whose evil spirit had returned without her knowing.

I had not known that could happen.

But the Prophet Mary Greenland was a pro. When Tilda Eubanks started grunting and snorting, out of nowhere, a couple seats down from me, I cleared the aisle in a hurry. The Woman of God marched right past me, confronting the devil without apprehension.

You filthy demon, she shouted, get out of there. How dare you return to this sanctified woman. Your hold on her spirit is severed. I rebuke you for eternity. Now leave her . . . *in the naaaaaaaaaaaaaaame of Jesus*!

Then she slapped Tilda Eubanks with both hands and held the Prayer Warrior's head still, and my mother's associate let out a long shriek that slowly turned into a sigh, and I swear I saw vapour or smoke pouring out of her mouth. She was slain in the Spirit, and two ushers caught her. They laid her down gently and covered her knees with a prayer shawl.

The crowd started clapping, and once I regained my composure, I joined them, unsure about who the ovation was for.

The Prophet Mary Greenland also blessed the Prayer Warriors with free copies of her newest warfare training manual, which wasn't even out yet, and they blessed her in return by covering the fare for her flight back to Anchorage.

But before she left, the Prophet Mary Greenland stressed the importance of breaking every demonic attachment at the abandoned cadet armoury. The Prince of Darkness knows that he's occupying the seat of the Great Revival, she said, and he's not gonna give it up without a fight. But when the devil declares war we declare victory in Christ—amen?

Amen.

So the Prophet Mary Greenland and the Prayer Warriors marched right across to the unpaved parking lot after church to let Satan know that he was already defeated, and from my perch atop the jungle gym, I watched the foursome consecrate the grounds by pouring nearly a quart of Kirkland Signature 100% Italian extra virgin olive oil into the dirt outside the armoury.

As soon as we got the keys to the place, Pastor Don hit up the Hotline, and the Prayer Warriors stormed the castle. It was a very exciting phone call, like one that Batman would get, and when my mother set out that night with her Bible and a broom, I imagined the three women suiting up and blasting into the building like the Ghostbusters, speaking in tongues like sonic screams, and rebuking a whole host of evil spirits in the name of Jesus.

When the dust settled, Yvette Rempel's husband, who would oversee the renovations, was delighted to discover the building still had its original wainscoting.

The next prophet was Black. He was already in the sanctuary when my family arrived. I saw him like a bright light and he caught me staring, starstruck, and came over.

He said: Hey little man, I'm Kevin, how about you?

I told him my name and I asked: Where did you come from? As one might ask a time traveller, or a visitor from a parallel universe. But he misunderstood me.

Inglewood, he said with a wide and welcoming smile. Listen: I'm gonna rap for y'all later. Wanna be my deejay, little man?

Kevin was a rapping prophet. His emcee name was Prophet K. The *K* was for Kevin. He was a large, round man with a buzz cut and a goatee. He wore baggy, blue jean shorts and an XXL T-shirt with the phrase MY WAY struck through and YAHWEH beneath it. An understated cross pendant dangled from a thin gold chain around his neck, and when I saw it, I realized that my own necklace was gaudy costume jewellery, so I tucked the chunky chain behind my collar while we spoke and I never wore the piece to church again.

It was kind of him to reach out to me, but I had no idea what to do with this man's kindness. I did not know what to do with this man. To me, Prophet K was another species, something else entirely, and I was distracted by his difference from the rest of us and ashamed to feel so thoroughly unlike him. We were both Black, but it seemed like only he was, and I found myself embarrassed to behold him as a stranger, for I knew that he could tell. I knew from experience. I watched him shift, and strain to give me grace, the same way I responded any time white people seemed to panic in my presence, and in that moment, I grew conscious of the gulf between my sense of self and Blackness. If there was a language for what I was feeling, or even a phrase, it was foreign to me. I was out of my depth, lost at sea, and in my disorientation, I blurted out that I didn't know how to deejay, because my parents were white.

He smiled, as if to forgive me, and said: You just push play, my man. Then he handed me a silver disc with PK BEATS written in Sharpie.

When the time came, Pastor Don introduced the congregation to his good friend Kevin from California, who used to ride with the Crips before the Lord called him out of the darkness and into the light, and now he rides with the Christians, and he's here today with a word from the Lord, a fresh prophecy for the congregation, so let's all give a Holy Ghost welcome to Prophet K.

Prophet K grew up in the ghetto surrounded by gang violence. But when his cousin was gunned down in a Black-on-Black crime, he decided to choose life over death. He surrendered himself to Christ and asked the Lord to guide his steps, and the next thing he knew, he was a rapping prophet in Canada. This was his testimony. Then came the prophecy.

Boot camp is over, the rapper declared.

I don't know if it's meaningful to y'all, Prophet K said, but I'm just being obedient to the Spirit, and this is the track that he asked me to share.

He signalled me. I pushed Play, and the prophet started spitting bars:

Boot camp is over, souljah
Hasn't anybody even told ya?
Put on the armour of God, be a farmer of God,
And sow seeds for the army of Jehovah

That was the hook. The first verse was more of the same.

But the second verse was unlike anything I'd ever heard, and it took a minute to even register what it was. Initially I thought he was just rapping really fast. Then it dawned on me, just as it dawned on everyone else, that Prophet K was doing something else.

He was rapping in tongues.

I was not the only person in attendance that Sunday to stifle a gasp. Across the way, I saw the Werther's Lady cross her arms in disapproval, and after church while I was eating her candy, I heard her talking over me that the performance was blasphemous. She did not return to Gateway.

As for me, I was inspired. The prophecy was on-point as usual, but it was the performance that stayed with me. Prophet K had come to my church and done something so Black it was a scandal, and I chose to believe he'd been sent by the Holy Spirit to reconcile the parts of me that seemed to disagree. Somehow, I'd come to imagine my Blackness as something I must disavow to be righteous. But where did I get that idea?

What kept me from the gift of tongues, I realized that Sunday, was my struggle to accept the gift of Blackness. Rejoice in the Lord, always. That's what the Bible instructed. All of this shame and self-pity was blasphemous, really. I blamed God for making my life weird and hard, and hardened my heart to his blessings. I stunted my own growth. He made me this way for a reason, and my ingratitude made me unworthy of anything else He intended for me.

Get over yourself, I thought, gritting my teeth, and when the altar call came, I responded at once, for I knew I was finally worthy.

Pastor Don got to me first, and I raised my hands in submission as the ushers pressed in once again, but with Prophet K now standing in place of my father.

And that's when a word came to my mind: *shattah*.

But still it seemed to me that the word was not imparted at all, that it was just a nonsense word rolling around in my head, where it originated, and moreover, it struck me as suspiciously similar to the *shamolo* sound my mother made. So I swallowed my tongue.

Pastor Don grew downright indignant this time, and in his righteous anger, he left me and he marched right over to the woman in the wheelchair to demand that she stand.

Sister, he said, God is telling me that the time has come for you to walk again. Do you believe me?

She nodded.

Then get up, sister.

She got up, and Gateway went wild for her.

Hallelujah! Pastor Don shouted. Hop and jump for me like this.

The woman did a bunny-hop to deafening applause.

Shamolo, shamolo, said an energized Pastor Don, and when he was done with the woman, he put a hand to her forehead and she collapsed into the arms of an usher. Then the Man of God spun around, antsy for more action, and did the same thing to Prophet K, who staggered three steps back like he'd been smacked by a bat before falling into a chair, speaking in rhythmic tongues.

Then it was my turn. With a head full of steam, Pastor Don returned to unleash his fury on the boy who could not be baptized, saying: The Lord your God has opened your mouth! Speak this instant, boy, in Jesus's name!

Intimidated, I obeyed. *Shattah!* I shouted. *Shattah! Shattah!*— and the rewards were great indeed. The crowd went mad around me, and their acclaim was an electrocution that sent my heart racing and slivers of cold ecstasy through to my fingers and toes, a sensation I truly believed to be the Baptism of the Holy Spirit, at long last. So I received it, what a relief, and I said: *Shattah talimama, tallio-mama shattolio shattah*, before my voice began to tremble and the room started spinning, and I allowed myself to fall into somebody's arms.

But we have all done this.

What does it feel like to speak in tongues? It feels like belonging. It is a universal experience to learn the languages we must, no matter how irrational, so that we may live and find love in irrational worlds.

Some languages belittle us, and still, we must adopt them to assimilate. These languages are said to edify. They only stultify. They bind us to realities in which we are diminished. We come away not civilized, but colonized, held hostage by a new vocabulary, where the world implied is one that has no love for us, no place for us to go. We internalize these languages like drinking deadly potions, and delude ourselves, believing that the language of our captors has a set of magic words that, said aloud, will set us free, for it is better to believe we have been Baptized by the Holy Spirit than poisoned by the people we are bound to love as family.

Whiteness has all of us speaking in tongues. None of it makes any sense.

• • •

We moved to the new building two Sundays later. After the service, our last in the gym, we collected our chairs and walked down to our new digs, then circled the armoury multiple times, just like the

Israelites outside the Promised Land. In lieu of a ram's horn, we whistled and shouted, then marched inside, clapping and singing.

I was a real somebody at the abandoned cadet armoury.

Right away, Gateway launched a new Saturday service, to reach those who worked Sundays and to take a second offering, and this created several new positions to be filled. Soon I had a hand in everything.

First they named me an alternate usher, and I took that velveteen pouch by the handle with gusto. That morning, I felt ten feet tall, at least. Then I was invited to rejoin Children's Church, not as a child but as Officer Frost's helper on alternate weekends, and I was over the moon to find myself in middle management so soon. When the bassist left the church, Jameson Crock asked if I would replace her. I didn't play the bass, so I had to decline. But it was an honour just to be nominated.

I even joined the Outreach Team, in search of new recruits. We went out one afternoon in the Outreach Van, a purple Plymouth Voyager that seated seven (eight if we squished), and we knocked on doors and put Gateway stickers on lampposts all along South Fraser Way.

The Outreach Team also placed ads in the *Abbotsford News* because it was free for religious groups unlike the *Abbotsford Times*, and we staged a very visible pro-life rally (explained to me as a pro-adoption rally) one Sunday after brunch at Swiss Chalet.

I sat that one out. I did not like the sign I was given—it said GOD KNOWS WHAT YOU DID LAST SUMMER TO YOUR BABY, a real sign of the times—and it seemed cruel to intimidate women into giving their children away. So I ordered more ribs than I could eat in one sitting, and stranded myself in the restaurant.

Soon after we sent the Outreach Team to Riverview Mental Hospital, the old insane asylum in Port Coquitlam, about forty-five minutes northeast by Outreach Van. A 1996 update to the *Mental*

Health Act enshrined patient rights into law in the province and suddenly a whole host of residents committed against their will were free to leave. But where would they go?

To Gateway, we hoped.

These lunatics were looking for deliverance in all the wrong places anyway—liberal ideas like medication, meditation, and trauma therapy, where it was always the mother's fault. The Bible was clear that there was nothing wrong with these folks but a little demonic interference, so it was time for them to leave the insane asylum behind and find God at the abandoned cadet armoury.

After all, Pastor Don said one morning, *asylum* is a synonym for *church*.

I wanted to go with them, but my mother said it wasn't safe—these people can be unpredictable—so I was made to miss a legendary mission.

The next Sunday there was a strange old lady in the maple grove behind the armoury. She was facing away, humming quietly to herself and swaying, and she was wearing a baby bonnet, which did not seem at all age-appropriate. But she did not come inside, and I was too frightened to introduce myself outside, behind the trees, so we never met. I wondered if the woman in the bonnet had boarded the Outreach Van by mistake.

The other new recruits seemed happier to be there. There were several fresh faces at Gateway that morning, including a Black woman named Esther Stratford, who seemed to know me. I saw her staring all throughout the service, and after church, she came right up to me and said: Hi, Harry, it's great to see you again.

But she only looked sort of familiar and I was mostly put off by her sorrowful gaze, especially after she urged me, out of nowhere, to never forget who I am. So I was glad when she moved on, and gladder still to learn after church that I was right to be wary of her.

Pastor Don had better be careful not to let Esther get him alone, my mother said on the drive home, or she'll falsely accuse him of something just to hurt him. The Jezebel spirit loves to use women like her to bring down powerful men like him.

You know her?

Of course, said my mother. You don't remember Esther? Her dad is Pastor Milton, from Stone Rolled Away, the church we attended when you were just little. She babysat for us a few times, but then she got all into drugs, so watch out for her, Harry. She is not to be trusted.

I looked for Esther the next Sunday, prepared to shun her, in full view of my mother, but she never came back to Gateway.

The rest of the Riverview folks stuck around, and several were rewarded for their loyalty to Pastor Don with brand-new suits and leadership positions. Before long, the inmates were running the synonym for asylum.

Pastor Don said that our muscular new youth pastor, Shawn Powers, might be a baby in the family of Christ, but that was his greatest strength. Those are the ones you want leading the way, he explained, the ones who aren't jaded, the ones still on fire for God. Ditto for Bernie Pendleton, a tall, earnest man with kindness in one eye and madness in the other. But it used to be madness in both eyes, before he was Saved. Bernie played the bass, and they made him the deputy youth pastor, too.

Youth group had two pastors, but it didn't have a name, and I was honoured when Pastor Don asked me if I had any ideas. You bet your bippy I did. Get this: Generation Exousia.

Pastor Don loved it, and he thought my logo was rad too, where the name stood over two knights in a swordfight, and the X was their swords colliding. It was just a little something I whipped up with a cool font and some clip art and it was actually one knight, but I used Photoshop to flip him horizontally, so that he was at war with himself.

Generation Exousia was an overnight success, and I had to imagine my top-notch branding didn't hurt. There were thirty teens the first night, when Prophet K gave a performance and another youth group came to see him, and I guess the Holy Spirit was really flowing afterward because Pastor Shawn got a fresh word from the Lord. It was a new name for the youth group, which was a little disappointing, but you can't argue with the Holy Spirit. After that, the youth group was known as Unite!, which was fine.

I wasn't old enough for Unite! yet. It was for ages thirteen and up, and I was just twelve then. But I could hardly wait. Few of the families who crossed the playground had boys my age, leaving only fuzzy memories of ones I once knew. Soon they began to blur together, and when I think back to the first days at Gateway, I see a whole bunch of boys that slowly dissolve into one boy named James, who disappears.

There were, however, five girls my age. They hung out by the swings, and moved and thought as one, and sometimes you could see their underpants when the wind hit their church skirts. I tried not to look. I didn't want to lose the gift of tongues for being lustful, and I didn't want the girls to call me creepy, so I stayed away. But the girls would come to me, for there was no one else to like, and Raquel Crock, the pastor's daughter, made it her mission to keep me abreast of new crushes.

Destiny likes you, she would say. And then the next week she would say: Destiny doesn't like you anymore. Miriam likes you now.

Well the feeling was mutual with Miriam, so I found her swinging by herself. We held hands for an electrifying instant, and at the Sunday brunch buffet, the dalliance continued. Going around me to the tater tots, she landed the whole of her palm in the small of my back, and I nearly spilled my macaroni salad.

I spent the week infatuated with her. But the following Sunday, Raquel said that Miriam's crush had expired.

So, who likes me today, Raquel?, I sighed in response, and something about my response made her laugh. It became an instant catchphrase, much to my embarrassment. Some Sundays I had to say it or she wouldn't tell me anything, and I was ashamed each time I went along.

Friendlier girls were on the way, though. Gateway was growing, and the devil was growing frightened.

One Saturday night, the Man of God was attacked by a devil woman. I immediately recognized her as the bonnet lady from the maple grove, since she was still wearing the bonnet, and I wondered if she'd ever gone home. Had she been out there all month? Either way I was glad I'd kept my distance behind the church. She was a very scary lady, especially that night, when she burst into the building wide-eyed and furious, and ran down the aisle at Pastor Don, flailing her arms and screaming: This is fucked! You're all fucked!

The woman was demonized. It was classic demon nonsense, after all, just foul language for its own sake in the house of the Lord, and I was glad that there were larger ushers in attendance that night to overpower her and take her away, blathering and blaspheming God on the way out the door.

Stay in the Spirit, the pastor's son said while the bonnet-wearing woman was delivered in the parking lot. But we knew what to do. This was not our first rodeo. Jameson Crock hit the chorus as hard as he could, and we screamed at the top of our lungs, and the madness outside was no match for the madness within.

• • •

The Man of God's sermon on Sunday was all about breaking generational curses.

I was intimately familiar with the topic—yes, yes, there are evil spirits and soul ties gumming up the bloodline, standard stuff—

and still I was not prepared for the direction Pastor Don would take the service.

He spoke about inheriting the sins of the fathers, and of how these curses are passed to the third and fourth generation, according to the book of Deuteronomy.

But it goes even further back than that, he told us. Church, it goes all the way back, and this is why the peoples of the earth are how they are, because they have all descended from sinners. Each of us is born a sinner, and we all have to stand firm against a cursed lineage. This is our burden. White people can be bullies. We see the big picture, and we always want to be the ones in charge, and this goes all the way back to the original sin of Adam. Now sometimes that's good. But sometimes, well, the white man can be rash and reckless and make a mess of things. Then you've got to send the gospel in afterward to do clean-up, hahaha, hallelujah, *shamolo*.

He paused and picked up his Bible.

People don't like to hear this. It makes them uncomfortable. It's not politically correct. But it's right here in the scriptures. The Man of God flipped through the book and the microphone amplified the sound of pages turning.

Amen, someone shouted, when things got too quiet.

Black people!—Pastor Don broke back in with a shout—are sexually promiscuous.

He lowered his reading glasses.

And this goes back to Ham. The story of Noah does not end with a rainbow. There's more. What happens next?

Reader, I'll tell you. Noah plants a vineyard. After the flood, the patriarch takes up winemaking, and wouldn't you? There is but one thing to do upon witnessing that sort of devastation, upon leaving so many to drown while you shut up your boat, the only boat, and sail away, and that's to drown oneself in booze. This is what Noah does, and he falls asleep, drunk, with his junk hanging out. And this is what Ham does: he looks upon his father's shame and goes to tell his brothers, laughing.

Shem and Japheth aren't amused. They enter their father's tent backwards, out of respect, and cover Noah with a blanket. Later on, they tell him what his son did while he slept.

So Noah awoke from his wine, Pastor Don read aloud, looking out at the whole congregation, and knew what his younger son had done to him. And he put a curse on Ham. Now, the Bible does not get into the details of what Ham actually did to his father, and neither does it say what the curse was. But the answer is in the original Talmud.

It was an act of homosexual rape, he declared. The curse was the skin of the Black man.

I hadn't been paying attention, but I definitely heard this and I felt it too, as every eye in the abandoned cadet armoury landed on the lonely Hamite sitting with my family.

Pastor Don continued: From these three the whole earth was populated, and Genesis 10 tells you where they all went. Ham became the father of Canaan, who persecuted and corrupted God's chosen people until they were driven from the land. The Bible says his descendants eventually settled in Africa and Arabia. The Black man's legacy is a never-ending struggle with sexual sin.

Amen, someone said, and I looked across the aisle to see the man who understood his mother, standing in agreement, and a tumour of shame and sorrow surfaced in my stomach like a U-boat. The man was a paragon of holiness, who often spoke not only for his mother but for all of us. If he agreed, the armoury agreed. I was humiliated.

My former flame Miriam's family was shocked to hear Pastor Don employing the very language used to justify slavery, which they were against, so they slipped out and never came back. But none of the others objected. My mother and father were silent beside me, and nobody reached out to me but the deputy youth pastor sitting behind us.

You can beat this, Bernie Pendleton said, giving my clavicle an encouraging squeeze, and he winked at me with his good eye.

I was encouraged. I had to believe that other Black people were like this, perhaps, but I was not like *them*.

The girls kept their distance that Sunday. I stood by myself, and I started to worry. Concerned that the sermon had ruined me for them, I went to the swings and I asked the pastor's daughter what I always asked her after church: So who likes me today?

Kicking her legs, she went higher. Today was the day she swung over the bar, I could feel it. I looked away, out of respect, and Raquel, who was almost on top of me now, shouted down.

No one.

• • •

Nobody spoke to me. Nobody told me the Ham doctrine justified slavery, which was its primary purpose, to justify slavery everywhere, dating back centuries. The people oppressed by this nonsense changed multiple times, even before it was used to mark slavers from slaves, cleaving the whiteness from Blackness, establishing clear lines of trade. Nobody mentioned the hate and the horror the doctrine enabled to thrive, or said it was poor exegesis, a misread, or even a lie. I was desperate to disagree with it, but it felt like defying the Lord God himself, and nobody told me it wasn't, or else, that it was, but you must defy God, or you'll never be free.

It took me a lifetime to figure it out for myself.

The Sunday after that, I came to Gateway on a mission. I would show them I was something else entirely, something better. I worshipped aggressively, shouting back demons. I made myself sweaty from dancing. I spoke in tongues the loudest, faking solemnity differently now, and I sprinted to the altar like a little boy on fire.

The effort made a difference.

Destiny likes you again, said Raquel, after church.

But I didn't like Destiny, and I didn't like the way that my performance made me feel, or that I had to go bananas every single, bloody Sunday.

I was glad when we finally left Gateway some five or six months later. I didn't even ask why. My parents never offered to explain. One morning, we were back to watching *Superbook*, and that was that. Best as I could overhear, another new treasurer turned up the usual problem—the money was missing again—and the church had no choice but to say it was bankrupt.

Pastor Don Crook is more like it, my mother said under her breath to a Prayer Hotline caller.

And this gave me licence to see things anew. If the Man of God was crooked, then his every word was suspect.

I thought about Pastor Don's sermon again, the doctrine that held that all Black people were sexual deviants and their skin was a curse tracing back to the days of Noah, and that the people of God were well within their rights to fear these people, and to despise and distrust and have dominion over them, because the Hamites were wicked beasts with so little impulse control that we could not keep from sodomizing our own fathers.

And I thought: That's racist.

PART II

THE PATH

Yet, if we dare to awaken, the path is before us.
—bell hooks, *Loving Blackness as Political Resistance*

5

CAMP

(or The Boy Who Ruined The Kid *for Everybody)*

I n the summer of 1999, I went to camp.

My mother signed me up, for a fourteenth birthday present, and I took it like parole from Hades. After years of feeling captive, like an indoor cat, I was out on good behaviour, I imagined, and I had to make the most of my reward. I had to get my act together and get a group of friends, a lifeline to the outside world, a safety net, if I should fall from grace.

This would be my final endless summer.

The millennium was ending, and it might have been the world. There was a sense that we were living at a turning point in time. On *The 700 Club*, they said the Lord would be returning any day now, and the Rapture was nigh, and the numbers added up: counting from Adam and Eve made six thousand years that winter, and the Bible says one thousand years is like a day to God, and on the seventh day, He rested, there you have it. The unsaved were calling it Y2K and trying to fix their computers, the fools. The prophets on TV knew better. These are the Last Days, they said, so get right with the Lord while you still can, the show's almost over. The End Times are upon us.

But really, we were somewhere in the middle of our story, much like the book that you hold in your hands. This is but the latest instalment of an ongoing saga, and the place where it begins is at the camp where I unravelled.

• • •

Camp Squeah was a ninety-minute drive upriver, nestled in the Lower Fraser Canyon. Our counsellors told us that *squeah* was an old Coast Salish word, loosely translated as *place of refuge*. But this was pure nonsense. The Mennonite camp merely borrowed the term from a mountain nearby. They never consulted the Nation who named it, and they didn't know the history, so they were very wrong.

It sounded true, though, and it felt true, for me. After six years of homeschooling, I arrived a wide-eyed refugee from a lonely land, absolutely thrilled to spend a week with my fellow fourteen-year-olds, or maybe even longer if I played my cards right. I said goodbye to my mother. As the Aerostar disappeared down the highway, I felt like a diver who didn't know which way was up, but who managed to surface with seconds to spare. I found myself gasping for air.

Chapel was held in the forest on the first night. Just as the sun was setting, the counsellors led us along a series of switchbacks to an outdoor amphitheatre above the campground. We sat down on logs bisected into benches, with the worship leader perched on the big rock beside the fire pit. For over an hour, we praised the Lord like Moses at the burning bush. It was a sublime experience, so moving that, at times, I was tempted to speak in tongues, but I never felt like I had to, or that anybody even wanted me to. After five years at Gateway, I was surprised to be so soothed by this freedom from expectation.

But now was no time to start backsliding. If the world is ending any day, I thought, I can't be losing my head now. I promised to speak in tongues next time, to stay true to God, and the boy I'd become.

The next day, I learned about Courage.

I was standing at the front of the breakfast line with my bunk-mate, Joel DiPrentis, when Nathan, the bully of camp, cut the line.

Nathan said: Move it, nigger cocksucker.

That's racist, I said.

Yeah, he said.

And unclear, I continued. Are you calling *me* the N-word or saying I suck some *other* N-word's dick?

Don't know, don't care, *Carlton,* he said.

Make up your mind next time, I said, before you come picking on the only Black kid at camp.

This drew a laugh from a blond girl with black bangs who stood just a few feet away from us.

You're *not* the only Black kid at camp, Nathan the Bully said. Then he gestured to a Blacker boy somewhere down the line, and I was rattled.

Luckily, my bunkmate intervened.

Fuck *off,* Nathan. Harry is my friend, said Joel DiPrentis.

Nathan backed down and I was relieved, and delighted by Joel's declaration of friendship. But I kept looking back at the other Black boy, feeling equally threatened by him.

Courage was Nigerian, and this kid was Black like a crack in a stone. He was midnight, the person. His cabin went streaking that night. The other boys sprinted by, and their pasty bodies reflected the moon like the Lake of the Woods. But Courage was practically invis-ible in the dark: all you could see were his teeth and tighty-whities, everyone said, floating behind the others like a ghost.

When Courage's cabin left for their overnight hike, I was glad to be rid of the boy. But as soon as they were gone, they were back, raving about the big cat that had stalked them for miles. Apparently,

Courage saw the cougar and shouted: Run for your lives! It was a very endearing thing to say with the hindsight of having survived, and repeatable too, especially if you mimicked his Nigerian accent. It soon become the catchphrase of camp. In no time at all, everybody knew Courage, and I was eclipsed by his presence.

I knew how to be the only Black kid. I did not know how to be the other Black kid. So I set my mind to being the better Black kid.

Courage could speak English just fine, but he didn't have my way with words. He couldn't rap. He wouldn't do the dance. He was too reserved, too timid to debase himself. I leaned into my self-effacing sense of humour, besting him by showing I was better at belonging. Courage might have been nice, but he wasn't entertaining, so I was, all week long, all the time, every day. I lived to make the other campers laugh, and I was never not performing. So what if I wasn't the Black kid this week? I'll tell you what I was instead: a very funny guy. My quiver was bursting with quips, and I became the undisputed king of comedy at Bible camp. I charmed the girls, disarmed the bullies, beating myself up before them, and I even developed a hilarious catchphrase of my own: It's because I'm Black, isn't it?

Big, big laughs.

Somebody sounded the gong. The cougar had been spotted by the archery course.

We went into lockdown. For the next several hours, counsellors scrambled to herd all the campers into the cafeteria. The last to be accounted for was Daniel Wagner, the smallest kid at camp. As time passed, we concluded that Daniel was eaten alive, and some began to mourn him prematurely, RIP the boy who died. Did you know him? I didn't know him, but he was cabinmates with Courage, which only made my rival seem more fascinating. Typical.

Daniel Wagner would survive. The counsellors held hands in a line from the cafeteria to his cabin, Red Rover–style, and found him hiding in there, certain that the cougar had killed us all.

A member of the BC Conservation Officer Service came to speak
with us. The sergeant explained that the cougar was likely a juvenile
male who had lost his mother and didn't know what else to do but
come down to the camp.

The cougar was destroyed.

It sounded a little excessive to some of us, but the sergeant
explained that *destroy* was a British legal term, meaning *to kill
humanely*. That's definitely not what I pictured when I thought of
destruction, but I took his word for it.

Camp Squeah was not the same after the cougar. Only Nathan
the Bully actually saw the cougar in the campground and he was the
one to sound the gong, but for a time, in our minds, we were all on
the verge of a mauling. We huddled together, afraid and confused,
and we were shaken by the death of Daniel Wagner, then further
inspired by his rescue, then inspired by the little orphan cougar who
had died without his mother, and we spent the rest of the week wide
awake to the tide of mortality.

The big winner was God. When the sergeant cleared us to return
to the forest for one final, fireside chapel, it was an uncharacteris-
tically spirited Mennonite service. We sang our hearts out and we
poured them out too. Some people cried, and at least one little boy
spoke in tongues beneath his breath.

The campers were invited to share what was on their hearts, and
the line for the big rock wrapped all the way around us. Most of
the notable characters took a turn, including Nathan the Bully, and
Daniel Wagner, The Boy Who Died, who spoke twice, and as the
night was winding down, we heard from Courage.

I want to thank Camp Squeah for being so welcoming of me,
Courage said haltingly, in that adorable accent of his. You have been
very kind. I was afraid because I am a refugee, and I did not know if
I would be accepted or rejected, because I am the only Black person
at camp.

Hey! I called out reflexively, forgetting that my voice, by then, was downright unmistakable and, in that moment, utterly expected, so the whole camp knew who said it. The campers couldn't keep themselves from laughing.

I'm sorry, Courage stammered. I mean: the only *real* Black person.

It was a legendary zinger, the joke to end all jokes, at least for this audience. They laughed until they nearly split their sides like the logs we were sitting on, and Courage became the new king of comedy, and to my great horror, I became Daniel Wagner, the smallest kid at camp, the boy who died.

I did not feel like myself in the morning, and as the other kids exchanged Hotmail addresses in the pick-up area, I checked out early, sitting on my suitcase. Several campers stopped by in search of one last laugh, and some even brought their parents. But I was in no mood for jokes, and I was beginning to suspect that the other kids saw me as something, rather than someone, to laugh at, a popular act or a jack-in-the-box, in lieu of a real boy worth knowing.

This is Harry, the girl with blond hair and black bangs told her father, who came to collect her. He's hilarious.

Her father was a heavy-set man with a big red nose, and when I did not immediately make with the funny, he seized the conversation for himself.

You must be mulatto, he said. Mulatto means half-Black. Correct me if I'm wrong.

You got it, I said, feeling like a zoo animal.

I thought so, he said. You don't have overly Negroid features.

Guess I won the *mulottery*, I said, and I didn't mean it to be funny, but the girl with blond hair and black bangs laughed so hard that she snorted.

My reward was her AOL Instant Messenger handle. She wrote it on a Post-it note and said: Don't be a stranger.

And her father said: A quarter-Black is a quadroon, and an eighth is an octoroon.

My getaway driver arrived in the Aerostar. I dove in headfirst, and we turned right around. But I didn't want to let my mother know that I had not enjoyed myself, or I would never get to leave the house again. On the highway home, I tried to make it sound like I had fun.

Camp was a blast, I insisted. I met this one girl. She had blond hair and black bangs. She was really kind. She wants to keep in touch.

This was the wrong place to start.

It's always girls, girls, girls with you, my mother said. Well, you can't date anyone until you're sixteen, and then you'll have to be chaperoned. We don't want you slipping up and getting some rebellious girl pregnant. It's up to you to break that generational curse, don't forget that.

I don't like her like that, I said, ashamed. She was just nice to me.

Hmm, said my mother, declining further conversation.

We passed a roadside sign for the Cheam First Nation and my mother scoffed. First they were Indians, she said, and then it was Aboriginals. Now they want us to call them First Nations, because they were here so long before us, they say, ten thousand, twenty thousand years, they say—it's ridiculous. Nothing was that long ago. The real problem is that they refuse to assimilate. Instead, they just want to cause trouble.

Her opinions became mine by osmosis, but I was only paying half attention. Mostly I was stewing over Courage.

What did he know, anyway? Courage was just fourteen too, and that jerk barely knew English. He wasn't even a real Canadian. Who died and made him the arbiter of all things Black? Every nickname the kids gave me at camp had something to do with being Black: black lightning, black magic, black ice, and it was the same thing everywhere else, all day, every day, black, black, black, like a noisy old crow I couldn't shake. If I wasn't Black, then what in the world was I, and what did it even mean to be Black if other Black people saw no Blackness where white people saw nothing but? It didn't make any sense. *The only real Black person?* Newsflash, Courage: there's such a thing as *too* Black, I decided then and there, and the very idea made me feel better about myself, so I stashed it away in my heart for safekeeping.

There was another Black boy named Courage, I said, as we emerged from the canyons. He was from Nigeria. He told me he was the only real Black person.

Well that's racist, my mother said, glancing over at my bare right foot. But it's true that you are only half—*where* is your shoe?!

I looked down to become suddenly cognizant of only wearing the one. That didn't make any sense either.

I liked to be barefoot. If I had my way, I'd never wear shoes at all. But my mother was embarrassed by this. People will think we can't afford to dress you, she would say. Or: Put your shoes on, this isn't *The Jungle Book*. Eventually, I only went without when I was somewhere else. Away from my mother, I'd be barefoot the whole time, and it would have been fine and she wouldn't have known, except that I often forgot to come home with my shoes. It seemed I had an uncanny ability to disconnect from my own body.

But not my mother. She always noticed.

You big ninny, she'd say as she turned us around, you'd lose your head if it wasn't attached.

It hadn't happened in years, though, as I had few opportunities to lose my shoes anywhere but the yard these days, and I had never come home with only one shoe before. It was weird. But we were too far down the road by then for me to confess to not knowing how or why I was coming home, half-shod.

So I said: It's in my suitcase.

And she said: Those are expensive shoes, Harry. You just *had* to have the fancy ones, didn't you? You always do this. You'd better have it or you're in big trouble.

I have it, I said, but I didn't know for sure and the suitcase was in the back, so I spent the rest of the drive afraid that I didn't.

• • •

Home was not a place of refuge either. In my absence, I'd been moved across the hallway.

I used to share a bedroom with Ben. We slept in L-shaped bunk-beds handcrafted by our father when we were still very young. Ben was on the top. I was on the bottom, beside a massive dresser made to fit beneath, and that was my choice. The bottom bunk was a sleigh bed—I had asked for that, Curious George had a sleigh bed—and the walls on all six sides were like a cozy cocoon made custom for me. When Ben got his own room and Mike moved in, I did not want to leave my special spot, and at camp I called dibs on the bottom bunk so I could fall asleep in the most familiar way.

But the cocoon belonged to Tom now.

This was according to Tom, my youngest brother. As soon as we got back, I went upstairs to find that shoe, and I'd thrown everything out from my suitcase and onto the bed when my seven-year-old sibling came in after me.

This is my room, he said. Get your crap off my bed.

I ignored him and I kept looking for the shoe. But by then I knew I didn't have it.

This is my room, he said again, coming closer as if to challenge me. I was confounded. Tom was half my age; he had no power over me, at least until my mother and Mike appeared in the doorway to back him up, and suddenly, he did.

So I asked: Since when?

Since you left, my mother said. You're across the hall now.

Why didn't you tell me? I asked, weakly. To my mind, there was lots of time on the long drive home to mention it.

But my mother only rolled her eyes and said: You never called.

Mike had gone to camp earlier that summer. He lasted one day, and he spent most of it in the office, begging to go home, until we went to retrieve him around midnight. There was no way I was going out like that. But I got the sense my mother was upset that I hadn't. Was I being punished for lasting the week?

I didn't ask. I took my crap off Tom's bed, brushed away the pine needles, plant litter and other bits of camp that fell from my bag, and I went where I was told. I looked back to see my youngest brother on his Game Boy, sprawled across a brand-new, plaid comforter that I hadn't even noticed.

My new room had a bunch of new stuff too, all from IKEA, and already built by my brothers: a sizable credenza desk, white; an empty bookshelf, white; and a white bed frame with white drawers along the base to match the white walls, white closets, and the aging, off-white carpet.

Surveying my new digs, I thought of the padded cell at Arkham Asylum where they keep the Joker until he escapes.

The bed was made with a black blanket, still wrinkled from its plastic packaging.

It's a reversible comforter, my mother explained. The other side is tan. And what do you think of these? She pointed to a rainbow curtain set in the kids' bedroom section of the latest IKEA catalogue. I thought they looked fun—we could get them for you if you wanted to brighten the room up a bit.

The curtains were hardly my style. I thought they looked tacky. What's more, they were so age-inappropriate that the suggestion struck me as thoughtless, and I was bruised by my mother's outdated view of me.

I tried to mask my agitation. A room of my own was a milestone; I should have been happier about it. But I did not appreciate being displaced without my consultation or consent, especially after four-teen years in one place. It was almost as if my input didn't matter at all. So why even bother asking me about the stupid curtains? Just put them up.

And that's what I said.

My mother got mad. You're so ungrateful, she said. You're so selfish.

I just wish you would have included me, I said, retreating.

Well we could move you back, she sneered, but it's been a whole week, so your brothers are already used to the change.

Casting about for a safe response, I spotted Mike, who was ten, on his way to the Big Room. He carried a bottle of Windex. My brother was cleaning the house.

That was my job.

When I was little, we had a housecleaner. Bobby was a pack-a-day smoker. I used to sit with her on the front steps, on her break between floors. But then she died suddenly—lung cancer, my mother said, never smoke—and when a suitable replacement could not be found, the job fell to Ben and me. We were each paid fifteen dollars a week. But when Ben got a real job, the whole house became my responsibility.

It was a tall task, especially for a boy with *the brilliance*, and what took Bobby two hours often took me two days, even after my mother tried to motivate me by banning trampoline time until I could get the job done. Mike and Tom should have to help, I argued more than once, frustrated to hear them playing outside when I couldn't. But my mother countered that thirty dollars, split three ways, meant a pay cut for me, and then I would have less to spend on books and Christian music at the House of James. So I backed off and, for years, I worked alone.

Mike and Tom took over the housecleaning while you were away, my mother said. Just this week. They started yesterday and they're finishing today.

It sounded reasonable enough. I was glad for a week's reprieve anyhow. But something seemed off, so I asked: Fifteen dollars each?

And Tom said: Thirty.

I was instantly aggrieved. That's sixty dollars! I shouted. What, are Mike and Tom worth twice as much as me?

Now my mother was furious, and she came at me with such ferocity that I hit the empty bookshelf backing away.

You made thirty dollars *too*, so it's the *same rate*, she said, jabbing the air before me like a one-finger typist until her fingernail clicked against the bridge of my glasses, surprising us both. You always have such a nasty little attitude when you come home. Did you even miss your family? Where's your shoe, Harry?

Then she went to her room and slammed the door.

I sat cross-legged on my new bed and tried to make sense of what had happened. The sun was shining through the window, lighting every airborne bit of dust, and when it settled, the black blanket showed it all.

Maybe I overreacted, I thought. Maybe if I say I'm sorry, she'll see where I'm coming from.

Soon she was back. Here, my mother said, coldly, flinging a clear package into the room.

It was the rainbow curtain set: 100 per cent polyester, cold-water wash, hang to dry.

Her door slammed again.

I crawled into bed, but drawing back the comforter revealed a technicolor top sheet made to match the polyester panels.

• • •

Maybe if I put up the curtains.

I set my mind to making the new room feel mine, and I was still working on it the next day around lunchtime when my mother shouted at me from the kitchen. I rushed downstairs to answer her, hoping there were sandwiches or something.

Where's your shoe, Harry?

I'd forgotten all about that, and I was still not ready to admit I came home without it, so I lied. Upstairs, I said.

You're so full of crap your eyes are brown, she said. Your little buddy Joel has it.

My eyes are brown because I'm Black, I said.

Oh, don't play the race card with me, my mother scowled. Just find out where your friend lives. Then she put the cordless phone down on the counter and stood there, her arms crossed, impatient.

Joel lived so close I couldn't believe it. If you got lost on the way to my house, you might have knocked on his door for directions. My mother drove me over, but you could stumble coming down the hill and tumble right into his driveway. In a sense, that's exactly what happened.

As soon as we left, we were there.

Joel was sitting on the front steps in his shiny blue basketball shorts, rubbing my sneaker like the lamp in *Aladdin*. To make him laugh, I jumped out of the van with just the one shoe on and I hopped toward him and said: Pardon me, sah, but you seem to be holding my ground!

He laughed. Then he invited me to stay and go swimming in the neighbour's pool.

I looked back to the van. So soon after camp, this was certain to trigger the Fun Limiter. My mother was not going to go for this, and I didn't have a bathing suit—a ready-made excuse. But it was a sorely needed, nearly miraculous opportunity to make a real friend of a camp friend and she was already mad at me, so I approached the driver's side to ask anyhow.

When she wouldn't roll down the window, I waited. Eventually, she granted me a sliver—just enough to hear.

Joel invited me to stay, I said. I can walk home. Can I stay?

No, she said. You just got back from camp.

I asked what else we were doing.

And she said: Is he Saved?

Well I met him at Bible camp, I said.

There's that attitude again, she said, putting the Aerostar into reverse. Whatever, Harry. If your camp friend matters more than your family, do whatever you want and walk back.

Then she left.

So I followed my new friend inside, hiding hurt feelings behind a fake smile.

Joel was a young Jack Nicholson, right down to the arch grin and devilish eyebrows, and to me he seemed like the same brand of natural leading man. He had that It Factor: he was so charming, and just so good to look at, the type of boy you see and have to sigh. I was utterly spellbound by him.

Joel took me upstairs to the master bedroom and began rifling through the dresser like a burglar. My stepdad has some shorts that you can borrow, he said. Here we go: black shorts for the Black kid. He threw a pair of faded trunks behind him, blind. I caught them and laughed to give permission for the joke.

I couldn't believe it when Courage told everyone I wasn't really Black, I said.

He shrugged. *Pfft.* Courage isn't Black either, he's African. Now help me with this.

Joel handed me a stack of pornography, one of two stacks he'd just unearthed from the dresser's bottom drawer, and we lugged the whole collection across the hall to his room—save for one issue of *Asian Fever*, which he left on his mother's bed.

Maybe she'll kick him out, he said, grinning like the Clown Prince of Crime.

Joel sat down with a *Hustler* and encouraged me to help myself to whatever, so I sat down cross-legged with the *Best of Beaver Hunt*, volume 22, a special expanded edition promising a beaver bonanza. I opened to a random page and there I saw a fully nude woman for the first time ever—Mia, according to the magazine. Whatever youthful lust I felt was quickly overcome by shame, and then disgust, which only deepened when I realized that Mia's page was stuck to the page behind it.

That was enough porn for the moment.

Let's go swimming, I insisted.

We cut through an alley that led to a block where the houses were larger, and soon we stood before a six-foot cedar gate with a keypad lock. Joel knew the code. He punched a couple numbers, and we followed a cobblestone path to a massive swimming pool around the back.

You can change in there, he said, pointing to a Rubbermaid storage shed the size of a small house.

The shed was full of unpainted *Star Wars* ceramics—spaceships and robots, mostly, displayed along handcrafted, wraparound shelving—and I would have asked about this, but there wasn't time. I was still tying my trunks when Joel came in, snatched a stark-white R2-D2 from a shelf, and smashed it on the concrete outside.

I threw my hands up in horror.

Don't worry, this guy sucks, Joel said. Now help me throw the barbecue into the pool.

I didn't understand why Joel wanted to throw the barbecue into the pool, and as we watched the big red grill sink into the deep end, I wondered why I'd helped.

We couldn't stick around after that, so we didn't go swimming.

Changing back in Joel's bathroom, I caught a glimpse of myself in the full-length vanity mirror on the back of the door. I saw a little gremlin—humanoid but not quite human, with a fat little face, a head too small for his big Black butt, an uneven smile, unmanageable hair, and glasses crooked from a week at camp. Everything I saw looked wrong to me, so preposterous it must be a joke, like a toddler in high heels or E.T. wearing people clothes. I was just as revolted by my own body as I had been by Mia's. Was I always this ugly or was this some kind of cruel, carnival mirror? Either way, I put a towel over it.

Let's go to Wonderland, Joel said, out of nowhere.

Wonderland was a family amusement park on the outskirts of Abbotsford, just off the Whatcom Road exit at the base of Sumas Mountain, not far from the tree where the boy Louie Sam had been lynched. It was a fifteen-minute walk from Joel's house, which meant it was only a twenty-minute walk from mine.

I had no idea, and it made me feel dumb as a doorknob. Marooned on Glenn Mountain since boyhood, it used to seem so far away. I could have gone down every day.

Wonderland was mostly known for minigolf. The black-lit, basement courses had a theme—you chose from coral sea or jungle—and the outdoor course was built around an old medieval castle, a roadside attraction with white walls and royal blue beavertail shingles and spires. It was a popular destination for birthday parties, as there was little else to do in Abbotsford. Wonderland had everything: a full arcade, a go-kart track, batting cages, tables for rod hockey, air hockey, pizza, and pool, and now, a new name: Castle Fun Park.

Joel was outraged. What happened to Wonderland, he ranted, checking the coin slots for loose tokens. What happened to *my childhood*?

Copyright infringement. There was another Wonderland in south Ontario.

We came across a string of tickets hanging from the Pop-a-Shot and we took them to the prize wall to see what we could get. Joel rang the bell rapid-fire until the manager emerged from the kitchen.

What can I get you?

My childhood back, Joel said, still mourning the erstwhile name of a party place constructed in 1989. He punched the glass countertop. I will not submit to the tyranny of Castle Fun Park!

How about three sour keys, the manager said, opening a jar of rainbow candy.

Deal.

But as soon as the manager left us alone, Joel reached across the counter and snatched the whole caboodle. He took off running, and I had no choice but to chase him, all the way through the long parking lot and across the street to the little block of stores with a gas station at one end and a Burger King at the other.

We went behind the strip, where the drive-thru looped around, and we sat along the chain-link fence that kept us from falling some twenty feet, fatally, into the excavated lot next door—the future home of Sumas Mountain Village.

Back then, there was nothing else around for miles. The Whatcom Road exit was an outpost, just two tiny castles at the edge of the world, one you played through, the other you drove through, and farmland as far as the eye could see. But something was coming. Across the vast cavity, the mountain rose majestically, dense with conifers except for a bald patch ascending along its spine like a shiver. Future development.

Staring up at what I did not know was stolen land, I got the sense that God himself had reached down like a shearer and shaved a strip in the earth, for in a way, He had. The strip was full of signs for Christian construction companies—a cross or fish in every logo.

There used to be another Sumas Mountain village, right where we were—a whole, entire nation even, living around a lake. But the lake was drained in 1924 to near-unanimous approval, according to recorded history. The only archived argument in opposition belongs to Sumas Chief Ned, who told the McKenna-McBride Commission: I am against the dyking because that will mean more starvation for us.

You stole! I said to Joel as soon as I caught my breath. I was scandalized and frankly frightened by my complicity, especially with my back to the abyss, so I shifted to one side.

You're allowed to steal if you're white, Joel said. And besides, they stole from me first. My childhood, man! I've been to, like, fifty birthday parties at Wonderland! So it's not stealing. It's *justice*. Why don't you take a little justice for yourself, as a treat.

No thank you, I said. Thou shalt not steal.

Punch buggy! Joel socked me in the shoulder. It hurt but I didn't say anything.

I spotted the Beetle in line for the drive-thru, and my eyes followed the little red Volkswagen around to the Burger King pick-up window, then past a blinking OPEN sign I never would have noticed otherwise.

I had no idea there were businesses out back. But there was a small salon tucked away there, next to a sandwich shop. Each was about the size of a wardrobe. Haircuts were just fifteen dollars at the salon, Emotional Rescue Hair, and at the sandwich shop, footlongs were five.

Looking back, based on where it was, I'm sure it mostly serviced truckers. But the name spoke to me and I was so desperate for a sign that I saw the one behind the Burger King and imagined a portal to my own private wonderland, or perhaps a magical gift shop run by my guardian angel, special guest star Della Reese, and I would drop in, desperate to be made beautiful, and Della would say: Oh my baby, you are.

Emotional Rescue Hair? I said to Joel, with a scoff. Surely they can't be serious!

Think it's Narnia in there? Joel said, stuffing sour keys into his mouth.

Wouldn't that be something.

I wanted a fade. Will Smith had a fade. *The Fresh Prince of Bel-Air* was on all the time that summer. On Thursdays, I'd watch old episodes back-to-back on WGN Chicago, then two more on TBS Superstation, before switching to the CBC for a new episode. You could tell a new episode by the new Aunt Vivian. I liked the old Aunt

Vivian, personally, but she was gone now, and no one ever bothered to explain where she went.

No matter. Most of all I liked Will, who was by far the show's coolest, Blackest character, and the only one, to my mind, worth aspiring to. Will was born and raised in West Philadelphia. He was from *the streets*.

I was not, and people could tell. More often I reminded them of Carlton, Will's rich, clueless cousin, a child of such wealth and privilege that he was completely out of touch with how to be a real Black person, and that was the joke. Carlton's entire existence was a punchline, like Steve Urkel from *Family Matters*, another common comparison because I wore glasses. Carlton had a dance. Come to think of it, they both had a dance. Of course they did. The whole performance was a dance. They were clowning: their ill-performed Blackness was a strange ballet; the comedy was in their movement, so their entire existence was funny, and it was humiliating and demoralizing to be told that I reminded anyone of either character.

I wanted people to see me and think of Will.

But that's not what happened when Joel and I entered. I wasn't touched by an angel—just a racist hairdresser, a thin white woman with no chin and no backside, blond, who saw me and immediately thought to say: Do you know who you look like? The guy from *The Fresh Prince*. The nerdy one.

And she asked me to do the dance, and I had so little self-respect that I agreed to before I even sat down. My heart wasn't in it, but she didn't notice.

You're hilarious, the stylist said, and reigning over me, she remarked, I'd pay good money for these curls. She advanced as though she had. She grabbed a handful and fingered my 4c hair like it was bubble wrap, stimming off the texture—It's so spongy, she cackled—and she cut me into silly shapes like a Wooly Willy, making herself laugh, wringing me dry of all hope for this haircut.

I might sweep this up and keep it in a bag and just touch it, she said to herself, although it's probably not as good when it's dead. What am I thinking? All hair is dead. Do you know what you should try? Dreadlocks. Like Bob Marley, mon! I bet dreadlocks keep better.

And she asked me how I felt about the N-word, and when I said it didn't bother me, it's just a word, she said it three times in the mirror, too eagerly, summoning something that did.

Still I stayed until the end, and when she asked, I said I liked the cut, pretending I could see without my glasses. Then I gave her the whole twenty dollars and let myself out.

Can you believe her? Joel said, laughing as we left. What a cougar.

But I ran away from there, reminded of why I rarely left home. Later, in Joel's room, I looked at women who looked just like her but without any clothes on, and I ate sour keys for hours until my tongue began to bleed. I left around dinner, feeling disgusting, and I made my way back up the mountain on foot.

On the way home, I tried to reorient myself, to make sense of my surroundings so I knew where I could go if I was left behind when everyone was raptured.

Probably Joel's house, I thought, and after misspending the afternoon, sprinting from sin to sin, I came home ashamed, and afraid it would come to that.

My mother saw me right away and said: Whoever cut your hair did an awful job.

I hadn't even noticed.

She took me to the mirror so I could see it for myself, and I beheld a shapeless mess: irregular lines, uneven edges, and what's worse, a strictly surface job. Either she didn't care or she never looked closely, and she stayed away from the roots completely. The stylist's mindless cuts found layers of neglect, all buried underneath, and she left them there. The woman made a fool of me. She let me leave, helpless, when I came to her for help. She should have been ashamed of herself.

Fortunately my mother knew how to fix it. It was not my first bad haircut—just the first since she learned to give her son a basic shape-up. So she did it again.

It wasn't ideal. By then I was broiling with an adolescent shame I wanted my mother nowhere near. But I was afraid of her; it's why I went to someone else, and why I hung my head and said nothing when she came at me with the cordless clippers.

Alone in my room with a head full of the furthest thing from emotional rescue, I made a new plan: no more cuts. No more trips to the shearing shed, no more strangers standing over me. I would just let it grow more and more massive each day until it became the most majestic afro in world history—a nimbus of glory, like the halo of a patron saint.

Then nobody would call me Carlton.

They'll call me Black Samson, I thought, forgetting that they put out his eyes.

• • •

What am I thinking? All hair is dead.

The new millennium didn't amount to much. Y2K was a tempest in a teacup. Not a single plane fell from the sky, there was no Second Coming of Christ, and nobody was raptured.

Which meant that I had to keep trying to grow this ridiculous afro. I thought it would be rounder. Instead, it was malformed and matted and there was no majesty in it—just knots and gnarls, enough to make picking more painful than ever.

It had always been painful. Early on, somebody told my mother about a special comb for Black boys. They called it an afro pick— aptly, I often thought, as it pulled my curls right out, in cottony clumps. Stop crying, my mother would say, when I started. Later I learned it was easier after a shower. By then, though, I hated the pick, and the way that it made me feel, inside and out, was too gruesome to do to myself.

So I put it away, and soon my so-called afro was a nappy crown of nettle, stinging all over. I wondered, at times, if I'd come down with head lice again. I had lice in first grade. It was awful. I thought of the nit comb, the worst kind of comb, and I scratched my head over the bathroom sink, looking for eggs, every time it was itchy. I shampooed daily—Johnson's Baby No More Tangles—but my hair was no good. Nothing made it feel better or clean. It came out smelling like wet wool, and the odour outlasted the water, and then it was too dry and it broke easily, like a tumbleweed.

The overall effect was to disgrace me so thoroughly that my hair might have been a dunce cap. It was a bush of burning shame, and when perfect strangers asked to touch it out in public, I cringed, which only presented it, and they took the shame in their hands and said: It feels like a cloud!

This was not the nimbus I was going for.

At the end of the ski season, we went up to Whistler. At the hat shop in the village, I found a big black Stetson from the Outdoor collection, constructed of crushable wool.

And I thought: Now *that's* black.

It was the type of hat you only buy on vacation—away from the place that holds your identity like a captive—where you feel free, at last, to transform. I bought it, of course, and I tried to become the sort of person who might wear it. But I did not know what sort of person that was. It was the hat of a Blaxploitation hero—Sweetback, Shaft, Superfly—but I knew nothing of these men, and nothing about how to wear a hat sold by the gallon except that it went on my head. So I hid my ugly afro underneath it like sensitive information, redacted.

It's not just hair.

The hair is the flower that speaks to the health of the roots. More than a mere decoration, it stands for the life underneath, for its present condition—its history, too, as the colour and shape of each flower attest to its reason for being. Transplanted or potted, removed from its context, it struggles to thrive, for it lacks what it needs from the natural world. Consider the bold bird of paradise, otherwise known as the crane lily, famed for its multi-hued flower that looks like a half-submerged heron. That's not what it is, though: the beak is the tail, and the crown is the wings of a sunbird in flight. Did you know? Do you know it looks inward, not skyward? Do you know that it grew, over time, to resemble the cape weavers that feed on its nectar, its pollen, its pea-like black seeds; it was taken from South Africa, and now it stands in suburban gardens, baffled and sterile, like half of what makes it is missing?

I had no idea.

Neither did I know that the hair is the body, and its treatment is felt from head to toe. So the rest of me was redacted as well.

That day I became a ghost, and suddenly I needed a whole gimmick just to have any definition at all. Back at home, in the foyer coat closet, I found a faded leather jacket, greenish-black, that belonged to the man my father used to be. I completed the costume with my magnetic clip-on sunglasses.

I went out dressed as the invisible man.

But the invisible man becomes a villain overnight. Unseen, he forgets himself, and the next thing you know, he's a thief.

I wasn't a thief. That's what I kept telling Joel.

Me neither, he'd say. I'm a shoplifter.

By the spring, he was practically a professional. Anything you wanted, be it candy, condoms, comics, Joel was the man that you needed to see. At Yale Secondary School, they called him Hustler Kid, like the character on *Recess* that he already resembled, even before he stole a trench coat from Value Village. He spent the weekend lining it with double-sided duct tape.

Sticky fingers get more sprinkles, Joel said, throwing the jacket open like a flasher.

Joel would have made a good flasher. He was downright shameless. I envied that about him. He was fearless too, and sometimes it seemed like he lived in a world in which there was nothing to fear. A classmate inquired about a didgeridoo. The next day, Joel walked the instrument right out of the music store like it was nothing. Nobody came after him. Nobody cared.

And I thought: No one is watching. If Joel can stroll in, dressed as two tots pretending to be tall, and leave the music store with a five-foot horn in his hands, what's the harm in helping myself to some Skittles? A Coffee Crisp? A Crispy Crunch? Will anyone miss this orange roll of Mentos?

Fruity Mentos?! I scoffed, upon seeing the new flavour, you must be putting me on.

I knew Mentos as mints. They were the Freshmaker, and that made sense. Freshness was a mint thing. This was well-established. Fruity meant candy. To my mind, there was a world of difference between mints and candy—it's what separated the men from the boys—and suddenly those worlds were colliding in the checkout aisle. I had to know how a fruit-flavoured mint made any sense.

So I stole them, but only to try them. They were not the Freshmaker.

This is just a big Skittle, I told Joel.

Now the thrill of stealing—*that* was the Freshmaker. The rush was incredible. The surge of panic; the avalanche of shame; the fear of damnation. And then the triumph of shoving it all down like a pillow between your legs, deep, deep, deep, down, down where it feels so good, and the thrill that comes with getting what you actually want is a thrill so fulfilling that it becomes a need in hindsight, oh wow, oh wow.

I relished my season as a shoplifter, and this paragraph is a montage (set to "Give It to Me Baby," by Rick James) in which I steal all kinds of candy from every unattended checkout aisle in town. Gobstoppers and Popeye Sticks, Werther's whenever I wanted. Give it to me. Any chocolate bar but Bounty. Safeway sold Cadbury Mini Eggs in bulk; I scooped them right into my pocket. Give it to me. My most brazen theft was two bulging handfuls of sour keys from a bin at Blockbuster Video while my father was renting *Mystery Men*. I took anything and everything. Give me that sweet, funky stuff.

I had it all wrong, though: I was not the Invisible Man—more like Invisible Boy, from the movie we rented, who can only disappear when no one is watching him.

Mr. Furious asks: So you're only invisible to yourself?

No, says Invisible Boy. If I look at myself, I become visible again.

The Blue Raja asks: How can you be certain you've achieved transparency?

When you go invisible, the boy explains, you can feel it.

You can feel it when they see you, too. One day I was spotted.

It must have been April. We did not shop at Funk's Foods, usually. The Mennonite grocery was all the way out on Clearbrook Road, the edge of the white side of town. We only stopped in at Easter, for lilies and a loaf of paska—the white bread frosted to look like white cake, which is said to represent the Christian tradition in some way or another.

That day, we were a family of five. My father was over the Atlantic, flying home from Amsterdam; he was travelling back through time, having departed tomorrow to land in Vancouver late tonight.

My mother, Mike, and Tom made a beeline for the bakery, toward the back, while Ben hung a right, down an aisle. Me, I wandered aimlessly for a while, then I lingered by the checkouts, and when the white-haired ladies finally stopped eyeing me suspiciously, I slipped a roll of fruity mints up the sleeve of my coat. Later, feeling seen, I moved the Mentos to my glasses case. Who would ever think to look in there?

The one who saw me: a brown man about thirty. He met us at the Aerostar. His arms were crossed and he wore a homemade police uniform, navy blue slacks and a sky blue button-up, and his thinning hair was combed to hide a bald patch.

Excuse me, he said. My name is Sunny. I'm the loss prevention officer. He tapped a badge that looked like it came from the dollar store. Would you mind emptying your pockets?

At first we thought he was talking to Ben. I was dressed as a bad boy but he was the real one.

Ben was on weed. He got a used car for his sixteenth birthday; our parents paid a penny more than half to retain ownership, and when he was caught hotboxing the little red hatchback with a friend, my father cancelled the insurance until Ben agreed to go to rehab. To keep tabs on him once he refused, they turned the Prayer Hotline into a kids' phone, and tapped it, warning me—and only me—that they were listening, and that every conversation was recorded.

I couldn't imagine smoking weed. Drugs opened your mind, and that's how the demons got in. But my older brother seemed to enjoy getting high, and he seemed to enjoy breaking all kinds of other laws, too.

So the four of us turned to my brother.

Sunny shook his head. Not him. *You.*

Well, okay, but I don't know what you think you're going to find, I said, turning my pockets inside out. It's just so typical to look at me and think—

The glasses case, he interrupted. Open it.

So I opened the plastic clamshell, nervously, tilting away so the candy might fall, smoothly, invisibly, back into the sleeve of my jacket. But I had no sleight of hand. Instead, the stolen Mentos fell between my feet, unfurling like a red carpet.

Follow me, please.

Back through Funk's, there was a small, square door behind the bakery: the Loss Prevention office, a partially renovated storage closet with a ceiling so low the adults had to duck. The little room smelled like sweat and spicy lamb, and there were only two chairs for three people. Sunny sat down at the desk in front of nine screens stacked up like *Hollywood Squares*. It must have been new equipment. The label maker was still sitting out. The other chair was meant for me. It was full of lost coats, as though Sunny had torn a layer off every thief and kept it as a trophy. The pile was intimidating, but I squeezed in beside it. It was that or stand next to my mother, who was half-hunched between us, by the door, strangling her purse strings.

That's you, Sunny said, tapping at the shadowy figure on CAMERA 03. There you are, buddy.

There I was. The resolution was so low you could hardly identify anything else. Filmed from above, beneath the fluorescent lights, the white-haired ladies could barely be distinguished from the tile. Everyone was indistinct but me. Everything was right where it belonged until I got there. All is well at the market, until a sinful blackness creeps in like a human oil spill, black as all hell, this thing, downright demonic, lurching about in search of something to possess. It was a low-budget horror, a creature feature from found footage, which is scarier, because it's easier to forget that it's fake. Even knowing that the monster was me ten minutes ago, I was afraid of it; my instinct was to rebuke it.

I'll tell you what *you* are, Sunny shouted, rewinding the tape. A good-for-nothing thief!

And beyond Sunny—for as he continued to berate me, he lost opacity like a window defrosting, and I looked through him, watching the screens again—I saw myself differently.

I saw my older brother too, on CAMERA 05. Ben was standing at the wall of European candy with a big bag of his favourite: double-salted liquorice. Then he dropped it into his shirt. He went to the next aisle over, right past Sunny—right through him, according to the low-res footage—and found the latest issue of *For Him Magazine*. He put it down his pants like it was.

Meanwhile, my every move had been watched. I came through the big doors on CAMERA 02 and the little doors of the Loss Prevention office opened on CAMERA 04. Sunny was never far from me. As I reviewed the footage a third time, it occurred to me that he was always going to follow me, even if I hadn't come in dressed as the villain from "Satan, Bite the Dust," and I felt like the biggest idiot ever.

I could send you to juvenile detention for this, Sunny said. Do you know what would happen to you in there? To you? To *you?* He picked up the phone to intimidate me further.

I don't want to go to jail, I whimpered.

The dial tone was deafening. But that's when Sunny saw my mother's fury in full, and the intimidation game was won. One good, hard stare was all it took to put the fear of God into him. He hung up the phone.

You're lucky, he said.

Sunny took my name and banned me from the store for two years. But that was it. We were dismissed, and for a moment, I was glad to have come in with a Prayer Warrior in my corner.

For a moment.

You humiliated me, my mother whispered viciously by the marbled rye, and she fled the store as if to leave me behind.

Speed-walking to keep up with her, I thought: If she backs over me in the parking lot, Sunny will see it on CAMERA 01.

• • •

I went straight upstairs to my little white room, awaiting an all-out assault on my conduct. My mother might actually kill me, I thought, and I began to read my Bible, as a shield, to show repentance in the hopes she might show mercy. Then I got a bit excited. This was sure to be an all-time eruption, and once my mother really let me have it, we could talk for real, and reckon with the reasons I had done it. It could be good for us. In the calm after the storm, maybe I would meekly say: I put up the curtains.

And maybe she would say: I saw that.

My mother might see me. It was so perfect, and so necessary, that I wondered if I'd wanted to be caught.

But she never came upstairs.

Just before midnight I heard the garage door, and I assumed the confrontation had been outsourced to my father. That was exciting too. What was he going to do—spank me? I was much too old for that, and no one had been spanked in several years.

My parents retired the practice for Mike and Tom. I saw it all. They were fighting in the car until my mother shouted: Five bare-bottom spankings! But even her weak palms were too much for them. Mike suffered two swats and fell to the floor in hysterics, dry-heaving and gasping apologies. Tom did the same in advance of his turn to be punished. They bellowed like two public mourners until they were blessed with a pardon.

That seemed unfair to me, and while I did not want to argue that my brothers deserved the abuse, I did want an acknowledgement that, in hindsight, I hadn't either.

My mother explained: It hurts them too much. And unlike you, they demonstrated real remorse.

I wanted to circle back to that. Whoever knocked on my door was going to have to answer for it.

But nobody knocked. Around midnight I realized I'd been sent to bed without supper.

No one knocked the next morning either. I didn't know that anyone was even awake until I heard the garage door open, and from the window in Mike and Tom's room, I watched the Aerostar pull away. My family returned in the late afternoon with two bags of leftover movie popcorn.

What did you see? I asked.

The Road to El Dorado, Tom responded.

The silent treatment struck me as a special kind of violence. When you hold the power to set someone free with your words and you choose not to speak, you take their distress by the hilt and drive it deeper into their guts. My father used to offer reassurance after spankings. You know that I love you, he'd say, while I cried, and it took away some of the sting, and the shame. But this new approach left me in anguish and offered no path to relief. It was worse, exponentially worse, to my mind, and the physical suffering lingered for longer.

It took a week to make the torture stop.

I'd been reading the Old Testament, but it was a slog—there were so many genealogies, and God was much more genocidal than I remembered. Still, I knew better than to question Him. I switched to the New Testament, and there, in the Gospel of Matthew, where Joseph encounters an angel, I found the way forward.

My mother was at the kitchen table, reading the *Vancouver Sun*.

Mom, I said, Did I ever see an angel?

And she looked up from the newspaper and said: You don't remember?

So my mother reminded me about the big tent revival in Mission, the night I looked above me and beheld a bright light—an angel, delivering blessings to all who called on the Lord—and she swooned in recalling our onstage encounter with the Holy Spirit, and how she always knew that God had something special for me, but from that day forward, she was certain.

So don't be your brother, she said. Cut it out. You have a higher calling.

I looked down at the newspaper. The front-page headline asked:

Whose baby is this? A child had been abandoned at the hospital. They found the baby bundled in a grocery bag. It might have been me, if not for my mother's benevolence.

I'm sorry, I said.

I saw a skookum outfit at the mall the other day, my mother said. I thought of you. But it was very loud, and you're wearing all black these days.

I'm changing my look, I said. This one gives the wrong impression.

I'm happy to hear that, she said. It was Hawaiian print. Such a dynamic design. I almost thought about getting it for your birthday, but I wasn't sure.

And I said: Show it to me.

We went into town that afternoon, to Sevenoaks mall, and at a store called Off the Wall, my mother pointed to the display. The mannequin wore a bright-red aloha shirt and matching shorts.

Isn't it fun? Do you know what an outfit like this says to people?

Hello *and* goodbye, I thought, fascinating myself.

Bold and confident, my mother said. But you tell me—maybe it's not your style.

And I said: It's my style. It was a little gimmicky, but gimmicky seemed like the way to go. If I could not make any sense of my difference or make it go away, at least I could make it intentional.

We bought another aloha shirt from Bootlegger and, at home, my mother pulled two more from the back of her closet, along with a tan Panama hat that used to belong to her father.

I was glad to have a different hat. The Stetson didn't match the new look, and my hair was still redacted. The shirts were ghastly. One had marlins and the other had flamingoes, and the fabric was a cheap polyester that clung to me like plastic wrap. But I did not want to squander the goodwill I had earned that afternoon, so I lied through my teeth, to us both.

These are great, I said. Such a dynamic design.

• • •

The transformation happened overnight. One day, I was the Man in Black. The next, I was a brand-new kind of boy, in technicolor.

Out in the world, no one seemed to know what to do with my unexpected rebrand, and I was delighted to present such a conundrum. I felt in control, and I didn't much mind when they snickered at what I was wearing. My livery was yet another artificial shield, just like my glasses, and a better shield than any hat or haircut. It allowed me to believe it was the colour of my clothing, not my skin, that made my every interaction so uncanny.

You'd have thought I was obsessed with Hawaii. It wasn't me, of course; the obsession was my mother's. She even started paying me in shirts instead of cash. By the summer of 2000, I was a reluctant collector, with a closet of many colours. Every new top seemed like overkill, but the outfits made my mother start to see me. Dressed like this, you couldn't miss me, and it is useful to pretend to love the things your captors love, and thus be loved by association.

Two weeks before I turned fifteen, and six weeks from my second year at Bible camp, I was even invited to see Disney's *The Kid* with my mother and two younger brothers. I leapt at the chance.

I don't know if you're interested, my mother said as they were leaving, and when I assured her that I was, of course I was, she said: Then hurry up and get yourself together.

So I threw on my red aloha shirt and tucked it into matching shorts. I clipped on my magnetic sunglasses and put on my Panama hat. Then I beheld my ensemble in the mirror and I said: The king of camp.

I ran down the hallway, afraid that they might leave without me.

I fell down the stairs. Rounding the corner at the landing, the fourth of fourteen steps, my right ankle buckled and snapped like a candy cane. I tumbled down the other ten, somersaulting to the bottom, and landed in the old wooden cradle.

Are you okay? My mother shouted from the kitchen.

I'm fine, I'm fine, I whimpered, and I hobbled out the door.

My red right ankle was a melon. It was broken and I knew it in my heart. We had to go to the hospital. But I did not want to be the Boy Who Ruined *The Kid* for Everybody, so I said nothing more about it until the movie let out. I simply chose not to believe it, refused to accept there was anything swelling within me. I followed my family into the theatre, and I sat there in the dark, trying not to think about it.

6

=

HOW DO YOU DO?

(or The Boy inside the Echo)

The Captain will initiate the descent.

For a time, this was my father's favourite phrase. He'd been passing the message along to air traffic controllers for more than two decades, always in reference to somebody else. But in the summer of my broken ankle, he was finally promoted to Pilot in Command, and on his first flight from the 737's left seat, when the co-pilot asked who had the stick on approach, my father responded thusly, and was delighted, at long last, to mean himself.

He said it all the time after that: leaving upstairs, driving me downtown to my dishwashing job, and several times that September, when my mother decided there was too much else on her plate to supervise my last two years of high school. Mike and Tom needed the extra attention—someone to sit there and keep them on track—so I fell to my father, who was glad to have fresh context for his catchphrase.

The Captain, he told me, taking me under his wing, will initiate the descent.

But really, he left me on autopilot. My father wasn't senior enough for four stripes in Vancouver: to keep his captaincy, he was deadheading to Edmonton—or Bad-monton, as he came to call it that winter. The man was around even less than before, and with my mother focused solely on my siblings, nobody noticed when I dropped out of school.

Six months later, having done nothing, I said that I was done for the year.

Harry, I'm taking the first birdie out of Bad-monton, my father said weeks afterward on the phone from Leduc. When I get home, let's do your report card.

I forged the whole school year that Saturday. I unboxed my Grade 11 classroom videos and put them all back, out of order. I made my textbooks look used by breaking every spine, folding a few corners, and spilling water on everything. I wrote the quizzes and exams with the answer keys open, aiming for A-minuses, and to be safe, I used twenty-seven different pens and pencils (I counted), to imply that the coursework was completed over time. The only math I did was to determine which assignments I could skip without failing, and when my father got home, I gave him everything, except the essays. It would have taken forever to write them all.

Instead, I broke the printer.

Gee, I hope Mitchnick is further along, my father said, sitting down to a year's worth of homework assembled in a day.

Morton Mitchnick was the arbitrator hired, following the merger of Air Canada and Canadian Airlines, to create an integrated seniority list for the pilots. Somehow, this had taken six months.

It should only take six seconds, said the Captain. Date of hire, that's all that matters.

Seniority determined salaries, scheduling, even assigned aircraft, and my father was deeply concerned that an unjust award, due any day now, could cost him his 737 captaincy, and tens of thousands in take-home pay. He might never be able to afford a motorhome.

It's a merger, not a takeover, my father said. A merger of equals.

Air Canada pilots disagreed. What mattered most from their perspective were the rival airline's destinations in Asia-Pacific. The accompanying pilots were simply excess baggage—the human lives caught up in the enterprise of seizing a bankrupt airline by the routes—so they weren't entitled to any seniority at all. Canadian's guys should start from the bottom, Air Canada's guys argued, histories erased, beginning again as second-class citizens, grateful to have jobs at all.

To me, this was nonsense. Inside each cockpit was a wide-body pilot, just the same, and it seemed downright un-Canadian to enshrine the supremacy of Air Canada's airmen by prioritizing their careers at another group's expense.

It's actually very Canadian. But I didn't know that then.

Where are the essays?

They're on my computer, I lied, but the printer is broken. I could try putting them all on a floppy disk, but that old Macintosh has never met a file it couldn't corrupt. Probably better for you to come upstairs or, I mean, I guess, honestly, you could just take my word for it and give me B-pluses across the board, since I'm sure that's what they'll average out to anyway.

And my father said: Hmmmmm.

I knew he'd fall for it. The Captain was an easy mark, easier even than the good grades I earned by lying to him, and he hadn't been up to my room since it moved across the hall. These days, he only took the stairs to go to sleep.

But something was bothering him. He sat up straight and raised an eyebrow, and for a moment I was nervous, until finally he asked: What are we listening to?

DC Talk's *Jesus Freak*, the 1996 Grammy winner for Best Rock Gospel Album.

My father made a face like something stank. Harry, this is rap, he said, and you know what I always say: rap is crap.

This was another of my father's favourite phrases. The Captain only listened to classical music. The shelves in his office were full of Brahms, Bach and Handel, his favourite, and there was a bronze bust of Beethoven up there too, presiding over everything.

Dad, Beethoven looks Black, I said as he ejected my CD.

He wasn't, my father frowned. He was a German.

I'm a German too, I said.

Well you're no Beethoven, he said.

My father opted for Mendelssohn's Violin Concerto in E Minor, one of the great concertos, he explained. The fiddler opens the moody first movement alone, unconventional for its time, before the orchestra comes in hot, restating the theme. But the fiddle is known for its fitness, Harry, so the soloist becomes an accompanist, playing along until the quiet climax—an extended solo this time, surprise—and it sounds like the fiddle is falling apart from the dissonance. The darker, middle section introduces a contrasting countertheme, and now the fiddler must be nimble enough to accompany himself. Then it's off to the parallel major for an effervescent finale. It's the cat's ass. You're gonna love it.

My father explained all of this to me without a single stammer, which only made it stranger that he couldn't hear the difference between rap and alternative rock.

The Mitchnick award came down around midnight, mere moments before April Fool's Day on the east coast. Fitting, as it seemed like a cruel prank: instead of going by date of hire, Mitchnick used a variable ratio model that placed six hundred Air Canada pilots in the top eight hundred, and just as my father had feared, he found himself one spot below a Mr. Wright, hired seventeen years after he was.

Even if he wasn't relegated to first officer, my father would never have the seniority to captain a 767, which was his dream: it was twice the size of a 737, and the cockpit was all digital. But it was worse than that. Ben was seventeen. In his bid to build seniority, my father had missed all kinds of precious moments in his children's lives, and now there was little, career-wise, to show for his sacrifice.

Admittedly, the Captain mostly fathered from afar—even at home, he seemed to stay somewhere else—but suddenly there was nothing to show for any of it. So he started over immediately, with me.

How's your handshake?

My father spun around and held his palm out. He was testing me. But it was a weird thing to do all of a sudden, and I wasn't ready. I flinched and shook his hand fearfully, looking up, ashamed, and it seemed to make him sadder for some reason.

Standing, he said: If you want to land that dream job at the House of James, you'll have to do better than that! A man's handshake says it all—it's the difference between first class and coach.

The first time I applied to the Christian bookstore, the cashier threw my resumé away. Her nametag said Deb, and she was shaped like a budgie.

Deb thought I had a bad body, I could tell. It was probably the limp. The cast came off in August, three days before camp, but the ankle was sensitive well into September. Walking around, I developed a double-step, and the woman seemed to blame me for it.

Or maybe she hated Hawaiian print.

You don't have any work experience, she said, glancing down with a scowl, completely disregarding my half-decade as a Sunday school helper.

That's your fault, my father said. Always ask to speak to a manager. If someone else tries to take your application? He shook his head. *I will leave after speaking to Lando.* And when he arrives, you hold out your hand like this, making eye contact, and squeeze, good and firm for two seconds, how do you do, sir, always sir, one Mississippi, two Mississippi, my name is Harry Mooney, and I believe I could be an asset to you.

The two-second rule was useful; however, I could not imagine myself saying *How do you do*. I'll come up with something else, I said, something that sounds more like me.

Yo, bro, what's happening, man, my father said, mocking a manner in which I did not speak. That ain't gonna cut it, homeboy.

That doesn't sound like me either, I said, practising a firmer handshake. Hello, Lando, my name is Harry Mooney, and I could be an asset for you.

You have to say *How do you do*, my father said.

I'm not gonna say that. How about *Nice to meet you*.

And that's when the Captain, who was doing a very fatherly thing here and would appreciate if I just went with it, flew right off the handle.

No! he shouted, clapping the table, and a stack of quizbooks filled with lies fell over and spilled off the side slowly, hilariously, like it was raining dumb stuff I didn't need to know. It was so distracting that I jumped when he kept talking, forgetting I wasn't alone.

You think you're Joe Cool, my father said. Get over yourself and listen to me. You *have* to say *How do you do*.

I assented to end the conflict. But secretly, I still meant to improvise. Standing by the Bibles to see Lando on Monday morning— bright and early, so he knows we're not lazy, the Captain insiste ̇—I fully expected to come up with something better. I was wearing my red aloha shirt, tucked into khakis from Costco.

But Lando emerged from a door I didn't know about. I panicked. Searching my thoughts, I heard the hiss of blank tape, and, lost for words, I found only the ones I walked in with.

How do you do, sir, I stammered, surprising us both. My name is Harry Mooney and I will be an asset to you.

The bookseller seemed to suspect some kind of joke. But suddenly, he decided to take me seriously. Lando looked down, examining my application, then past it, further down, at me, and after a moment, grinning greedily, he asked: What's your availability?

Sir, I'm homeschooled, I said, selling myself. So I'm completely free.

• • •

My mother made me go to youth group that night. I tried to get out of it, but I had nowhere else to be.

I'd been going with Joel on Mondays to Northview Community Church. We were regulars there for months. The richest congregation in Abbotsford boasted the best youth group by far, and the sermon was short—ten minutes, tops. After, it was all fun and games: balloon tag in the bonus room, basketball in the double-wide gym, and finally, a free-for-all at Checkers—the fifties-era milkshake place built into the building, across from the gift shop, where Jones Soda sold for a buck.

Just before Valentine's Day, I split a root beer with a girl I liked. Her older brother cornered me in the parking lot.

Hey doink, he said, pushing me up against a lamppost, stay *the fuck* away from my sister. She won't be dating some shitlegs like you, I promise.

And on the drive home, my mother said: That's what you get for chasing girls.

I was more of an irregular after that, and I'd stopped attending Northview entirely when a competing youth group was launched at my current home church, Stone Rolled Away Christian Fellowship.

Several former Gateway members had migrated there: Tilda Eubanks, Destiny's family, the Werther's lady, and us—returning, it turned out, after more than a decade away. All were absorbed into the Fellowship, which was actually a family church. Adam and Amos Schumacher, the associate pastors, were brothers who married sisters, Eileen and Ellen Stratford. Their father, Milton Stratford, was Stone Rolled Away's main Man of God. He was a pious and obdurate man who commanded respect from the rest of the Schumacher family. The whole clan lived together in a huge duplex near the airport, along with their nine children, five white, four Black.

The Black kids came courtesy of Eileen and Ellen's adopted sister, Esther Stratford, the woman from Gateway who swore that we knew each other. My family had first attended Stone Rolled Away when she was just a teen and I was just a wee one, learning how to use my legs. She used to take me by the hand and guide me down the aisle.

But those days were long gone. Esther was a drug addict now, a lost soul, and she couldn't stop having her drug dealers' babies. Eileen and Amos adopted each one. It was their obligation and somehow also to their credit. The fourth was brand new, and Esther's tubes were tied after delivery to prevent any more surprises. She returned to a drug den, no doubt, on Vancouver's Downtown Eastside; the baby, whose name was spelled strangely, remained in Abbotsford.

The spelling was amended once the adoption was official.

Eileen and Amos believed the best form of birth control was abstinence, and right around their fourth adoption, they launched a care cell just to say so, meeting Mondays at their house, where the majority of Stone Rolled Away's young people already lived. But everyone was encouraged to bring their friends.

I'll stick with Checkers, Joel said, when I asked him. Our first text was the *I Kissed Dating Goodbye* youth study guide. He wasn't interested.

But Destiny brought a friend. We picked her up from a house at the base of Glenn Mountain and the girl whose house it was came with her.

This is Ashley, Destiny said, climbing into the back next to Mike.

Ashley sat down beside me in a low-cut white tank top, showing serious cleavage, and high-waisted denim shorts, showing legs. We met. Destiny's friend was curvy and her hair was very curly—a wild mane of ropey black locks. She had light brown skin, too tan to be a tan, and, finally, finding her brown eyes, we met again, this time with feeling—the feeling of falling, not into love, not yet, but into the same oasis.

Tell me, Ashley, I said, turning on the charm, are you excited to kiss dating goodbye?

And Ashley said: Oh, I'm gonna kiss dating goodbye *with tongue*.

I overlaughed. In the rear-view, I saw my mother roll her eyes and turn up the radio—Praise 106.5, blasting worship music in a bid to drown us out. Ashley and I leaned in closer. Soon, we were fused at the knees like a three-legged race, and the prickle of her calf through my lime-green polyester pants felt like sparks flying between us.

Ashley was Persian. Her father was born in Iran. Her mother was a German, raised in Abbotsford's deeply devout Holdeman Mennonite community, whose members lived modest lives, shunning technology, and made their homes among the other Anabaptist sects on Bradner Road. Ashley's mom grew up just down the hill from Gateway Christian Centre, attending elementary school where I attended church—at Aberdeen. As a young woman, she rebelled, and she fell for a Muslim who worked at a greenhouse. Soon she fell again, pregnant. He abandoned her with a secret that she kept for seven months, and when she couldn't hide it anymore, she was shunned by her family and expelled from the Church of God in Christ. But she left with her head held high, and her baby.

True love waits, Pastor Amos told us at youth group, wrapping his wrist in Scotch tape. When you have sex before marriage, guess what?—unbinding himself like a mummy revealing its true face, the Man of God raised the adhesive strip, spoiled by detritus and flecked with his body hair—the mistake sticks to you forever.

That's how you get a *tapeworm*, I joked, ignorant about sexual health. Nobody laughed.

I'm not a mistake, Ashley said, not to me but to everyone, and suddenly, it seemed, all eyes were on us. We were sitting on the couch together, our fingers almost touching behind an accent pillow. But now she was sitting upright.

My mom was an unwed mother, she said. How can you say I'm a mistake?

It was a challenging question from a relative stranger. Eileen cut in.

No one is saying that you or anybody here is a mistake, she said. The mistake is premarital sex. Actions have consequences, sometimes lasting ones. That's why the Bible calls us to be in the world, not of it—to flee youthful lust, to turn your back on sexual immorality and follow the righteous path. It's tough to stay pure. But you won't go unrewarded.

Eileen went on to explain that she and Amos met as teenagers, committed to saving themselves for one another, and never so much as lain down together before marrying, as teenagers. Look at them now. Look what the Lord has done. See how they shine, blessed in abundance, with room enough in their hearts and their home to adopt Esther's four children, and we thank God for that, because where would all these kids be otherwise?

With their mother, Ashley whispered, and she crossed her arms and sat there, disengaged for a very long time.

Eventually, I brought her back with a bit that never failed: ignorant about moisturizer, too, I drew a game of tic-tac-toe across my very ashy arm, and with my fingernail, I made the first move, placing an O in the corner.

Ashley smirked, and her bad mood went away. Pretending to pay close attention, she put her thumb inside my centre square and drew an X.

She'd fallen right into my trap, but before I could win, Eileen crossed the room, sitting between us.

I called Ashley on the Prayer Hotline as soon as I got home.

We had so much to say that we talked for hours more, asking big questions, hanging on every response, defying every attempt to derail us. Destiny called, complaining that we were her friends, not each other's. Eileen reached out, crying, hurt to be accused of calling anyone a mistake. And then there was my mother, who tried everything.

You've been on the phone all night, she said.

So what? It's a separate line, remember?

Well, Ashley has school in the morning, she said. Time to say goodbye.

Ashley says she's fine.

Well, you should go to bed, my mother said. You're up early tomorrow.

It's not even eleven.

So she turned off all the lights downstairs, and left me in the dark.

My mom is acting really weird, I said to Ashley.

Do you know your *real* mom? Ashley asked. Did she give you anything?

My *birth mother*, I corrected, teaching Ashley my language. My mom is my real mom. But I got my birth mother's Blackness, that's for sure. Her big butt. Her unmanageable hair. I didn't get her nose, though. My mom said it was one of those wide African noses. Luckily, I got my birth father's nose—a good German nose.

It's a nice nose, said Ashley, you're cute. But I meant like, did they leave you with anything?

Oh. Two stuffies, I said. A little brown bunny and a white unicorn. But I only have the bunny right now.

Where's the white unicorn?

My mom has it, I said. It's pure white, white as snow, so she knew it would be special to me. I guess she was afraid I'd get it dirty as a baby, so she put it away until I was older.

You're older now, Ashley said, and after a pause: She still has it?

I guess so.

Do you even know where it is? Have you seen the white unicorn?

What is this, roll call on Noah's ark? I don't know, have you ever seen the rain?

That's bizarre, Ashley said. Why would your mom keep it for herself?

She *isn't* keeping it for herself, I said. She's keeping it for *me*.

And Ashley said: It sounds like she's keeping it *from* you.

It was almost midnight and a figure emerged from the darkness to say so. Say goodbye, Harry, my father said. Ashley's got school and you're up early tomorrow for your big day.

I could see him standing in the kitchen, bathed in blue-green light from the house alarm panel. But I heard my mother. Unscripted, the Captain would say, *You've got an early departure*, and he'd call my big day *your whole hullabaloo*—that's how he spoke, with a bouncy imprecision and a great deal of pilot slang. My mother spoke tersely, as if to blame you for making her speak at all, and she gave orders. *Say goodbye* was very her. My father would have made the hang ten sign with his hand, turned it over and said: *Wheels down, Harry*. The ghost in the kitchen had his moustache, but it was my mother, astrally projected, piloting the pilot like a plane.

It was sound strategy. How could I defy my father after this morning? Come back tomorrow and bring a lunch, Lando had told me. Hired, just like that. I had landed my dream job, and it was all thanks to the Captain. Landings were his speciality, and he's the one who told me what to say.

So I said goodnight.

• • •

The next day, I found myself in the upper room at the House of James, sorting summer sale brochures with a young man named

Jordan. There were deals in every department, and it was up to us—
me and Jordan and a woman called Rachel, back from a mat leave and
deeply unfriendly—to get the word out. The task was to unpack box
after box, enough to block us in until Rachel made us make a path,
and stick a mailing label on each flyer. It was an all-day job, even
before the printer came to life, spitting out thousands of sky-blue
inserts: there was a concert at the coffeeshop, and a new gelato flavour.

Jordan was deeply distressed by the insert. It meant we had to
start all over. He stood up, ready to fight about it, then closed his eyes
and took a breath. Smiling, he said: Do you think we're competing
for one position?

I hope not, I said. Let's just be such a good team that they have
to hire us all.

I'm actually still on maternity leave, Rachel said. I only came in
for the day so I can buy a nicer stroller. You guys are probably competing for a temporary summer job until I'm back to work.

If you come back, Jordan said. Statistically, many mothers don't.

Jordan had arrived under the same impression I had: that the
job was already his. He told me on the steps outside, waiting to get
in. But when Rachel arrived and Deb finally unlocked the door, we
were led upstairs to learn we were temps. They'd pay us for the day,
and we should think of it as a kind of audition—hopefully for more
than one position.

Jordan walked with his hands in his pockets, and the swagger
of someone who knows God is on his side. He reminded me of
Gladstone Gander, Donald Duck's lucky and debonair cousin. The
guy was obviously worthier than me: three years older and wiser,
six inches taller, and much better looking. Jordan looked like whatever you're supposed to look like, and he was dressed for success,
in Buddy Holly's black-rimmed glasses, a stylish sweater-vest and
brown bellbottom pants.

You've been to my house, Jordan said to me, smiling.

Jordan had three brothers, just like I did, and I knew the one my age from Northview—not well, but well enough to fill out the guest list at his fourteenth birthday party. I only stayed a few hours. I remember entering a house that felt familiar, with a frightening, maternal presence downstairs and the children hiding upstairs, and I was relieved when my mother wouldn't let me spend the night. I told him so. Better the devil you know, I said, and Jordan agreed, so with nothing else to do to pass the time, we spent the day bonding over difficult mothers.

I hope my son never talks about me this way, Rachel said.

He probably will, Jordan said.

Your only hope is to buy him the right stroller, I teased.

Rachel took offence. You know, your mother didn't *have* to adopt you, she said.

Yeah, he *definitely* will, Jordan said, and the upper room fell silent for a while.

The hot property at the House of James that year was *The Prayer of Jabez*, a self-help book urging Christians who covet prosperity to pray like a very minor character from 1 Chronicles. Jabez was said to be more honourable than his brothers, and his prayer went: O that you would bless me indeed and enlarge my territory!

God granted his request—and the author's, only strengthening the book's thesis—so the devotional text became an international bestseller, launching a whole pipeline of spinoff product: study guides, journals and Jabez-scented candles; Christmas ornaments, mousepads, and wall art; Jabez for Women. All of it was on sale at the House of James, while supplies lasted. And that's not all, the brochure boasted: certain books were half price and came with leather bookmarks, and every Saturday in June was Buy One, Get One on all products, save for Bibles.

On the back page, I noticed an ad for the new Raze album, which wasn't coming out anymore.

Do you think they know the Black guy's a kid-toucher? I asked aloud. It was in *Christianity Today*. He was arrested last month for sodomizing a thirteen-year-old girl.

That's appalling, Rachel said. Does Lando know?

He did after I told him. He wasn't happy to hear it. It was far too late to amend the flyer. It would have to go out with a picture of a pedophile. Nothing could be done about that.

But we should take all their product off the floor, Lando said. Do they have any other albums?

Their 1999 debut was called *Power*, I said. There's a couple copies downstairs. And the lead single, "Always and Forever," is on *Wow Hits* 2000 and *Wow* 2000: *The Videos*, if you want to be thorough.

Harry, run down and pull *Power* from the shelves.

I did as directed and when I got back, Lando took me to his office for an interview. He asked why I wanted to work at the House of James. I told him I loved everything he sells, especially Christian music; that I read every issue of *CCM Magazine*, cover to cover, and knew everything there was to know about the industry. For me, I told him, this Thursday's must-see TV isn't *Will & Grace* or *Friends*—it's the Dove Awards, Christian music's version of the Grammys, live on the Nashville Network.

You start Saturday, Lando said.

Sitting back down beside Jordan, another artist jumped out of the flyer: Philo Percy. His newest album, *Hymns Acoustic*, recorded live at the Global Worship Academy, was just twenty dollars this summer—allegedly a great savings.

Whoa, this guy sucks! I said. He came to my old church, and we all had to pretend to like his music.

Jordan asked: Why did you have to pretend?

Because it wasn't about the music, I said, sarcastically. It was about the outpouring of the Holy Spirit.

So you had to clap for him or God wouldn't show up? Sheesh—

Jordan said, tearing into a fresh box of brochures—imagine feeling like you had to pretend that something was good, when it wasn't.

I came home with cracks in my fingertips, paper cuts all over, and a full-time job.

We'll have to start thinking about getting you a car, my mother said, sitting with my father in the kitchen, and you should book your N-test right away. I don't want to get stuck driving you to work all summer.

The brand-new law in British Columbia required young people to put a big green *N* on their vehicles—*N* as in novice driver—for the first year. The *N* magnets were truly unfortunate. Kids liked to hold them over my head like bunny ears, or giggle if I found myself standing beside one. Eventually, I made a habit of snatching the joke right out of their hands—and often, from the back of their vehicles.

The *N* stands for Nubian, I would say, wrongly assuming that Nubian simply meant Black. It was a guaranteed laugh. No one else knew what it meant either. Sometimes I'd switch it up and shout: They want a Black guy to drive around with an *N* on his car—what is this, *The Scarlet Letter*?

Laughs and laughs. We all knew what I was getting at there.

I promised to book it right away. Maybe I'll take Ashley out for dinner, I said, waggling my eyebrows.

No dating until you turn sixteen, my mother said, scowling.

That's only a few months away, I responded.

I thought you were doing *I Kissed Dating Goodbye*, she said.

I don't want to kiss dating goodbye, I said, I want to kiss Ashley. I waggled my eyebrows.

I don't think Ashley is right for you, my mother said. God has someone better in mind.

How would you know? What's wrong with her?

She has a single mother, for one. Those girls are always unstable, she said. Their mothers think they can be best friends, so they never learn to respect authority. That's why she was so rude to Eileen.

Eileen told us we were mistakes.

She did not! My mother was angry now. That's a lie and you know it, you liar. Do you take your marching orders from a teenage girl now, your little girlfriend, who just wants to cause trouble? She was very rude to me in the car, you know. She didn't even thank me when she got out. You can tell a lot about a person by the way she treats your mother.

Yeah, whatever, Mom, I said, I'll make sure she sniffs your butt next time.

You shut your cotton-picking mouth! My mother exploded to her feet and her chair went flying out from under her. Don't you dare talk to me that way!

But I was used to being menaced, so this time, I gave it right back.

Hey Mom, I said, can I see the white unicorn, the one you put away for me until I was older? Because, guess what, I'm older.

She left the kitchen. I'll have to see where I put it, she said, halfway up the stairs already, and for a moment, I thought she was coming back. But then I heard her slam the bedroom door.

• • •

Ashley threw her arms around me coming up the driveway. Sunday after church, I took the catwalk down to her house, and there she was, dressed to impress only me. She'd straightened her hair. Whatever it took to kill those curls left them smelling like burnt peanuts, and the scent was at odds with her perfume. Still, it was one of the best hugs of my life. After a week of phone calls from a conflict zone—intimate conversations followed by little fights with my mother—it felt like coming home to my sweetheart, from war or from jail. I took her embrace like a man, standing stiffly, but I'd just as soon have collapsed into Ashley and cried like a baby. Two magnets, swallowed separately, can find each other in the intestines. It sounds painful for a person but think of it from the magnets' perspective. This was like that: a hug so unstoppable that everything between was torn apart. A hug so unforgettable, I'm still talking about it.

What are your intentions for my daughter?

Ashley's mother was behind her now, arms crossed like a cop. Laura was a very heavy woman, with knees that bent like PVC pipe, as though the weight had fallen on her all at once. She flashed an authoritative glower, so I thought of my own mother and quickly introduced myself, for fear she would say I was rude when I left.

Nice to meet you, I said, cracking her mask with a smile, and beneath it, a much smaller woman emerged, like when Samus takes her helmet off in *Metroid*. Uncrossing her arms, she seemed unsure of what to do with her hands.

Mom, get the frick out of here! Ashley shouted, embarrassed.

And I thought: That's no way to talk to your mother.

But it produced the desired result. Laura retreated into the house, then returned with car keys, as if to apologize. Go and get your *N*, she said. No speeding. No parking.

We raced into town and we parked at the mall, behind Sport Chek, where no one could see us.

Unbuckling our seatbelts to face one another, I thought I knew what Ashley wanted. But crossing the console, I ran into an invisible partition: What did I want? To touch Ashley everywhere, first and foremost. I know I've been meaning to abstain, but from what, exactly? Now that we're here, I might be willing to have a little sex, just to see if I want to have it all. Then I grew ashamed. Black people struggle with sexual sin—isn't that what they say? They're wrong, but after giving in so easily, how could I say I was different from Ham or the rapper from Raze? What if she gets pregnant? Our curses would continue and our mothers would be crushed. Mine would disown me. But I didn't want Ashley to abandon me either. Plus, it might feel good to simply swallow these anxieties, and put my tongue to better use in someone else's mouth.

Or maybe I was overthinking it.

We need to talk, Ashley said. We can't have sex. There's too much at stake. My mother gave up everything for me and I won't throw it all away for you. If we start dating, we have to agree, right here, right now: no intimacy without marriage. Promise me we won't push things too far.

And I said: That's exactly how I feel.

Then we kissed. Oh wow, oh wow.

But how far is too far?

I don't know, Ashley said. I guess we'll know if it feels wrong.

So we spent some time exploring what felt wrong.

Heading home, holding my hand across the console, Ashley said: My grandparents will be at the house. Grandpa might grill you. He can be pretty intimidating but he's just a big softie, like my mom. Oh! And he's Holdeman. It's sort of like the Amish. So don't tell him we have a TV.

It's right there in the living room, though. Won't he see it?

We hide it in the closet, Ashley said. That's why it's on wheels! And don't mention movies or music at all. You'll only annoy him.

What else is there to talk about?

The conversation starter was on plates around the table.

Have you ever had head cheese, Harry? It's a kind of meat jelly, made from leftover animal parts, like tongues, Ashley said.

It looked like a big batch of novelty fake rubber vomit. What's the gunk around the meat? I wondered.

A natural gelatin produced by the skull when you boil it, Grandpa answered, with a mouthful of pig mouth. He was a stocky man with a big round belly, a square head, and an even squarer beard, wearing a white shirt, thoroughly buttoned, black pants and suspenders.

Grandma sported an ankle-length floral-print dress and a small black prayer cap bobby-pinned to her hair.

So you're the boy I've heard so much about, he said, still chewing. What are your intentions for my granddaughter?

Grandpa, don't, Ashley said.

All of you, out, he responded. The women obeyed him, and left for the living room.

Alone now, the square-headed man stood up, towering over me. In turn, I rose to shake his hand, one Mississippi, two Mississippi, smiling uneasily and saying: How do you do, sir? My name is Harry Mooney.

His palm grew three sizes, swallowing mine like a snake. Let me be clear, he said, cracking my knuckles. My daughter's life was ruined by a deadbeat coloured who left her to raise a baby alone, and I'll be damned if I let another deadbeat coloured, pardon my language, do the same thing to my granddaughter. So I'll tell you what I told him: treat her right, or I'll gut you like a pig and serve you cold.

Yes sir, I said. I respect your position. I come from a good Christian home and I would never do anything to threaten your granddaughter's chastity. We're considering purity pledges ourselves.

I like you, he said, letting go, suddenly coming off kind. Try the *sulze*.

So I ate a little head cheese and said: Not bad.

• • •

I wanted to work in the Music department, but so did the rest of the House of James staff. As the youngest and newest employee, my preference mattered least, and my expertise was neither here nor there. It was not fair for me to get the plum assignment, I was told, just because I knew the most about it.

But I didn't fit anywhere else. Lando didn't trust me in Bibles, Deb didn't trust me on cash, and I had no barista experience. So I spent the first few months as a floater, unboxing product, dusting shelves, cleaning the bathroom, and doing the work that my colleagues avoided.

Anytime I floated through Music, however, I tried to look available, just in case anyone had any questions. An opportunity to prove myself was sure to come along.

But customers kept me at arm's length. I saw them see my nametag and still go somewhere else. They took their questions to co-workers who didn't know the answers and often sent them back to me. Then people would say: Oh, never mind, it wasn't that important, as if they would rather leave with nothing than allow me to assist them. It felt like a grand conspiracy to keep me from proving that I could be useful.

I'm looking for a song, a woman said to Jordan one morning. I heard it on the radio. It goes: *I give my life to you, so I can gain it back again.*

Jordan was stumped. He sat down to search for the lyric online.

I know the answer, I said. I can help you.

It's all right, the woman said.

The song is by a band called All Together Separate, I continued. But before I could tell her its title—"Paradigm"—she cut me off.

No *thank* you, she barked, brushing me off like a beggar.

So I backed away, embarrassed.

She must have felt bad about it. Ten minutes later, the woman found me again, hoping to clear her conscience. My son is into rap, she said, sighing heavily. Are there any *good* Christian rappers?

I was stumped. Apart from what I learned skimming a *CCM* article about John Reuben and KJ-52, two white rappers vying to become the Christian Eminem, I knew nothing at all about the genre.

But maybe I could wing it. The House of James only carried about ten hip-hop albums anyway.

Thumbing through the rap CDs, I found myself suggesting stuff I'd never even seen before. Preachas in tha Hood? The Cross Movement? Grits? *Muzik Ta Ride 2, Vol. 5*? This one's a sampler.

All of this might be a little too . . . *thuggish* for my son's tastes, the woman said. Do you have anything else?

There were only a few other options.

How about this one, I said, holding John Reuben's *Are We There Yet?* It was the first album I showed her with a white guy on the cover.

This one looks promising, she said, convinced in an instant. Then she paused, like it was my turn to say something. I kept quiet. She placed five dollars right in my pocket—Thank you so much for your help.

Who gave this stranger permission to put her hand down my pants? I thought to myself, and the answer came back to me: You did.

The woman was racist. You knew it at once, from the way that she handled your first interaction. She came back to clear up her conscience, in search of a tacit assurance of goodness from someone who saw the true shape of her heart, and you gave of yourself. You shrugged as she showed you that Blackness was nothing to her, that her son was above it, and she would not pay for it, except as an indulgence, if you smiled as she unmasked herself again. She waited for you to recommend a white rapper, to let her believe she was not who she was. She outsourced the shame and the labour to you. She asked you to dance and you danced, like the clown that you are. You didn't sell her anything but absolution, undeserved; you acted blind to every disrespect, and you sold it so well that she tipped you a fiver, and that's what they all want, for you to keep your head down and their comfort top of mind, and that's what you're best at: debasing yourself to make white people happy.

Before I could blame myself further, the owner appeared, out of nowhere, annoyed by my outfit.

That's not a collared shirt, Lando said. Are those sturgeons?

They're marlins, I told him. And respectfully, sir, the collar is by far the biggest part.

A real shirt tomorrow, Lando said. Now, what are you doing back here? I thought you were a floater.

I explained that a customer asked for my assistance in selecting a good Christian rapper and, speak of the devil, she's back now.

Everything's on BOGO today, so I should get two, she said, smiling as if we had a special bond now. Can you recommend any other good rappers?

Of course, I said. You're gonna want this one.

I handed her the new KJ-52 album with absolute certainty, never breaking eye contact with Lando. The woman glanced at the cover for all of three seconds. Then she thanked me again and went off to buy both.

Lando was impressed. Maybe we can find a spot for you in Music after all, he said.

A week later, I opened the department. To celebrate my achievement, I played some Mary Mary, one of the few Black gospel groups to cross over into mainstream Christian music. Their poppy lead single, "Shackles (Praise You)," had Auto-Tune like Cher's "Believe" or Eiffel 65, and it was the first Christian album to offer a sound that was all over secular radio. I couldn't get enough of it.

Take the shackles off my feet, so I can dance
I just wanna praise you
I just wanna praise you

But Rachel, back from mat leave already, was not in the mood for Black gospel that morning. Can you change the music? It's too energetic, she said. Maybe your people like it this early, but I have a headache.

• • •

172

By the summer, I was working nearly forty hours a week, and with the money I was making, my father convinced me that I could afford a new car. I thought we would buy something used, and my parents would pay for their half, plus a penny, the same way they did for my brother.

Not if you're raking it in, said the Captain. If you can count on steady shifts, let's get you building equity.

I was surprised by the hostility of the Abbotsford Automall salesman. He was a massive man, the largest to appear in this book, with a shaggy grey goatee and gold aviator glasses. He had hair, but only some. He wore a blazer, a long tie and shorts, and the contempt that most people hide in their hearts on his face. Even from a distance, making his way across the rolling hills of cars for sale in every shape and colour, you could tell he despised us.

Or maybe it was just me.

Hey Harry, he's wearing *aviators*, my father said, elbowing me as the man approached. I wonder if he likes airplanes.

What do you want? said the salesman, while scowling at me.

I struggled to answer the question, so my mother stepped in. My son is looking for a car for his birthday, she said. Something small.

The salesman lit a cigarette and walked through us, stopping behind a Toyota Echo.

This one's black, he said, dryly. Do you like this one?

The car was pre-owned, but so new no one would know, and it was priced to sell. Suddenly, we were inside, my mother and I, with the front doors swung out wide like wings.

It's got a pretty small backseat, I said.

You don't need a big backseat, my mother said. You won't be going back there.

Outside right behind us, my father and the salesman began a tense negotiation disguised as a friendly conversation. Looking in the rear-view, I overheard only snippets. *What do you know about motorhomes?* I witnessed a strange kind of honeybee dance, where much more was communicated than said. The whole thing was in code. I knew this sort of man, and I knew what he needed from me to be fair to my father. The Captain was clueless. The salesman's evil eyes met mine in the mirror, and it was painfully clear that my agent, the person who went to bat for me, did not understand the game we were playing. He was focused on the cost of the car. The salesman was stuck on the value of the boy inside the Echo.

I had no language for what my father could not see, and one cannot speak up without words. Powerless to prevent a quick transaction, the negotiation became a negation, and suddenly I came with the car.

We paid sticker price for the base model with nothing else thrown in—not even intermittent wipers. My father provided the down payment and took out the loan in his name. I owed him three hundred dollars each month for half a decade, happy birthday!

Driving home from the Automall, struggling to see through light rain, as I would for the life of the Echo, I asked to go by Ashley's house. I wanted to show her my fancy new car.

You're seeing her after you get your *N*, my mother said. You need to go home and study.

It's a driver's exam, so I'm studying right now, I said, faithfully checking my mirrors.

I don't want you driving your new car all over, she said. Every time you do, it loses value.

But what could she do, riding shotgun? I was the one at the wheel. So we popped by, in spite of her protests. My mother refused to get out of the car.

Then came the N-test. The examiner got into the Echo, and I could swear he was the same man from the Automall. I recognized his square goatee and glasses, not to mention his hugeness. A week ago, I was glad to get away from the man. Now, here he was again, granted unconditional authority over a boy he clearly despised.

Watching the big man struggle to sit down, it struck me that the Echo was a clown car, unusually tall and unusually narrow. I looked like a fool in it. So did the salesman.

Nice to meet you, sir, I said, inviting a handshake.

My examiner kept a two-handed grip on the clipboard. Looking straight ahead, he told me: Hands at ten and two. When it's safe, start the vehicle and back out slowly.

But it never felt particularly safe, not for the next half hour, and I was relieved when our serpentine route brought us back to the lot where we started. Neither one of us enjoyed the other's company, and we disagreed on whether I deserved a driver's licence.

You didn't pass, he said. You can retake the test in two weeks.

What? I was shocked. What did I do wrong?

You missed a shoulder check changing lanes at Hillcrest, he said. That's an instant fail.

He was lying. I was certain, because that shoulder check had me looking back at the business where Joel stole a didgeridoo. I was outraged, and I spoke without thinking. That's not true and we both know it, I said. I signalled, noticed the music store over my shoulder and even saw you, writing nothing down, because I did it correctly. And then we turned right at Emerson.

You think you're so smart! The massive man shouted. Spittle flew everywhere. He slammed his hands down on the dashboard, and I flinched, expecting the airbag to deploy. Don't you talk down to me, you arrogant little prick! I might have changed my mind, but not anymore. Take your L and get the fuck out of here.

Then, with great effort, he stood up from the car and threw the door closed so forcefully that the window crank fell off.

They call it an Echo, but it doubles as a soundproof booth. For a while I sat there screaming, and I came home with a sore throat.

I told you that you needed to prepare more, my mother said.

I don't think that's why I failed, I said. The examiner was a racist, that's why.

Enough with the race card, my mother said, get real. I tried to tell you we didn't have time the other night—that you needed to study. But you just *had* to see your girlfriend, didn't you? And look what happened. You'd better call Ashley and tell her your plans for tonight are cancelled.

They aren't cancelled, I said.

Who's going to drive? Ashley isn't registered to drive your car. Pass your road test, and then you can take her wherever you want.

I'll walk down or she'll pick me up, I responded.

What's the point in starting something now? You'll be leaving for college in a year, and didn't you say you wanted to continue with Abeka at Pensacola Christian College? Your father just bought a motorhome so we could road trip down to Florida and tour the campus.

I didn't ask for that, I said.

And my father said: Harry, this thing is a *beast*. We're leaving in March. We'll be staying at KOAs all over the States. We'll go to Disney World and stop at SeaWorld on the way back. It'll be a sky-high adventure.

Ashley has two years before she graduates, my mother said. Don't tell me you'd throw away the chance at university *in Florida* to hang around here with some high school girl.

I haven't decided where I'm going, I said. Why are you trying so hard to separate us?

I don't want you slipping up, she said. You're the same age your birth mother was when she got pregnant with you. Don't go repeating her mistake.

Do you think I can't help myself? What mistake—do you mean me?

I think you have a tendency to get carried away, she said. You're not dating Ashley. You two can *court*. Get to know each other in groups or take Mike and Tom along to chaperone.

Absolutely not, I said. *No.* You said I could have a girlfriend at sixteen. That was *your rule*. You can't just change it now because you don't like who I chose. What's your problem with Ashley, anyway? Why do you hate her so much?

Because she's a bitch, Harry, she's a *bitch*!

I took the long stairway down to Ashley's house, my mother's words still ringing in my ears. She was the wisest and holiest woman I knew. She only wanted the best for me, and she'd never said the B-word before in her life. How could she say it now, about Ashley, unless there was some truth to it?

My sweetheart met me on the driveway, as usual. Her hair was curlier than ever.

But I thought it looked better straight.

• • •

The morning of September 11, my mother burst into my bedroom, shouting: The bastards blew up the building! She said it like I knew who we were talking about. For a moment, I thought she meant Ashley and me.

Turned out, it was Muslim extremists. Ten men, who hijacked two 767s and crashed them into the World Trade Center. On the TV, I saw the two towers collapse, killing thousands, and I sat up in bed, speechless, as a tidal wave of grey matter filled the frame, leading the way like the pillar of a cloud. Afterward, even Abbotsford's air seemed toxic with whatever was released.

Tom's tenth birthday party was ruined. No one but the Schumachers showed up that afternoon at Castle Fun Park.

It's Air India all over again, my father said, as Castle Fun Park's animatronic rat band serenaded us. They hate our way of life, you know.

Who's *they*? Air India was Sikhs, I said, and these guys were Muslims.

What's the difference when they do the same thing?

The difference between India and Afghanistan is Pakistan, I said. They're totally different people, different as you and me.

And my father said: I wonder how those nitwits knew to put the bird in Heading Select?

Maybe they went to flight school?

The second guy almost missed, he said. The wings were banked.

But even after we knew who did it, why, and even how, people treated Ashley like the tragedy was her fault. On a walk around the local lake, a woman spat on her shoes. A jogger saw it and stopped to ask how we were, then how we met and where we were from, and when Ashley said, I'm Persian, with the same pride as always, he responded: Iran, you mean? Jesus. You people are sneaking in all over the place.

I saw how someone's knees begin to bend.

Even at my house, it was no longer off-limits to blame her for her heritage.

What if her father comes back? My mother asked. Are you prepared to deal with her Muslim family? They cut off your hand just for stealing, you know. He'll want her to marry a nice Persian man. They kill women who marry the wrong men, and they hate Christians, so they definitely won't approve of you.

Ashley's not a Muslim, I said.

They convert you at knifepoint, she said.

At the same time, my parents appeared to experience a renewal of faith. They weren't alone. Stone Rolled Away was full of familiar faces that Sunday—familiar scenes as well: a woman prophesied in tongues; her son translated after. The Rempels attended. Tilda Eubanks too. There was talk of a Prayer Warrior reunion.

My father wrote a letter to the *National Post*. Nine days after the tragedy, it was included in a round-up of recently received calls for revival, all published under the headline Whither God? Something was happening everywhere—the Second Great Awakening, they said on CBN, and all the prophets who'd been wrong about the End Times coming last year claimed that they had been right all along. They'd simply forgotten to carry the one.

But to me, it seemed this so-called outpouring of the Holy Spirit was really an outpouring of anti-Muslim sentiment. I began to wonder what prejudice had powered the First Great Awakening.

The new bestseller at the House of James was a book called *Answering Islam*, by the lead witness for creationism in a famous US Supreme Court case. The book taught Christians how to confront the worldwide challenge of Islam. It was a guide to defending the faith, steeped in hateful language.

My parents mostly used it to debate my girlfriend's worth, and after each heated debate I would wonder if Ashley was being pressured to hate me too. In fact, I just knew it: she was back in Grade 11, with all those white boys, and I bet they were telling her to dump me for them. Destiny had her ear all day and she was against us too. If her high school had a Black guy, he was probably better at Blackness than I was. How could I compete with a Real Black Person, and how could she resist a fellow Persian, if she found one?

Nothing can come between us, Ashley reassured me.

By then, I knew enough to know that she was wrong. The whole world stood between us. I wanted to cut her off completely from school, to sever every tie that failed to strengthen hers with mine. I'd have homeschooled her myself, if I could have.

But I was too busy with work.

Tonight I need you to dust the Southern gospel section thoroughly, Lando said.

I did an unthorough job. The section was enormous: six entire carrels full of off-putting, old-timey crooners and yodellers, bad bluegrass, endless quartets, and everything ever released by Bill & Gloria Gaither. Only old people went back there.

Dusting sporadically, I found the Black gospel section—only a few CDs, mislabelled and lost behind a disgraced televangelist. Kirk Franklin. Angie & Debbie Winans. The Brooklyn Tabernacle Choir. Donnie McClurkin's *Live in London*, bringing down the house.

It was the best album in the bunch, marked in inventory as missing.

It was hard to feel passionately about the House of James anymore. Everything we sold was like a weapon formed against me; everyone we sold it to, too.

It wasn't just the anti-Islam stuff: on the shelves, I found Dr. James Dobson's *Dare to Discipline*, the timeless paperback classic that taught my parents how to beat me. Nearby was the Mary Greenland book that filled my childhood home with evil spirits. And I personally assembled the cardboard display for *Boy Meets Girl*, the sequel to *I Kissed Dating Goodbye*.

Why do we even sell Bibles at all? Jordan asked. That seems like a huge conflict of interest.

Yeah, I said. And why are so many Christian bands just clones of secular bands?

It's like we're consciously constructing an alternate reality where everything is worse, Jordan said, but the one thing we all agree on is that, actually, it isn't.

Definitely constructed without consulting a single Black person, I said.

Just before closing, Jordan sent me an email on the internal server: The Top Ten Ways to Get Fired at the House of James. The list was only partially completed.

10. Replace all the Thomas Kinkade paintings with the work of A Serious Artist.
9. Four words: Bibles Free For Homeless.

The other eight slots were left blank.

Add a couple more and send it back, he wrote. P.S. Don't show anybody!!

Chuckling to myself, I looked behind me to ensure that I was all alone, then made a pair of clever contributions.

8. Point to stuff and say: This book here enabled my abuse.
7. Inquire as to why the Southern gospel section is so sprawling, while the Black gospel section got lost.

• • •

I got home late, expecting a dark kitchen. But my mother was waiting up. She handed me the unicorn, wrapped in a tea towel.

Here it is, she said.

I took it like a newborn baby, afraid to get it dirty or disturb it in some way. Pulling back the towel, I saw a part of myself that I'd never seen before, and even imagined all wrong. The unicorn was a foal lying down, eyes closed, head resting on its forepaws, asleep. All my life I'd pictured some loose-legged thing, or a stuffie sitting upright, like the bunny.

Somehow this was sweeter. I honked its little horn and felt a sudden surge of loss, as though the unicorn was wired to change the channel in my heart.

If you want, I'll put it back, my mother said, reaching for it almost right away.

In her eyes I saw sheer terror, and my heart broke for a woman so racked with insecurity that she could barely stand for me to look at the little piece of myself she kept locked away. Overcome with guilt, I let her have it. I never meant to make her this afraid. I wanted her to let me go a little, not to leave; returning the unicorn was my way of saying so. I never found the nerve to ask again.

Somewhere in that house, the little foal is still asleep.

• • •

Lando found the list.

Just before my shift began, he called me to his office. I found him reading the final two entries aloud.

2. Ask Deb what her problem is.
1. Kick Lando in the butt and run away.

He put down the printout and paused to control his emotions. And then he said: You and a co-worker have been exchanging comedic lists. These words are hurtful and disparaging to a business that I built from nothing. They violate your oath to conduct yourself in a Christlike manner. They have damaged our working relationship and it cannot continue. Effective at the end of your shift, you're fired.

Eight hours later, at home, I collapsed into my father's arms and wept. I didn't mean to: I'd have fallen to the floor but this time, he was there, and he hugged me so hard that I struggled to breathe.

It was a trap. The next morning, he still had me.

Harry, we're off to Florida in a month, he said, as soon as I woke up. You need to get a new job before we leave. After the Mitchnick award, I can't afford to cover your car loan.

You bought a motorhome, I said.

So we could tour a college in Florida *for you,* he said, and now you might not even go! Well, enough. You've been fighting all year to fly solo, and this is what that looks like. Sorry for the wake-up call, homeboy, but it's wheels up until you land a new job.

Unwilling to waste all day handing out resumés, I decided to lean on my previous work experience. I applied at just one store: Sport Chek. When people think of Black people, I said to myself, they think of athletics. Betting that the hiring manager was secretly looking for someone like me, a Black boy who knew that the art of commission-based retail was selling oneself, I secured my employment with minimal effort.

The manager's name was Steve. He saw me and his hungry eyes grew wide, just as expected. He came to devour me. I let him, and that's how I made my first sale.

Do you know who you look like? Steve asked me.

Carlton Banks, at your service, I said, and I shimmied a little, to put him at ease.

This is so crazy, Steve said, laughing to himself. Just the other day, my GM told me I needed to bring a more *urban* flavour to the staff. I was like: Are you kidding? In this town? I had no *idea* what to do. And then you walked in. I guess it's my lucky day! What did you say your name was?

Harry Mooney, I said. How do you do?

7

PEOPLE CAN TELL

(or The Boy Could Be a River)

The motorhome was enormous.

We paved a second driveway through the front lawn just to put it somewhere, and the white Winnebago resembled nothing so much as the house next door—a kind of family resemblance, as if the building gave birth to it following a tryst with a twin-engine jet. It was a laneway house with a cockpit. A 34.5-foot, Class A spare residence, wide enough for a king-size bed and wider still, at will: the wheels were fixed but the wings were retractable. Flip a switch and the living room tripled in size, grinding and groaning, expanding like the iron lungs of some asthmatic monster.

The beast killed the yard. Most of the grass became concrete and rocks, and the trampoline covered the rest. A mesh trampoline might have kept some space green, but the rubber one smothered the clover. The RV blocked critical mid-morning sun, and the Captain was too taken with his new toy to trim the hedges throwing shade all afternoon. Ever in darkness, my childhood arena dissolved into dirt.

By the time we were packed for our cross-country journey, the front lawn was just a big mud puddle. I couldn't believe that we just let it happen, and part of me couldn't accept what was lost. Leaving the landing we called Puddle Lane, I prayed that the grass would grow back over six weeks of sunrise.

We set out for Florida in the spring, all six of us, two months before the public schools let out for summer break. First we'd go to Iowa. Then we'd go to Florida. After touring Pensacola Christian College, we would carry on to Disney World, anticipating better crowds and shorter lines than in June and July, when classes were out.

This autonomy was just one of the benefits of homeschooling. The other, of course, was the gullible Captain: I fooled my father again that year, graduating at the top of my class, to the fanfare I deserved, which was none.

In February, I came downstairs and shouted: I'm finally finished!

I don't believe you, my mother said, without looking up from the *National Post.*

So I went back upstairs.

Anonymity was the obvious downside. Alone in my room, I named myself valedictorian and crowned myself prom king. I elected my girlfriend as prom queen, but Ashley was not invited to the cross-continental homecoming parade, let alone the future my family envisioned for me.

My mother's aim was clear: to put as much distance between us as possible. She denied this, naturally, but when I floated the idea of attending somewhere closer to home—Trinity Western University, the Christian school in Langley, one town over—she grew agitated.

I thought I knew why: Trinity was a liberal arts university.

Abeka defined liberalism as the rejection of Christ and His principles. It was a final exam question, three years in a row. Surely this was her main concern. But it never came up.

You just want to be closer to Ashley, she said, suggesting, to me at least, that she meant to break us up geographically, if not literally.

She all but admitted it to Ashley on the night before we left. In the kitchen, left alone with the girl for only a moment, wringing the life from the bags in her tea, my mother remarked: Do you know that my people would have killed your people if we were back in the day with our ancestors?

That night, my girlfriend said goodbye as if I were never coming back. It was a baffling show of dismay—I'd be home by the summer—but her disheartenment stayed with me, even as we left her behind. I mentioned it along the way. My mother said Ashley was being manipulative, using her wiles in an effort to make my decision for me. It seemed like a scurrilous characterization. Suspecting manipulation on both sides, I disqualified all others from impacting my decision and determined to go where God willed.

Looking down from my window seat at the smaller, less luxurious vehicles on the I-90 eastbound to Iowa, home to my family's family, I imagined myself a first-class passenger on a transatlantic flight, taxiing on the tarmac, gliding above the ramp rats and bag throwers in their little lifts and luggage carts. Any moment now, we'd be cleared for takeoff, ascending, transfiguring with the sun, and, finally, forgetting the world shrouded under the low-lying cloud we got over.

The RV never left the ground, of course. This was a modern-day Noah's ark, built for a fallen world, flooded with road. But all along the way to Pensacola, the westernmost city in the Florida panhandle, the Captain was drawn, perforce, to gas stations branded to suggest flight—Pilot Travel Center, for instance, or Flying J Travel Plaza, aviation-themed roadside villages offering much beyond motor fuel: restaurants, gift shops, game rooms, and sometimes even internet kiosks. Flattered by the illusion of having arrived at some higher station in life than a gas station, my father refused to refuel anywhere else, and he rarely had to. These chains were all across the country, and seeing little besides, I came to regard America as a land of truck stops pretending to be airplane stops.

My mother was quick to dismiss this as a short-sighted stereotype. You're clueless, she said. You don't know anything about America. I grew up here.

I thought I knew a little about the place after eight years studying American history, but even I understood that a bit of book learning was no match for lived experience. And, after two nights in small-town Iowa, at the old farmhouse where my mother grew up, sitting among my so-called family on sofas covered in clear vinyl, making small talk with strangers acting strangely, like a bunch of body snatchers or ghosts hiding head wounds under their hats, I had to concede that I was out of my depth. I didn't know these people at all, and their efforts to treat me as family rang false. Stranded among uncanny aunts, uncles, cousins, and Grandpa, whom they feared but feigned respect for—they congratulated him just for speaking to me, implying it was hard for him to see me as a grandson—I found kinship only with Gloria, Grandpa's new wife, whom they all pretended to accept but clearly resented, especially once we seemed to hit it off.

Leaving the state at long last, I was forced to admit that I would never know this country like my mother knew this country.

In Missouri, she had to admit it as well. Southbound along Interstate 55, on the outskirts of St. Louis County, we passed a roadside sign that read:

ADOPT A HIGHWAY
LITTER CONTROL
NEXT 1 MILE
KNIGHTS OF THE KU KLUX KLAN

For a moment, the motorhome fell quiet, the entire party sitting there, blinking, wondering what lay ahead and what peril I put us in, just by existing.

Finally, Tom asked: Is Harry going to get us all killed?

And my father said: Eh, probably not.

Probably not, right? I knew the KKK mostly in abstraction—a bunch of bygone bad guys in white sheets who faded away after everyone saw they were silly. On television and in movies, Klansmen were comic relief, buffoons and bunglers mostly, never meant to be taken seriously, and certainly not a present-day threat.

But on I-55, I stood corrected. Looking back on the sign with bemusement, more afraid to show concern than to feel it, for how much harm could these bozos really do, I quipped: I wonder what they mean by *litter control.*

And my mother shouted: Harry, *get down*!

Stung by the order, I fell to the floor, frightened, lying flat like a war correspondent caught in crossfire, a Klan speciality, and I stayed down for more than a mile, awaiting an all-clear that never came.

They forgot about me down there.

My terror grew exhausting; eventually, I army-crawled to the RV master bedroom and took a nap. On the king-size bed, I dreamt of a blockade. White-hooded villains boarded the vehicle, surrounding me, appearing closer each time I opened my eyes, until I jolted awake from a nightmare that felt like a memory. All out of sorts, I sat up, unclear as to whether we were still on a racist road.

Are we out of Missouri? I asked.

We're in Harrison, Arkansas, my father said, chuckling at the name of the place, or maybe at my apprehension. It's probably safe to come out.

But I didn't feel safe. We stopped at a diner. The patrons regarded me grimly. I felt their eyes burning a hole in my back. My mother said I was imagining things. We ordered as one, but my food came out last, after everyone else was done eating. I took it to go.

The sun was setting, and as we pulled into the suspiciously named Harrison KOA for the evening, the threat of the Klan seemed more present than ever. My paranoia reached a fever pitch that night. Surrounded by giant white RVs, I saw myself beset by monstrous, metal people-eaters, and with anxious eyes, I recognized the conspicuous spelling of *kampground*, with a *K*. Why would they do that, if not to signal some sinister affiliation? And why was this town named after me, as if I was going to die here?

Harrison was a sundown town. White riots in 1905 and 1909 erased the Black community with menace and murder, and nothing had changed in the century since. Census records show that there were no Black people living there as late as 2001. I might have been the first to spend the night in several decades.

No one else was dumb enough to dare. Harrison has often been described as the most racist town in America. A warning at the city limits used to make it clear—*Nigger, don't let the sun come down on you here*—and even now, the signs of white supremacy are everywhere. Welcome to Harrison, read a 2003 billboard sponsored by area business owners: Beautiful Town, Beautiful People, No Wrong Exits, No Bad Neighbourhoods. As recently as 2020, roadside signs have advertised white pride TV and radio stations. A Confederate flag flies outside of the Harrison Chamber of Commerce. The KKK's national headquarters is just a couple miles from where we parked the motorhome. They call it the Christian Revival Center.

We never left the racist road. We followed it, right to the end, into hell, and we spent the night camped among Eaters of Men, in the Cave Where They Spit Out the Bones.

But I didn't know that then. Only my body did.

My meal at the diner was poisoned or something. I woke up after midnight, violently sick, and I staggered outside, into pitch-black darkness, to vomit on the grass while my family slept soundly. Spilling my guts offered little relief. Alone in the night, I grew terrified. Something was stalking me here—I could swear I saw eyes in the bushes—and something else stirred in my body, a chill beyond illness, a sense of grave danger I felt in my spirit, my bones. I thought it was the Lord trying to warn me. Go back before it's too late, screamed the voice in my head. It's not safe for you here—get inside, lock the door. But the poison was still in my system. Convulsing, I crawled back inside and knelt at the motorhome toilet for nearly an hour, puking my guts out and begging my God, make it stop, make it stop, make it stop.

Somehow, despite all my retching and weeping, no one but me was disturbed.

I felt right as rain by morning, and I wondered if maybe I dreamt the whole ordeal. Leaving the kampground, however, I spotted the puddle of throw-up I left on the lawn. It was real.

I think I was poisoned, I said, but I knew that I sounded insane, and nobody believed me.

There you go again, painting the whole country with this sinister brush, my mother said. You just had a bad quesadilla. Stop living in the past.

This is why I hid my fear, at first. Assuming any danger was the same, it seemed, as assuming the worst about America, and my mother took offence on behalf of her country.

Don't generalize, she would scold.

But to me, it's like critiquing a cake for being too sweet. One might beg to differ: don't lump the flour in with the sugar. Ah, but that's how you make a cake, especially in America, where racism is baked right in, like a leavening agent. Without it, the empire never rises.

Arkansas changed me. The fear that consumed me that night calibrated my radar. Whereas before I had been sensitive, I came away sensitized, and now every aftershock tells me the truth about places and people that mean to destroy me. I knew what it was, despite every denial. I knew what my body was trying to tell me. And once I recognized it there, I felt it all over, both abroad and at home: Klansmen had come north into British Columbia from Washington State to found a klavern in March 1928. A week later, they were parading through old Abbotsford, dressed in full regalia, accompanied by a drum and fife band. After the sun set, they ignited an enormous cross on the hillside where Old Yale Road descends into the beating heart of my hometown.

Klansmen Give Impressive Display, wrote the *Abbotsford Post*. The first new recruit, they reported, was a member of the Trethewey family, local leaders whose name marks the Abbotsford Heritage House. The city has pledged to rename the museum, but these things take time. It's a process.

The process is often the problem. The State of Missouri first sued to remove the Impressive Display on their highway. The US Supreme Court supported the Klan, who had freedom of speech on their side. So Missouri got creative, finding a way to revoke the group's adoption rights. Their argument was negligence. A state spokesperson explained: Groups are required to pick up litter four times a year in this program, and they have never picked up anything off the highway.

That particular stretch of road, one of the routes used to bus Black students to county schools during desegregation, was renamed the Rosa Parks Highway—a nice gesture, I suppose, as it's important to stand up to the KKK. But if the constitution rules in their favour, renaming the road isn't nearly enough. You might have to rename the country.

In any case, the sign was not up long, a couple months at best, and looking back, it seems a great coincidence to have seen it at all. But such signs are everywhere, all over the world, in plain language or in code, so we were bound to see something. These hazards are impossible to miss unless one is committed to the cause of missing them. Take my family, for instance, who forgot me on the floor of the RV, so determined were they to stay blind that I wonder sometimes if they'd have left me alone to get lynched by trash-pickers, and carried on, untroubled, to the Magic Kingdom.

Even I might not have noticed right away.

Coming out of a truck stop men's room in the Deep South, one of those long troughs where you go against the wall, I held the door for the gentleman behind me. It was a simple courtesy, the sort of affable act that served me well in Abbotsford, and likely couldn't hurt in Mississippi. Stepping to one side, I offered an earnest smile, the great big grin of a boy without a clue, and waited for the man to cross the threshold.

Instead, he looked at me, perplexed.

So I looked at him: this enormous, bearded trucker, with his trucker hat, John Cougar Mellencamp T-shirt, truck gut, and truculent gaze—a gaze so overwhelming that it turned me back, like a tidal wave turns back a sailboat, and both of us saw the creature holding the door, this dopey Black boy from out-of-town, with nappy hair and bent glasses, simpering stupidly in a bright-red romper.

To stop looking inward, I looked skyward.

The trucker rejected my courtesy. No, he said. No thank you.

I fled across the parking lot, humiliated, looking back from a safe distance to see him still standing there, waiting for the door to close completely before he would touch it; and watching him go, at long last, from the restroom to the cabin of a Fuso truck with a Confederate flag bumper sticker, I thought: That's the stupidest thing I've ever seen anybody do in my whole, entire life.

A little while down the road, still feeling self-conscious about the incident and desperate to invalidate the trucker's evil eye, I remarked aloud: Now *that* guy was a racist for sure!

Spare me, my mother responded. You're a little overdressed for the South, is all.

•••

The campus tour began with a brief introductory video.

We open in mid-air, soaring through blue skies above the clouds, softly strummed harp in the background. Slow dissolve to the stained-glass facade of the college chapel—heaven on earth, the transition seems to suggest—as a voice announces: *Catch the Spirit of Pensacola Christian!*

The whole thing had a distinctly retro vibe: early nineties, judging by the perms and khaki pants, not to mention the ubiquitous yellow font of the era. I recognized the title card from years of classroom videos. Nearly a decade and nothing much had changed.

While high academic standards are required, the complete development of an individual requires more than academic learning. Additionally, all people must develop their spiritual and social dimension.

Already dozing off, I scanned the footage for familiar faces, just to stay engaged. Tyson, the boy with big braces—but probably not anymore—or Brooke, my childhood crush, the one who wore a pink beret and sat beside the camera? I swore if I saw her again, I would take it as a sign and enrol. One fancy hat and I'd be sold.

But Brooke did not appear in this video.

By the end of the film, however, I was very well-acquainted with Jimmy, the slender Black man who made multiple appearances, reading a balance sheet, walking with classmates, playing fiddle for the orchestra, and twice above a title card that read: JIMMY—NASSAU, THE BAHAMAS.

Look at that cool brother on the violin, my father whispered. *Think he likes Mendelssohn?*

That's Jimmy, I deadpanned. *He's in Finance.*

Over all these years, as PCC has grown and expanded, the voice continued, *the foundation has remained the same.*

The word BELIEFS flashed onscreen in sparkling white text, as an international coalition of students recited the core tenets of the school, one by one.

We believe that God created man and the universe, said Karina from Mexico, and that He is the author of the order, reason, and reality that are reflected in the universe; we believe that moral conviction, self-discipline, and enthusiasm for Christian witnessing are as important as academic excellence, said Andrew from Colorado; we believe in the spiritual unity of the body of Christ, and that God has ordained the local church for the perpetuation of His truth and work in the world, said Jimmy from the Bahamas.

Above the clouds again, the students were superimposed in the sky, repeating the important part, in turn: we believe, we believe, we believe.

It was all a little much.

Asked to catch the spirit in the academic centre, I caught a flashback instead, returning to my last brush with this brand of fundamentalism, surrounded by cultists in the armoury.

Then the lights came on, and a long-forgotten face emerged, as if summoned: our tour guide was a dead ringer for Bernie Pendleton from Gateway, the man with one-eyed madness who boarded the Outreach Van at Riverview, was born again into youth ministry, and comforted me when the Man of God said I was cursed.

It couldn't be the same man, unless he aged backwards—this guy was younger. But I saw in his massive, blue eyes the same manic energy that defined his doppelgänger in my memory, and as he placed a hand on my shoulder in the hall, I bristled at a touch that felt familiar.

How are you doing, brother, he said. They call me Big Bern.

We shook hands, but after one Mississippi, Big Bern tried to snap it and pound it, and the gesture fell apart. The tension between us was strange, and each time we met eyes, we were totally baffled.

Big Bern led the group across the landscaped, mid-century campus to the library, where we ascended a spiral staircase to the fourth floor. In the Bible room, he showed us several King James Bibles under glass, including a rare one with a misprint—a pronoun error in the book of Ruth that suggested a same-sex romance.

You can see why they couldn't put it out, Big Bern laughed.

Then it was off to the sports centre.

We support our basketball team here, Big Bern told only me, and we're not above a little gamesmanship, let me tell you. Last year, we all brought newspapers, and when the visitors had the ball, we pretended to read the Sunday funnies!

I'm considering a career in journalism, I said. Do you have a student newspaper?

Not yet, Big Bern responded. There's an unauthorized newsletter going around, but it's banned on campus. One hundred and fifty demerits—anyone caught reading the *Student Voice* will have some explaining to do!

I had not known about the demerits. Hold up, I said, is this place super-strict? Be honest, Big Bern.

The tour guide feigned amusement, buying time, deciding how to answer. Well, you wouldn't be allowed to wear *that* shirt. And you'd have to cut your hair, he said, pressing a palm into my afro, enjoying its sponginess for a moment. Too bad. It's so soft.

Hands to yourself, I said, surprising us both.

You'll love it here, Big Bern continued. They're planning an expansion with an indoor water slide and double FlowRider surfing waves!

What's wrong with the beach? I asked.

Nothing at all, he said. Pensacola is an oasis. We have the world's whitest beaches, you know.

Not when I'm around, I said. Do you guys have any problems with the KKK here?

He chuckled again. Heavens no! PCC is very safe. The whole campus is walled, like Jericho, and there's barbed wire all around. It's a fortress. We've got security guards at the gate, too. Nobody gets in or out without us knowing.

This set my mind at ease a little, but less so the more I thought about it—nobody? Leaving for Orlando, it struck me that the barbed wire faced the students, not the street.

At Disney World, I Googled the school.

This had never really been an option before. Google was brand new then, and it changed everything. Prior to search engines, you had to guess what was available online, adding .com to whatever you could think of; prior to the internet, you had to take your family's word for everything. But that sort of blind faith was so last century. The truth was out there, so I went looking for it.

This is how I found the *Student Voice*. The rebel zine was squatting on the PCC domain with a tagline befitting a banned publication: Have I now become your enemy because I tell you the truth?

Short answer: yes.

The school did all it could to shut the website down, and when they lost in court—free speech strikes again—they punished the student body, throttling the on-campus internet and establishing a new rule against sharing the unflattering newsletter.

The *Student Voice* said this was pretty typical for PCC, among the most authoritarian schools in America.

The website warned: *When considering attending Pensacola Christian College, it is important to know that they have rules. Rules, rules, rules. They have rules to govern every area of your life, just like the Bible, only more.*

I scrolled through a long list of strange and draconian prohibitions. No television. No movies. No modern music. No disrespect or bad attitudes. No walking barefoot in the dormitory halls, or the lounge. You may not allow the end of your belt to hang down from the belt loops resembling a phallus. Chapel is mandatory—no falling asleep. No horseplay, and no indirect horseplay either, which might include watching horseplay from a distance. No hyper-Calvinism.

Campus was segregated by gender, with different staircases, elevators and sidewalks for men and women, who could only be seen together before sundown, in public, chaperoned areas. Neither could they venture into town together, and if they were spotted out in town —where the school had spies everywhere—expulsion was certain. Leaving campus was considered a privilege. Students were expected to scan out and say where they were going, and be back before the 10 p.m. curfew, if permitted to go out at all.

PCC was not so much a college as a prison, according to the zine's testimonial letters. Pensacola Communist Country, some called it. Others went with Pensacola Concentration Camp.

The testimonial that tore it for me came from a Washington woman who recalled the persecution of a popular student, since graduated but banished from campus and banned from visiting his fiancée because the school didn't like his attitude—or his beard.

They told him that he had to shave it off if he wanted to see her, the letter writer said. *It was ridiculous! This was a student who they featured in every publication they put out and covered pages of the yearbook with his photograph. He was young, handsome, happy and BLACK.*

That got my attention. PCC had been mailing brochures to the house for years. My mother delivered them directly to my room, and each one went, unread, into the cabinet of my desk.

I had to know if the letter was true; there was evidence stashed in my room.

Just picturing the stack of shrink-wrapped magazines in Abbotsford, I struggled to enjoy our stay in Florida. Nothing at Disney World managed to displace the image. The Magic Kingdom failed to fascinate me. I wanted to be home, alone, for once, and just my luck: Glenn Mountain might as well have been across the universe. The rest of the road trip was endless, like flying through space. We drove west through Texas, then up along the coast, stopping only at KOAs, more Flying Js, and the SeaWorld in San Diego, where I bonded with a puffin just as desperate for the north. As soon as we got back, I raced upstairs. I gathered up the magazines and leafed through every one, in search of the young, handsome, happy, BLACK man.

It was Jimmy from the Bahamas.

I found him right away and then in nearly every issue, dating back years, and as I came to recognize his face, I began to see the man behind it: the anxiety in his eyes, the uncertainty in his smile, even the ease with which he was exploited, striking pose after pose in service of a school that would betray him, in the end. I saw, in short, my future.

I rejected it.

I hated to defy my mother. Every instance seemed to throw my love into question, baffling her, breaking her heart, and mine too. Her love always receded in response. I went to Florida desperate for the school to win me over—to spark some inner certainty apart from her urging, to make me worthy of her love again while salvaging some sense of independence.

Impossible. It seemed to me the only way to please her was to climb into another cage. I wouldn't go to jail.

The matter was settled for her. PCC was where I belonged; it was my place, and she strove to put me in it. But how could she know where I belonged? She didn't even know where I was.

Train up a child in the way he should go, the book of Proverbs said, and when he is old, he will not depart from it.

Yet here I stood, dearly departed, despite my every effort to conform. Somewhere along the way, I got lost—dispersed, like white light refracted through a prism. Maybe in Missouri, maybe Mississippi, maybe before we set out, who could say, but stranded in this new dimension, torn away by rapture or by rupture, everything appeared in a different light. Seeing the world now in colour, I squinted back through time at the long road to Pensacola. This was no straight and narrow path. It was a sinuous, Escherian road that seemed to end right where it began, like the maze on a kids' paper placemat, solved in what I thought, at first, was crayon, but not quite: all along the winding way I found the bright-red trail of a boy bleeding out, dragged across the continent, unconscious.

If I did not wake up now, I would wake up in prison.

So I asked to tour the other university—the closer one. It wouldn't be difficult. Driving to Trinity from our house in Abbotsford took twenty minutes.

My mother was furious. I knew you'd throw your future away for Ashley, she responded.

But Ashley hadn't even been a consideration. Not for me, anyway, and as my mother accused me of single-mindedness, still failing to see my fractured identity, I knew at once that she was just projecting. Ashley was her obsession, not mine. The whole point in sending me down to Pensacola was to get me as far away from my girlfriend as possible, institutionalized in a maximum-security college with no access to email or the internet. As I made this accusation aloud, my mother's eyes became daggers. Seeing her fury, my whole heart hardened against hers, and up against an ontological resistance she'd never encountered before, the woman threw her hands up and stormed out.

The second campus tour was mostly a formality. My mind was already made up.

Over there, you'll see the bunnies, Trinity's tour guide said—a thin blond woman wearing a shirt that could have come from my closet. Last year, the administration released two white rabbits to impress the Asian students. But then they started multiplying like, well, rabbits. So now we have the cutest infestation! And over here, we have the gymnasium where the students go to chapel.

Is chapel mandatory? I asked.

Of course not, the tour guide said. Though it is encouraged.

I chose Trinity. My mother was outraged. But in the summertime, she had a change of heart. I received one big present for my seventeenth birthday: room and board for my entire freshman year. Rather than commuting in the Echo, I would live at school.

I think maybe you need to get the full student experience, my mother said, and I was touched, until she gave the game away: You never know what kind of girls you'll meet around campus.

Hearing this, it sure seemed to me like my parents were paying a great deal of money for me to meet someone else and leave Ashley, or maybe even cheat on her, as if they still believed, after all this abstinence and obedience, that I could be so easy to upend. My mother was manipulating me. Inferring that she thought I couldn't help myself, my radar pinged, and I was outraged. But I didn't want to fight about it—just to get away. This trap disguised as freedom could still be my ticket out.

Thank you guys so much, I said, smiling as wide as I could. Really, wow, this means the world to me.

• • •

Homeschoolers made up a special class at Trinity, so the school made up a special class just to accommodate them: University 101 was a compulsory course on student life, with lessons in note-taking, reading syllabi, and getting a library card.

Also included in the course pack: step-by-step instructions on self-care and sorting laundry.

It all seemed a bit rudimentary, unless you were coming from a commune or cult—uncommon upbringings everywhere else, I gathered, but not at Trinity, the largest faith-based university in British Columbia, a province infamous for its lax homeschooling laws. With no one to report to and no one checking in, many incoming students had gone years without a proper education—and it showed. Up from bunkers, out of the wilderness, steeped in silly ideas or, worse, sheltered to the point of incapacity, they wandered about campus, eyes wide and bleary, still in the fog of a culture war they knew next to nothing about.

Trinity went out of its way to welcome us. *We understand and deeply respect the home-based education ethos*, their brochure promised.

Among the student body, we were scorned. University 101 was a sore spot for kids from the usual feeder schools, who resented the homeschool contingent for wasting their time. Even the instructors didn't take the class seriously. The mandatory refresher was taught by seniors, not professors, from the school's BA in Leadership program. Each was assigned an octet of freshmen, save for my instructor, Danielle, a star pupil entrusted with nine.

Eight plus me, I assumed.

The first time we met as a group in the atrium, Danielle sat with her legs open on the back of a couch. She was a short, stout woman with a severe resting face. Her jeans had two small holes where her thighs rubbed together. She wore her hair in a big messy bun, mid-collapse: the sock inside was falling out.

Danielle asked: Was anyone here homeschooled?

No one would admit it if they were.

Thank God, she said. Listen, you guys, this is baby stuff. You should know how to do it already. I mean, if you can't handle simple crap like using a planner, or sorting your whites from your colours, go back to your idiot village, 'cause college isn't for you. Like, this week, the assignment is to read a chapter of a book, *any book*, seriously, and write two sentences on what it's about. Laughable, isn't it? So just email me your summaries by Friday and we won't have a problem.

Class adjourned. We made plans to meet again in two weeks.

But the work of defogging the lost generation extended beyond this one course. Raised in defiance of conventional wisdom, many former homeschoolers fought their liberal arts education every step of the way, unconvinced by simple facts and almost always adversarial. On the first day of classes especially, Trinity's professors came prepared to defend the very foundations of their discipline.

In Geography 101, Dr. Robert Jordan spent the first half hour arguing with creationists.

The earth is 4.5 billion years old, he began.

Twenty hands shot up, including mine, but seeing Dr. Jordan lick his lips, I thought it might be best to let him pick on someone else. I rescinded my question and sunk into my chair, embarrassed by my automatic response.

Others were not so intimidated. The professor called on a woman so indignant, she was standing.

How would *you* know, she demanded.

We know because of uranium-lead radiometric dating, he said. The geologic record doesn't lie. Your parents and pastors lie.

You're wrong, someone else said. According to the Bible, the earth is only six thousand years old.

Nope, Dr. Jordan said, switching to the next slide of his Power-Point presentation—a picture of the earth beneath the caption GEOLOGISTS ARE RIGHT.

Some students laughed. Others only smouldered in their seats.

Listen: I teach this course three times a year, and this is how it always starts, Dr. Jordan said. We've known the true age of the planet for half a century and you guys just keep coming. It's absurd. This is a faith-based institution, yes, but it's also *a real school*. I don't teach Creationism, I teach geography and geology—hard sciences, rooted in hard facts. I am giving you *the facts*. I know some of you homeschoolers and private school kids were taught one thing, and you were raised to be quite combative about it. But it's not my fault you've been brainwashed, and if you can't believe in God without also accepting the scientifically proven understanding of His universe, then your faith is not as strong as you think.

Nearly every class was like this.

In English 101, a group of Puritans objected to a swear word in Margaret Atwood's "Happy Endings," a sort of choose-your-own-adventure about two lovers, John and Mary. The very short story presented several ways the relationship could unfold: Option A sees John and Mary fall in love. Eventually, they die. Option B sees Mary fall for John; her love goes unacknowledged.

He merely uses her body for selfish pleasure and ego gratification of a tepid kind, said the student, reading the selection aloud. He comes to her apartment twice a week and she cooks him dinner... and after he's eaten dinner—the student paused, looking up, uncertain—I can't read the rest.

He fucks her, Professor Song cut in. And after that he falls asleep.

Several hands shot up, predictably enough, this time, for me to opt out in advance. I mostly sided with the scandalized students—there was *never* any need for foul language—but I kept my opinion to myself, sitting silently, watching the discussion from a distance.

Professor Song was a slight, Singaporean woman in a cardigan made for a much larger person. She fiddled with the buttons on her sweater and wrinkled her wide, freckled nose in response to the sticklers. The professor seemed caught off-guard at first, like she was new here too, but then she leaned into the controversy, scrapping her lesson plan to moderate the great debate.

Her patience was astonishing. After an hour, with nothing settled, she sent us home to think the issue over.

For class on Wednesday, she said, write a one-page essay explaining your position. Should this expletive be removed from the text? Is it inappropriate? Why or why not?

So I made my way back to my dormitory, prepared to condemn Margaret Atwood's poor choice of words.

Douglas North Upper was set apart from the other men's dormitories, on the far side of the lounge, above the mailroom. It was overflow housing; in lean years, the twelve rooms sat empty. When I arrived, the dorm was half-full, following a flurry of last-minute registrations from clever sophomores, who'd cracked the system freshman year.

Carter Rawls and his cohorts began arriving late, well after Orientation Week, just before classes began. They greeted each other with giddy congratulations and a curious gesture: two quick, high hand-slaps, followed by a sack-tap.

The misfits!, Carter shouted, every time. Slap, slap, tap.

Even beyond the ball-patting, the whole thing seemed bizarre. Somehow, my dorm had a history, a nickname, and even a secret handshake already. It didn't make sense. How had I arrived before they did, only to find myself still, somehow, behind? I couldn't tolerate any more trouble fitting in. I needed to show these boys that I was one of them. Naively assuming the ball-patting was typical behaviour among high schoolers—not old friends who conspired to reunite in my dorm—I set my mind to doing as they did.

To signal my belonging, I shall have to tap a sack, I thought.

Carter was the man I wanted to be. He was the bad boy of campus—a real Van Wilder type. He had a poster of John Belushi in his room; he read *Pitchfork*, the independent music magazine; he appreciated edgy comedy like National Lampoon and *Mr. Show*, and spent his first two semesters lashing out at stuffy seniors after being cut from the improv team for making insensitive jokes.

I aspired to be his sidekick.

On my way to class that morning, I passed a groggy, half-naked Carter in the hallway. He was headed to the bathroom in a pair of boxer-briefs. Desperate to befriend him, I attempted a kindly sack-tap, catching a handful of flaccid penis instead.

His crusty eyes sprang open and he punched me in the shoulder.

Mortified, I fled across the campus to my lecture. We never spoke of this again, though it was still on my mind when I returned from English class. Somehow, I had to redeem myself.

Arriving mid-shenanigan, I saw the other boys emerge from Norm's room, fully nude but for white socks hanging from their penises, laughing and high-fiving as they headed to the common area.

Norm was on an island at the far end of the hall. The reclusive, third-year student lived alone, and all he ever did was homework. No one included him either, but he didn't mind, and neither did he seem disturbed by the whimpering coming from Jared's room, three doors away. (Jared only spent a couple months with us. He said he missed his girlfriend. He would cry all morning, call her every afternoon, and cry her name all night, until he disappeared before the Christmas break. After that, Norm had the south end of Douglas North Upper to himself.)

What the heck was *that*, I asked him, looking down the hall, where I saw Jared—even Jared!—sitting naked, with the others.

Beats me, said Norm. They just came in here dancing with socks on their dicks. I think they think I study too hard?

Well, you do, I said, aligning myself with the cool kids. You should have joined in the fun.

To signal my belonging, I thought, I shall wear a dick-sock.

I figured it might be endearing if I walked in, barely covered, saying something like: How embarrassing, we're all wearing the same outfit, someone should change.

While undressing, I even rehearsed the line a few times in front of the mirror.

But the single step down into the common area shook loose the sock. Before I could deliver my line, it fell off, and there I was.

Nice *baby* dick, Carter said, as I scrambled to cover up, and a roomful of semi-nude men started howling.

To save face, I used an old standby: It's because I'm Black, I muttered, retreating to my room. At least it got big laughs, as I expected.

Not *that* Black, from what I saw, Carter quipped, to bigger laughs.

Regaining my composure, not my clothes, I sat down at my desk, besocked, and started on the Atwood paper.

John fucks Mary? Way too crass, I thought. There must be some more appropriate word that will evoke the same feeling.

But every verb I substituted seemed to flatter John. Screws? Humps? Sticks it to? These synonyms fell short and only served to soften the man's disregard for the woman who loved him, the woman who cooked for him and cleaned up after him, who put on lipstick to please him, who hid her despair and pretended to enjoy sex for his benefit. Soon I found myself identifying with Mary. It was a very familiar feeling to have my body disrespected and the rest of me ignored, especially by those whose love I wanted most of all.

Maybe *I've* been fucked, I thought, and finding no other word that could adequately describe the inhumanity of John and Mary's sex, I scrapped my first draft and mounted a defence of the essential expletive at the heart of "Happy Endings."

It took me all day. I couldn't remember the last time I sat down to write an essay, let alone how, and sitting there, fiddling with my hair, I couldn't remember the last time I did that either. Scratching at my scalp broke brittle knots, and dandruff flakes as large as finger-nails fell all about me.

Just outside my door, I could hear my dormmates, still carrying on in the common area. Somehow, the talk had turned to mastur-bation.

I used to smear it on my bedroom wall, someone said. Then it got all discoloured. One day I came home and my mom was repaint-ing. She threw a box of Kleenex at me and said: Next time you whack off, use *this*.

More big laughs.

Having never really touched myself at all, I briefly entertained the idea.

Maybe *I* should whack off, I thought, to signal my belonging.

It was a serious consideration, and I even took a break from Margaret Atwood to visit the only pornographic website I knew:

WhiteHouse.com. But that's when Matt, my sweet and sinless room-mate, wandered in. I closed the window as quickly as I could.

What's with the get-up? he asked, too distracted by the half-erect sock to notice the X-rated pop-ups still blinking on my monitor.

When in Rome, I mumbled, pointing to the hall.

Matt went out to investigate.

Weird, he said, returning with a grimace.

Late that evening, when the essay was finished, I got dressed and ventured out. The dorm was deserted. Carter and the others had gone into Vancouver to see the Dismemberment Plan in concert. I'd never heard of the band, but I'd still have gone along, if invited. I could only assume they didn't like me.

Somehow, I imagined, these guys knew that I was homeschooled, and they wanted nothing to do with me.

So I went down to the lower cafeteria, the only space on campus that was open after 11 p.m. There I found the night owls, seeking friendships just like me, and I was delighted when I spotted another familiar face: it was Daniel Wagner, The Boy Who Died.

He recognized me too: Did you ever go to Camp Squeah? And that's how I made my first college friend.

Daniel sat on a big couch, surrounded by girls. He seemed to have his own gravitational pull. I wanted to be *that* boy. So I sat down beside him, chatting up the girl to my left. I recognized her too, from youth group at Northview, but she didn't recognize me. That was fine. I wanted to start over anyhow, to reinvent myself as soon as possible, and I thought I was doing a pretty good job—until she raised a hand to interrupt me.

I'm sorry to pry, she said, but, Harry, were you homeschooled?

How did you know? I asked, deeply embarrassed.

People can tell, she said, patting my head out of pity.

• • •

I got an A on the Atwood paper. Professor Song said I should be a writer. So I am.

Everywhere else, I was failing—failing to wake up on time to make it to my classes, or, if I did, failing to remember to take notes, or bring a textbook; failing to stay organized; failing to stay clean.

A week went by before I bathed. Even there, in the tiny shower stall that smelled like twelve men's shame, I failed. No one told me Black skin could be so uneven. Hyperpigmentation—more specifically, melasma—is a very common problem, often caused by sun exposure. But my family always said the dark patches on my shoulders were just dirt, so that was my self-diagnosis, and I never considered a second opinion. After scrubbing until I was red and raw, desperate to come clean, nothing had changed; I went back to my dorm room, still feeling disgusting.

I failed to keep up with the readings, and what I read, I failed to understand. Sometimes it seemed as if the texts were in a different language. I had never seen an MLA manual. I had never even heard of literary theory. What's a theme? Define irony. Compelling counterarguments? Never heard of them. It was like I had no foundational knowledge whatsoever. I never knew what I was looking for; class discussions seemed to arise from a different book than the one I had skimmed. More than once, I found myself looking around, comparing covers.

In my home-based English classes by Abeka, the selections were the same, year after year —the same simple allegories from the same recycled sources. *Pilgrim's Progress. Of Plymouth Plantation. The Journey of Everyman. Sermons* by Jonathan Edwards. We just read the books. We didn't unpack them. We didn't delve into divisive topics. We read them, again and again, and moved on. I hardly remember the last two grades. I was an undeclared dropout by then. But from Grade 4 to Grade 10, the topics we covered in English, history, science, and probably math, in some way or another, were carefully curated to prop up a worldview that couldn't withstand even slight scrutiny. So the students were not taught to scrutinize. Writing that challenged our minds wasn't covered, except to disparage the writers as godless, or lazy. Karl Marx, I was told, never worked an honest day in his life. This bald-faced lie—he wrote a book!—was written in bold font, and it showed up again on the final exam.

I wasn't equipped for a real school at all. I knew how to look for evidence of my own worldview, and I knew how to lie about stuff I hadn't read. But that only got me so far.

Neither did I know how to spot a prank.

One morning, I received a notice from Student Life. Somehow, they knew I had visited a pornographic website.

Your IP address has been flagged for viewing explicit content, the email said. This is a direct violation of the Community Covenant. You are facing expulsion unless you bring a typed, double-spaced, apology letter to the Student Life office by noon today.

I skipped my first two classes just to write it and sprinted across the lawn, through the rain, to meet the deadline. At the office, though, I found a line of students snaking out the door, all with typed apologies in hand. The woman at the desk—Danielle with the thigh holes, come to think of it—seemed confused.

That's when I knew I'd been duped.

Walking back to my room, humiliated, I passed a Black student—a girl about as dark as Courage, and no less threatening to me. She walked arm-in-arm with her dorm mates, and I envied her success at fitting in. Most of all, I envied her insulation: who would dismiss her as some other, or pat her head in pity, when a dozen white girls vouched for her belonging?

As we passed one another in the rain, I found I could not even look at her. I was too ashamed of myself, and I was not programmed to speak to someone like her. I feared that she would see me for what I obviously was—a lost boy, Black in outward appearance only, so uncomfortable in his splotchy skin that he couldn't even tell it from dirt, so under-practised in speaking to anyone, let alone another Black person, that his homeschooling showed right away. Afraid to be seen by someone else who might see all of that, I tried to make myself invisible.

Another failure. Our eyes met by accident. I flashed her an insecure grin. She gave me the same look—precisely the same.

Back upstairs, I found my dormmates laughing. Carter had sent the email. Somehow, he'd stolen the freshmen mailing list and sent the same notice to everybody. From the window in the common area, the bad boys of Douglas North Upper—and a girl, in violation of the Community Covenant—marvelled at the long line of suckers across the lawn.

High fives and sack-taps all around.

Burning with bitterness, I threw my apology in the trash; desperate for comfort, I phoned home.

I was wondering when we'd hear from you, my mother said. Out of clean clothes, I assume?

I'm sorry, I said, shrinking, but you could have called *me*.

Good sons call their mothers, she said. Say hi to your roommate. That Matt is a mother's dream—I bet he calls home all the time.

Yes, he's a very good boy, I muttered.

Take notes, my mother said. Now when are you visiting next? Are you coming to the Stone Rolled Away harvest party next month?

Harvest parties were the Christian alternative to Halloween. Rather than indulging in the satanic holiday by dressing up as goblins, ghouls and other demonic entities, we fled into the church, dressed in wholesome costumes—cowboys and farmers, mostly—to collect candy at mini-game booths.

I hadn't planned to go, but after two weeks at Trinity, an evening among friends and family sounded swell. At least I knew what to expect, and how to act. So I said I would be there.

Good to hear, my mother said. Tom thought it would be funny to go as you this year. Is that funny?

Sure, I said, sounds funny to me.

Great, she said. When you come out, could you bring him an outfit? Something colourful, obviously.

No problem, I said.

I hope you're staying focused. But I'm sure you're spending all your time with Ashley, my mother mumbled.

I haven't even seen her, I boasted, I've been too busy with school.

Yeah right, she said.

But it was true for one more hour. Ashley was on her way. It was a school day for her, but with a free period after lunch, she decided to skip the whole afternoon block. I only had one more class to attend—University 101, set to meet for all of fifteen minutes in the atrium—and she could wait in the cafeteria while I did that. Then we'd have the rest of the day to ourselves.

Ashley arrived with the afternoon sun, and for a moment, I felt pretty good. It turned out it was cool to have a girlfriend—even Daniel Wagner said that he was jealous—and I could see the positive effect it was having on campus. Ashley seemed to validate my existence. She vouched for me, just standing at my hip. Now there were two of us.

But two's a crowd, for folks like us. Everyone saw us everywhere. Her huge hair. My bright clothing. My huge hair. We were too visible, and there was nowhere we could go to be alone together, even to let down our guard. People weren't just watching us, they were staring—and why wouldn't they? We were a curious, on-campus couple. Even the shadows we cast were ridiculous. We looked like two people disguised as a bush.

I asked if we could sneak into my room. Matt was home in Washington, dealing with a family thing. But my resident advisor, who chatted up the unauthorized girl in our dorm just hours earlier, reminded me the rules did not allow it, no exceptions, and he said if he saw us alone in there later, I'd be looking at a couple demerits.

So we walked into the woods in search of privacy, and somewhere off the beaten path, we found a little treehouse. Hasty and horny, we climbed into the cramped, wooden box to fool around. That day, Ashley touched me to the very point of climax, then let go, retreating to her corner—and I pressed my knees together to suppress the sensation, denying the urgency of my turgid vasculature until most of the genie went back in the bottle. That's how we did it in those days, edging closer every time, but never quite crossing the line.

This time, however, I resented her for it, and Ashley seemed to sense my aggravation.

You know we can't do that, she said, weakly.

Why *not*, I sulked, and I'd have kicked rocks, but we were too high up for that.

Our lives were so limited. Everyone around me was finding new lines to cross, and they were having a blast. But Ashley and I were bound by our generational curses, so determined to prove our goodness that even our most intimate moments were wasted performing identities crafted for others. Fooling around was impossible—slipping up, out of the question. We were terrified to cross the line. What if there was no going back? There was too much at stake for the two of us, too much humanity hung in the balance, and I knew that things would be easier with a girlfriend whose burden was lighter than mine. Some of these girls were determined to prove they were *bad*. That sounded more fun to me, and in my anger, I considered saying so—a white girl would have let me finish—but before we could get into it, we heard a crowd approaching.

Scanning our surroundings for the sound, I saw the ropes, dangling from the trees in all directions. This was no love nest: we were smack-dab in the middle of the Trinity Challenge Course.

We descended in record time. Whatever the real record is, I assure you, we beat it.

I don't think they saw us, Ashley said, as we ran off.

Then someone shouted: We see you, Harry and Ashley!

After that, we walked.

Ashley reached for me along the dirt path back to campus, but I buried my hands in my pockets, smouldering with contempt for the girl whose appearance on campus only heightened my visibility, and I was glad to get away for fifteen minutes in the atrium.

At the second meeting of University 101, the group had a stronger bond, as if it was actually the third meeting.

That's because it was. They'd met in secret. Making small talk at the outset, someone alluded to the popcorn incident, and everyone laughed—then they all stopped, like a pinched balloon, when they saw I was not laughing.

So what's the popcorn incident?

Oh, Tyson made a whole bunch of popcorn and spilled it, Danielle said, and I detected a movie night held in my absence. I assumed it was an honest mistake. She probably forgot that she was the out-lier, with nine students, not eight, how embarrassing for her. She'd be mortified if she knew. Kinder not to mention it. And I wouldn't have thought twice about it, but at the end of the get-together, Danielle passed around a contact sheet and there I was: my name, number, and email, not even halfway down an alphabetical list.

There was no missing me, unless she intended to.

And I thought: It's because I was homeschooled.

Wasting time before collecting Ashley, less enthused about our day together, feeling kept from fixing what was really wrong with me, I wandered through the library, remembering the boy in Arkansas, the boy in the atrium, the boy climbing down from the treehouse, and I decided I despised him. Who was he, anyway? Nobody. Just some jackass cut loose on campus, no more inconspicuous or native to the region than the store-bought bunnies hopping all around. This boy barely existed at all. Nobody would miss him, if he died.

University 101 was the one class you couldn't drop. I know because I stopped attending; still, somehow, I passed.

With nowhere to hide after dark, Ashley and I stopped by the lower cafeteria, finding Daniel Wagner and several other night owls watching Hayao Miyazaki's *Spirited Away* on the big screen. We pulled up an armchair to join them.

It's a beautiful movie. Chihiro, the ten-year-old heroine, loses her parents, and finds herself stranded at some sort of bathhouse for spirits. She bonds with a boy named Haku, who is also a dragon. It doesn't make sense, but his past is a mystery, even to him. A witch called Yubaba has taken his name, and the boy has forgotten himself.

I loved every moment except how the film ended. Chihiro is riding the dragon, when suddenly, high in the sky, she recalls his real name.

I remember falling into you, the little girl says. I think your name is Kohaku River.

Something magical happens, a shattering, of sorts, as a window between worlds is broken. The scales of the dragon explode from its back, and Haku becomes the boy he used to be.

To me, it didn't make sense. All throughout the ninety-minute feature, no one ever mentioned that the boy could be a river, and I ranted about this hole in the script all along the walk to Ashley's car.

I liked it, she said. It's a world where anyone can be anything.

On this, we disagreed, and I tried not to be annoyed, but our common ground was disappearing quickly.

When will I see you? she said, sensing something amiss beyond dissatisfaction with movies.

Already walking away, I responded: I'll see you at the harvest party.

• • •

I went home for a break from not belonging, and to do some laundry. The harvest party hardly even mattered, but I'd said I'd go, and Ashley was expecting me, and Tom expected clothing to complete his Harry costume. I brought him two colourful outfits to choose from.

Take your pick, I said. Lime-green polyester pants and marlins? Or the original red romper?

Tom went green; I went upstairs to change.

Neither look was coming back to campus with me anyway. I packed the whole collection of aloha shirts when I first moved. Two months later, I swore that I would never sport Hawaiian print again. I'd have burned every bright shirt that I owned in the backyard, if I had a barbecue torch and bucket. Instead, I stuffed them all in the back of my closet, replacing each with neutral shirts and sweaters.

Satisfied with my newly desaturated wardrobe, I went down to the kitchen. There, I found my brother and my mother, putting the finishing touches on his Harry costume: a healthy coat of Duracare Brown Paste Polish for his forearms.

This would be no pale imitation.

I don't know what I expected. Ever since I heard what they were planning, I pictured a bad wig, an old pair of glasses and a brightly coloured top—more than enough to suggest me. But the afro was insulting: they took the rainbow-coloured clown wig from the bottom of the dress-up box and spray-painted it charcoal black.

Now they were painting Tom's face. That was worse. The whole point of these outfits was to establish an identity louder than the Blackness. It hadn't worked at all.

Seeing my brother all made up, like some grotesque, carnival version of the ridiculous boy I now knew better than to be, something occurred to me: my mother was doing this for the second time. First, she made me, fashioned in her image. Then I sinned against her. Now she was building a better me, one less likely to rebel, and she was pleased as punch about it.

Have a look, we're almost done, she said. Pretty good, right?

I grimaced. Is that shoe polish?

Well, how *else* are we supposed to do it, she said, instantly defensive.

I don't know, I mumbled, feeling somehow this was my fault. I guess I didn't realize Tom's costume called for blackface.

Tom is going *as you*, she snapped. It's not blackface, it's *you*. And it's only a Halloween costume. I just knew you'd become a humourless liberal in no time at Trinity—get over yourself, Harry.

Mostly, I wanted to get away from myself.

Instead, I saw myself laid bare, irrefutable, overdetermined from the outside and still overdressed for the South. Staring at the other me, I thought of the evil demon I used to worry was inside me—the wicked one wearing my body as a disguise. I got over that. But here he was after all, grafted onto Tom, his second host, mocking me from outside, over there.

I'll take good care of the shirt, don't worry, Tom said.

I don't care, I told him. I don't wear that stuff anymore.

Too cool for school already, my mother sneered.

Not even hardly, I said. And I left to pick up Ashley.

Everyone at Stone Rolled Away thought Tom looked just hilarious, and I was inclined to agree. I was back in Abbotsford to bask in the familiar, but showing my displeasure or dismay would only serve to marginalize me, even among friends and family, and it would make for an awkward evening. I didn't want to mar the harvest party. I wanted to be the life of it. Neither did I want to bring dishonour to my family: Tom was my brother. My mother was *my mother*. It was my duty to defend them, especially from baseless accusations of, say, racism. How could they be racist? They had me. So I co-signed the costume, encouraging laughter, standing next to Tom to bring this travesty to life.

Can you tell we're brothers? I joked to anyone in earshot, smiling uneasily, frantic to signal approval. The resemblance is uncanny.

I was lying. I hated every moment of that harvest party, and I hated myself for my complicity, not only in that moment, but in every moment leading up to it.

Tom was named the costume contest runner-up that night. Called up to the stage, he took a twirl, to great applause, and someone said: He looks just like a real Black person!

No he doesn't, I thought, because I don't. I look like a fucking clown.

Time to die. Ever the child of my upbringing, I did what white men do when confronted with an other so unreal and so unlike them as to destroy their shallow sense of what a man can even be: I cursed the monster. I scorned him and I drove him out, at once.

Numb inside thereafter, I drove Ashley home in silence.

Tom's costume was so funny, she said, just to say something, echoing the lies I told all evening.

But the boy she fell in love with wasn't with us. Maybe she still loved him, but I didn't; he was dead to me, and so was his every allegiance. With no other outlet for my self-destructive rage, I glowered at the only living person I could hurt and I broke up with her, right there inside the Echo.

Only I was too much of a coward to tell her in person. What if she asked for a full explanation? Where could I even begin to explain how I needed to start my life over? I didn't have the language then; each sentence is a struggle even now. And so, outside her house, in the driveway, where she threw her arms around me once, and then again, I feigned affection to get away without a conversation. Speaking for the boy I would no longer be tomorrow, and believing, incorrectly, I was acting out of kindness, I said, Ashley, for the last time, I still love you. Nothing has changed.

PART III

INVISIBLE TO WHOM?

And the question for me was:
Invisible to whom?
—Toni Morrison, in *The New Yorker*, October 19, 2003

8

=

BURDEN BEARERS

(or The Boy Storming Upstairs)

E verything must change.

In my dorm room, I listened to Nina Simone's saddest songs in the dark, feeling miserable. No one and nothing remains the same, the High Priestess sang, and the ballad became my new anthem. But I didn't know how to change. I knew how to sit and feel shame. So that's how I spent the spring term, for the most part. Heartbroken after ending things with Ashley on the phone, and disgusted by the weak-kneed boy who victimized us both, I fell to pieces. I stopped attending classes and attending to myself. I spent my days languishing in bed, chugging Snapple after Snapple in another bottom bunk, buried alive beneath the rubble of my being.

A spirit of rebellion surged within me. At Chapters, I purchased a book on evolution and allowed it to shape my perspective. The first section focused on squirrels on both sides of a canyon, who grew into two separate species. The river between them kept each to its own population—its own kind, in time, for with each adaptation, the likeness eroded. Bisected, the rodents became incompatible.

I knew it was true, from experience.

I swore off Christian music, and at HMV, I bought a stack of secular CDs: Rufus Wainwright, Remy Shand, Jeff Buckley, the Dismemberment Plan, and Ms. Simone, whose incredible voice I first discovered, along with a whole host of white folks, thanks to Felix Da Housecat's Heavenly House Mix of "Sinnerman."

Frankly, I felt Blacker just for knowing who she was, and all the words to every track on *Silk & Soul* and *Baltimore*. I blasted these albums on long drives to nowhere, waging little revolutions in the Echo, finding solace in the sing-alongs, for singing is a kind of crying out.

But it's never enough just to listen to Nina Simone. You have to *listen* to Nina Simone.

Mostly, I was using her to signify a Blackness that I didn't really feel. My tears were white tears, and my ears were white ears, so the context of her protest songs was lost on me completely. I didn't know why Alabama got her so upset. I didn't know why Tennessee had made her lose her rest. I didn't really want to know. I wanted to restore the strained relationship with my mother, not exacerbate things by finding new reasons to be angry. A bit of liberal outrage was enough to make my point; militant Blackness was out of the question.

So my private reform didn't mean much: I doomed myself, for fear of something deeper than these changes.

Still, I was committed to a sweeping transformation, like a larva spins a small cocoon from silk. The caterpillar walks on six pairs of prolegs, at least, just to support the sheer weight of its fat, edible body. But even a dozen appendages buckle eventually, and I only had the one set. It was never enough, and each day I grew heavier. So I returned that summer to my old cocoon in Abbotsford, set to become a new moth.

I had to evolve. At school, I was barely getting by, barely passing my classes, let alone passing for a serious student. Apart from A's in

English and Acting 116, the letter grades my freshman year were ugly, none more so than D's in University 101 and Human Kinetics 110, where I slept through the final exam—a badminton tournament—and nearly failed the class.

My parents demanded to see a report card. But I was too ashamed to let them see.

That's my business, I insisted, and besides, the printer is broken.

To avoid follow-up questions, I retreated upstairs to a bedroom that attested to the boy I used to be.

Thus began the purge. With a dramatic sweep of my arm, I cleared the bookshelf, boxing up all faith-based content—every novel, every album, every Carman music video. I restocked the unit with Norton anthologies, course packs, and Nina Simone's *Greatest Hits*. I raided the closet of everything silly—the big-brimmed hats, the tacky, spotted garments of a clown—and stuffed it into two black trash bags, sentimental about nothing.

I drove it all downtown to Value Village. I left it by the back door, in the rain. There's a bell you're meant to press, alerting receiving. As a final disrespect, I didn't ring it.

Someone saw me anyway: a staff member rushed out to retrieve the items. Then she dashed across the parking lot to catch me by the Echo. Before I could get away clean, I was gifted a ten-dollar, store-credit coupon.

So I went inside and found myself a serious, secondhand jacket—a vintage trench coat of undyed cotton cloth, with a faux sheepskin, shawl collar, and six wooden buttons: the outerwear, I imagined, standing upright, arms down, flexing my fists in the mirror, of a Serious Person.

Exiting the dressing room, still wearing my new staple piece, I spotted the loss prevention officer keeping a close eye on me. I thought of Sunny from the supermarket just across the street, and in my anger, I considered lashing out by dashing out without paying.

But this could cost me far more in the long run, so instead, I flashed my wallet at the man and clicked my tongue in insolence, to let him know his presence was an insult.

Just doing my job, he said.

Get a real job, I responded, going by.

I was becoming someone stronger. The boy was beginning to fade. His livery discarded and his little bedroom gentrified, I had him on the ropes. He felt defeated, in my heart.

But I did not want to know how he felt. I wanted him dead, fucking *murdered*, splayed out in the street to send a message to his whole community. So I cashed in my coupon, paid the difference for the trench coat, and went out to have him beheaded.

Four years had passed since I last cut my hair at the truck stop salon by the freeway. I decided back then I would just let it grow, dreaming of a righteous afro, a burning bush, like the one that spoke to Moses, declaring: I am. But the Lord is a leave-in conditioner, and I'd never even heard of such a thing, and it showed. Mine was the bush once the spirit departed, all fried to a crisp and dried out in the desert—an unholy bramble that followed me like a black cloud.

Just thinking about it, sensation returned: a tingle, at first, then the throbbing of mange. For years, I ignored the discomfort. I tried not to touch it, see it, or feel it. But now that it had my attention, it hurt. Massaging my scalp, I found sensitive spots, sending shivers of pain through my body like shingles. Still, I scratched every itch like a flea-bitten mutt, too desperate for succour to stop, debriding the milk crust beneath all that hair, snow falling inside of the Echo.

My mind went to Disney's *The Jungle Book*, where the snake slithers into a knot before inching away, half-immobilized. Cheer up, Kaa, things could be worse: the knots in my being are legion.

Where do I go? Somewhere new, I decided. No more truck-stop hair salons; no more white hairdressers, period. With home to my right, through the white end of Abbotsford, I made a rebellious, dramatic left turn, to see how the other half lived.

I parked outside a brown barbershop.

I knew what it was from the posters out front: the Punjabi characters, people and print. Inside, the air smelled like Indian spices. The atmosphere frightened me, frankly. I struggled to breathe in. If anyone noticed, I'd struggle to fit in as well. I thought about running away. But I overruled myself, adjusting to the odour with deep, calming breaths as I sat down, awaiting my turn.

Thanks Raj, a customer said, at the door.

Raj nodded, then looked down at me and said: Next.

So I crept up to the chopping block, envisioning a simple execution, and I sat down with my back to my assassin.

Punjab?

English.

Okay, boss. What do you want? Raj asked, and his thick accent made him seem angry with me. I could only assume he was judging my appearance. The barber had incredible hair: a grand, black pompadour with nary a strand out of place. I saw the man comb through it twice in the mirror, sweeping it upward and over his forehead before setting it with several blasts of aerosol. Clearly, he took thoughtful care of himself; surely, he could tell that I did not.

With both hands, I snatched at the unruly afro, suggesting a wig that went rogue and took root.

Cut it off, I said. It's embarrassing.

What *number*, Raj said.

Having no idea what he meant by such a question, I repeated myself: Just cut it off.

Number one?

Yes, I said, feigning certainty, unclear on what I'd asked for until I saw the man attach a guard comb to the clippers. I realized then that I should have said zero, but it was too late to clarify.

To change my mind now, admitting that I didn't understand him before, would only make things worse for me, I figured. He might suspect I couldn't speak to barbers or brown men, and how could I explain myself when both those things were true? Better to just keep my mouth shut.

Whiteness prepares you for naught but more whiteness. A lifetime immersed in it left me with no understanding of what else was out there, and little appetite to lift the veil: encounters with the other were a crisis every time.

Freedom from this anxious, wimpy life is pretty simple: desegregate your spaces. Burst your bubbles. Get to know the unknown and the fear of what you don't know disappears. You'll see yourself in every face by the end of the week.

Raj's first foray into the thicket was fraught. The clippers jumped back like he'd hit a brick wall. The boy would not be so easily scalped. The next few passes found serious resistance, but the barber persisted, and after a struggle, the afro relented and seemed to exhale— or maybe the blast of cool air came from elsewhere, but it felt to me like breathing, and the barber's breath was hot.

The dead thing rolled over, revealing the rot underneath: a raging case of seborrheic dermatitis, otherwise known as cradle cap. The room erupted in whiteness, dandruff and internalized erasure bursting forth like airborne spores, surprising us both, and black clouds fell slowly, pursued by little flakes—a violent, winter storm, collapsing upside down.

It made an awful mess. A lady left.

I'm sorry, I said, upon seeing her go.

But Raj did not respond. A porcupiny layer had emerged from underneath—twisted dreadlocks, stiff as bed springs, embedded in a rigid mantle. The barber was at war. He ditched the clippers and attacked the thousand quills with a thick, metal brush. It was painful; I hid my discomfort. Then he switched to a tool I'd never seen before: a plastic dome with wide-toothed bristles on the bottom that cleared away much of the buildup and felt just incredible.

What is *that*, I asked him, suppressing a shiver of ecstasy, as another wave of fresh air hit the wound.

Horse comb, Raj said.

Was he naturally terse or just furious?

I asked: Can I buy one?

Have this one, he said, turning it over to show me the crime scene beneath. Bits of flesh and fungus were all over. The horse comb was ruined; he would have to throw it out.

I'll pay for it, I said, as an off-white chunk of offal hit my lap, large enough to make a little sound when it landed. I knew it was bad but I never would have guessed it was this bad. I didn't need a barber. I needed a doctor.

Squinting at the mirror with my glasses on the counter, searching for the one to blame, I saw a vague, brownish blob, and nothing more but for a red bead of blood that trickled from my forehead to my eye.

Harry died a gruesome and humiliating death. One last time, the little Black waif made me look like a fool.

I'm sorry, I said.

But Raj was giving me the silent treatment. That, or he was lost in his work. He scoured me again with the horse comb—what a wonderful, cold, burning feeling—and dutifully brushed the detritus from my face, unaware I couldn't see a thing without my glasses anyhow.

His clippers jammed. He changed the blade.

I'm so sorry, I whimpered, breathing through my nose to keep from crying. The last thing I wanted was to weep before a man I couldn't read.

The barber continued in silence until, finally, mercifully, he released me. The high chair fell. The apron clinging tightly to my neck was pulled away. I found my glasses and took a look: somehow I saw less than when I squinted.

At the cash register, I tipped twenty dollars plus an apology, offering to sweep up the mess before I left. Raj waved a hand to dismiss me.

You need to moisturize, he said, combing his pompadour, and as I turned away in shame, certain I was no longer welcome, he snapped his fingers twice and tossed me the horse comb. He smiled: I'll see you soon.

Safe inside the Echo, shaken up and soaked through from only a second in the rain, I inspected myself in the driver's side mirror. He'd given me a crew cut. I looked like a young cadet initiated with a midnight beating. And looking closer, with an overhead view of the volcanic damage, I surveyed clouds of ash, the craters the carnage created, and the awful red ridges like magma escaping the earth's molten core.

I looked away.

As I fastened my seatbelt, it got tangled in my trench coat. One final indignity. The shoulder strap slipped from my grip and retracted. I buried my head in my hands, and I cried.

• • •

You joining the military, G.I. Joe? My father was sitting at the kitchen table, drinking a Harry—which is what we called a coffee with two creams, sometimes, for laughs.

I think you mean G.I. Joe *Cool*, I quipped, still standing, to conceal my sensitivity. No, I'm not enlisting, just trying something new.

Well, maybe you *should* enlist, said the Captain. They pay for your college, you know.

You pay for my college, I said. From my college fund.

Not for long, Harry. You spent nearly all of it living on campus last year. Trinity is expensive, he told me.

What? But I thought—

So next year, my mother cut in from across the table, you can commute. She said it with a scowl, strangling her teabags as usual, and I saw that she was angry with me, which meant that they both were. For why?

I'm sorry, I said, did I do something?

Clearly, you do whatever you want, she responded.

What's *that* supposed to mean?

My father slid a piece of mail across the table. It was addressed to me, from Trinity. The envelope was slitted on the side. I squeezed it and shook; my freshman report card fell out.

You opened this? This is my business, I said, barely concealing my fury.

We're paying for it, so it's actually *our* business, my mother said. Account for yourself. Are you a dummy all of a sudden? If you're not going to take college seriously, why are we footing the bill?

I don't get it, I said. You have to formally request a physical copy. I didn't ask for this.

I did, the Captain said. I called the office of the registrar last week and said I was your father—and benefactor!—and that I had every right to see what I was paying for.

And they went along with that?

He shrugged.

How dare you? I hated that it came out as a question, so I added: That's a *massive* violation of my privacy.

Tough boots, the Captain crossed his arms and said.

How dare *you*, my mother erupted, better at this sort of thing, and before I could respond in righteous anger, she cut me off by shouting: I rebuke you in the name of Jesus!

I was stunned. Or maybe the demon inside me was stunned. Either way, I found I couldn't speak. Not knowing what else to do but flee, lest my backtalk see me any further exorcised, I went upstairs.

My mother stood up to follow me. I don't know what's gotten into you lately, but you've got a real spirit of rebellion! she shouted.

Not anymore, I said. You just rebuked it.

That's it! she said. You can commute from home next year.

So now it's a punishment? I laughed at her. I thought it was a money thing. Whatever, I'm sick of this. Maybe it's time to move out.

You can if you want. She shrugged. But once you're on your own, you're on your own, Harry. We're only paying if you live at home.

She had me. There was no way out but back into the rain.

Then I guess I'll be in my room! I said sarcastically, stomping up the stairs. I slammed my bedroom door with force enough to shake the house. I put on *Baltimore* and turned the volume up as high as it would go.

I went a little mad that day. Snarling like a caged beast, I snatched the technicolor curtains from the window—an act of violence so severe it snapped the plastic curtain rod in half. I stripped the wall of every single poster, leaving Sticky-Tack smudges and scars of Scotch tape in the paint. I emptied my desk drawers right into the trash. Much was recyclable. I didn't care.

After that, I rearranged the room. I dragged the desk over there and the bed over here. I rebuilt the bookshelf against the far wall.

Searching for more changes still, I remembered my beheading, still unfinished. So I found the cordless clippers, and I rose up against what was left of myself. Standing over the sink, before the bathroom mirrors, a triptych where one self becomes a thousand at the right angle, I shaved my head, not bald but raw, scraping at the remnants with a razor until the pain became unbearable, and I was halted by my own survival instinct.

Reborn in blood, I decided to take a new name—my given name, not some childish nickname. My name is *Harrison*, I said in the mirror, three times to summon him and once more, for good measure.

There I am, I thought.

Even trapped in my own home, I never felt so free. Harry was a victim, lost in confusion and fear, somehow segregated from his body. Let him stay lost. He was out of his depth. Harrison Mooney can take things from here.

But a new name alone would not save me. Ascribing new words to the same broken structure will not keep the roof from collapsing. There is work to be done, and instead, I was waging a spiritual war by the way my mother rebuked the Boy Storming Upstairs, attacking an actual problem with magical words. I was speaking in tongues.

I wanted to put the past behind me. But until we turn around to face the past, it's still the present, and our future is our history, rebranded. A name change would not bend the bars of my cage. What I needed was total regime change—to overthrow those who had kept me in bondage. Take the shackles off my feet, so I can dance.

• • •

The night I turned nineteen, I got a phone call. The woman on the other end requested Harry Mooney.

That's me, I said, but now I go by Harrison.

Oh sure, sorry about that, she said. This is Lynn Braidwood from the Hope—and she paused, bracing herself, before tiptoeing through the next two words like there were land mines everywhere— *Adoption . . . Agency . . . ?*

I laughed aloud, to fill the pregnant pause that followed. Such a careful introduction. Clearly, Lynn Braidwood had surprised a few people. Hello, Lynn, I know that I'm adopted, I said, to assuage her concern.

That's *good*, she said, exhaling for effect. It's nice to hear your voice, after all these years. Happy birthday! How are things at home?

Just fine, I said dryly. Everybody loves me and it's great.

Glad to hear it, she chuckled. Well, Harry, you're a legal adult today, and that means your birth parents are entitled to certain information, including your new name. If they ask, I have to tell them.

Okay, I said. Tell them it's Harrison.

That's right, sorry, Lynn said. You should know, though, once they know who you are, they might come looking for you. Just a heads-up! In your case, I wouldn't worry. Both of your birth parents have expressed a willingness to meet you—*but only when you're ready*. Every adoptee has a different timeline for these things. I've explained that to them.

Okay, I said.

After a pause, Lynn Braidwood asked: Is that something that interests you?

I was thinking of my mother downstairs, and how she might react if I seemed too keen to meet the other woman. I thought of the unicorn, stashed somewhere in the house. She trembled when she brought it out of hiding. Her biggest fear was losing her son to the woman who left it for me.

And mine? To be found unworthy of her love, and I knew that if I misspoke on the phone, that was a given. I wanted my mother to see that my foundation was firm—that I would die before I two-timed her with some replacement person, that I would sooner self-immolate than let the fire go out between us. *My mother* was my mother—not some random woman who gave birth to me.

What could I gain from an awkward reunion anyhow? Nowhere close to what I stood to lose.

I heard a bit of static. For a moment, I imagined my mother might be listening from the kitchen—or even recording the call. She'd done it before; she could do it again, and honestly, I wanted her to. She wasn't really speaking to me anymore. But if she wouldn't hear me, she could at least overhear me, so I spoke to Lynn as though I had an audience, and I hoped that my mother detected my ambivalence when I finally said: Maybe later.

Lynn Braidwood heard it. You can also choose to maintain your privacy by filing a disclosure veto, or even a written no-contact declaration, she said. It's all up to you.

I don't think *that's* necessary, I said. I can't imagine they'll be banging down my front door. If they wanted me that badly, they'd have kept me, am I right, Lynn?

Now, sometimes, she said, sidestepping the joke, birth parents leave messages for when everything is unsealed. Until today, these messages had to go through your parents. But now you're an adult, so you're entitled to hear them from me.

I have messages?

Yes, she said. Would you like to hear them?

I guess so.

Both your parents want you to know that they love you very much.

Oh, I said, suspicious of a love I hadn't earned. Are they still together?

No, but they still talk, she said.

And they both left the exact same message?

The exact same. Do you want to respond?

How dare these people even claim to love me. We were strangers. At best, they loved some bygone idea of me. They would probably resent me for not living up to it. Perhaps they would pressure me to become more like them. Well, it's too late, whoever you are, I already adapted to the place where you left me; I no longer need you, goodbye.

Tell them thanks, I said. I'll reach out when I'm ready.

• • •

Maybe after graduation.

Harrison was a work in progress, after all, and things were progressing quite well. My second year was more successful. I brought my grades up: A's and B's across the board. Commuting to campus made for fewer distractions—less time in the lower caf and lounges—and fewer friends, with fewer chance encounters to remind them I existed.

A lot of people made big changes that summer—dramatic transformations born of bloody, metaphysical battles, I imagined, probably not unlike mine. All they wanted now was to be taken at face value.

Before philosophy class, where I sat beside my crush, I asked Daniel Wagner, the Boy Who Died, my old friend from camp, if he had any gum.

Harrison, I don't have any gum, he declared, I'm a mint man now.

Daniel the Mint Man knelt like a knight. He popped a tin of Altoids like a ring box. I accepted. In a way, we were all mint men, the second-years, with brand-new acts and attitudes, and all our childish things were put away. But my adjustments met resistance everywhere.

Our essays were returned to us that morning. I got an A-minus; Colleen, my crush, got a B. Leaning across the aisle, she held up her paper and whispered: B . . . for *Black*. She reached out to give me a fist bump.

That's not funny, I said, looking away.

Colleen called me humourless. Harry, what happened? She asked, after class. Freshman year, you would have laughed at that.

Harry's gone, I said. He was a clown. I'm Harrison now, and I only laugh when things are funny *to me*.

Harrison's a jerk, she said. I liked Harry way better.

You would, you racist, I responded in my mind.

The next week, I sat next to Daniel the Mint Man.

A lifetime of tolerating bigoted behaviour serves as a kind of blackmail. The whole world rests upon your acquiescence, you'll discover, if you dare attempt to walk a little taller. Even the closest relationships are exposed for what they really are: uneasy alliances, like the one between Atlas and the terrestrial globe, broken just by standing up for yourself. The Titans have turned you to stone, and the planet is perched on your shoulders. Make no sudden movements. Arise, and it all goes to rubble.

I tried to be gentle with people, go slow, cut them some slack when they crossed my new boundaries. The only safe way, I thought then, was to inch forward, little by little. But at times it felt like bending over backwards.

At Christmas, I found a family pack of fruity mints in my stocking—the same ones I'd stolen from Funk Foods: a relic of bygone days, purchased in bulk.

If this is a joke, I don't get it, I said.

Oh please, my mother said, smirking. You love those mints. Or at least you *used* to.

That was, like, four years ago, I said.

You're so sensitive these days, Harry. It's not even fun to be around you anymore.

Harrison, I said. My name is Harrison.

No prophet is accepted in his own country. It's hard to see the new man when you knew him as a boy. I am the one prophesied, Jesus said, and the Nazarene Pharisees said: This is Joseph's dumb kid. So he went down to Capernaum, where a demonized man's demon mocked him thusly: Leave us alone, Jesus of Nazareth. Little wonder that he walked into the ocean after that. I understood the impulse, and I'm sure it really bugged him that the prophecies were true. He probably wanted to drown. Instead, he walked on water, and wound up saving Peter from the luxury of sinking.

You can see why he kept the disciples around. They didn't know a thing about his childhood.

People I met for the first time had no frame of reference either, so I preferred them, and I was glad when my father insisted I transfer to a secular school to save money.

I continued my slow transformation in secret at the University College of the Fraser Valley, the local school halfway between a university and a college, halfway between Stone Rolled Away and Glenn Mountain. They were on their way to full university status—a long process of petitioning the provincial government while building the brand of the school, and its reach. What they needed, amid the campaign, was to demonstrate strong community support, including representation from all regional groups. So they were more than glad to have me.

It worked out on my end as well. My transcript improved: University 101 wasn't a real course, they determined, but UCFV let me keep the three credits. Only the D-minus disappeared from my record; my GPA rose above three.

Indignities continued to abound, however. Abbotsford hadn't changed; I had, and not nearly as much as I thought.

My first day on campus, dressed sharply in an argyle sweater vest, brown slacks and shoes, and Buddy Holly's glasses, I went to register for a library card. The old woman at the desk was strangely wary of me. She took my driver's licence into the back, and after staring at the little piece of plastic for a while, she pulled a co-worker aside, looking back at me, suspicious.

That guy doesn't *look* like a Harrison Mooney, she whispered, a little too loudly.

She needed to know that her instincts were inane. What could she possibly think I was after—rare photocopies of CanLit short stories? It was inexplicable, and any thief *that* desperate to read a bunch of college course packs was clearly in the process of changing careers. Why embarrass him?

Admittedly, mine was a pretty white name—Irish-sounding, and the boy who it belonged to wasn't Irish-looking. But I could explain.

I'm adopted, I shouted across the desk, smiling.

This only embarrassed the woman. I wasn't supposed to have

heard her. She seemed offended that I'd spoken out of turn. So she rushed the lamination, and my library card came out crooked and peeling. She moved to dismiss me, as fast as she could.

I'm sorry, I said.

Next! she projected.

I backed away, embarrassed, passing a man who resembled me somewhat, but shorter and darker. It occurred to me that he might have a similar experience. I lingered to watch from a distance.

Sure enough: she studied his licence, suspicious.

Isaac, she finally said, with an air of annoyance. How do you pronounce your middle name?

Kulasekharapuram, he said.

That did it. The woman took her glasses off.

You people, she began, inauspiciously, you come to this country, you say you'll assimilate. But how do you expect to fit in when you've got names we can't even pronounce?

Isaac grinned. I actually *am* changing my name, he said, cheerfully.

Oh really? To what? I'll put it on your new library card, she said.

Isaac leaned in and said: *John Fucking Smith*. And then he just stood there, unblinking, as the librarian backed away, blinking rapidly. He seemed to relish her discomfort, as well as her struggle to enter every last letter of Kulasekharapuram into the database, and he kept his eyes fixed on the woman as she completed the deeply unsettling interaction by icily, silently, laying his card on the counter.

I was appalled. Isaac would never fit in with that attitude. And who dares to curse at a librarian? You'll never have a late fee forgiven again. For a moment, I thought of apologizing on his behalf, if only to claw back a little respect for myself. But the old crank took an unscheduled break, upsetting the long line behind us.

I introduced myself to Isaac straight away. I would not let another potential best friend disappear, and as we chatted in the university college cafeteria, I asked what had possessed him to lash out like that.

Anyone who thinks they can rename you thinks they own you, he said.

And so: he became my best friend.

By my third year, I was in the zone. I managed straight A's for the first time. I joined the English club. I started a blog, and I wrote a witty, one-act play that sold out every showing at the college's theatre festival.

Harrison Mooney was becoming a real someone on campus. But who was I off campus? I still didn't know, and as I ran out of runway at UCFV, I began to consider continuing on to graduate school. The time to sink or swim was drawing near, but I was not prepared to leave the fishbowl.

The real world was calling—my birth parents too. Someone left a comment on my blog, *Harrison Exists!*, beneath a post I wrote about Angelina Jolie.

The Academy Award–winning actress adopted kids from Africa and Asia, and the glowing press she got for this had left me unimpressed. Transracial adoption was suddenly trendy; on TV, the pundits were all but insisting that racialized babies were Hollywood's new must-have items. To me, it seemed, Jolie and other rich white folks who followed in her footsteps were adopting for themselves, to feel like saviours. But the lives that they uprooted in pursuit of their progressive vision seemed to be an afterthought. These children were more than collectibles. They would grow conscious, in time, of how they were really seen, if they were seen at all, and each of them would draw their own conclusions. Adoption was not necessarily good.

Black children are not Beanie Babies, I wrote to no one in particular. The Oscar winner may look saintly now, but wait until these kids grow up. Eventually, they're bound to learn she did it all for clout.

An anonymous reader responded: This made my day. You do

exist, and Harrison, I'm glad. I thank God every day for the great man that you're becoming. I can't say who I am, but just know that I've been watching your life from afar with great pride.

I hoped it was my mother, but she never read my blog, even when I emailed her the hyperlinks. Fearing that she'd start today, and see this, I deleted it.

My mother was opposed to a reunion—for my sake. So much could go wrong, she'd often tell me. Be careful. A lot of people say that they regret meeting their birth parents. They can bring a lot of drama into your life. You can never trust them; they might abandon you all over again. And some folks are just out for money. It might not be what you think.

Once, she clipped an op-ed from the *National Post* that supported her point. She left it in the kitchen, where I'd find it, and I felt that she was making herself clear: don't do it—not unless you're ready for the consequences, ready to be on your own forever, if your mother feels the slightest bit betrayed.

I wasn't ready. I didn't want to be alone; I wanted to earn her respect. So I applied to several master's programs, hoping validation lay ahead.

Just before graduation, set to claim a bachelor's degree in English with a minor in Media and Communication Studies, I received a letter from the school. The Captain delivered it, opened as always. It was an invitation to a special convocation day event: for having the highest GPA of any graduating student minoring in Communications, I would be honoured at a luncheon, pre-ceremony.

A luncheon, Harry! That's so impressive, my mother said. I didn't know you were getting good grades. I thought you were just screwing around, as usual. Why didn't you tell us?

Because it's still my business, I said. And *my* name is *Harrison* Mooney. See it right there on the label? Stop opening my mail. But please, be my guest, by all means.

On the big day, the three of us entered a classroom arranged as a banquet hall, and after filling my paper plate with cheeses, meats, and melon cubes from lukewarm Costco platters, I took my seat at the centre of a long table, amid a wedding party's worth of school officials, to be treated to a trio of laudatory speeches from professors that I didn't really know.

Afterward, I stood with Dr. Beverly Best, a white woman in her early thirties whose expertise was in decoding media messages. She came to every class with advertisements clipped from magazines, unpacking the violent intent behind each. Her critical eye was an X-ray machine. Nothing got past her. She saw through it all.

You must be very proud, she told the Captain.

We are, we are, my father said, piling his plate with salami.

And once he sat down, Dr. Best turned to me. Is this weird for you?

I didn't quite follow.

The highest GPA of any student *with this minor*? I mean, congratulations, she said, but I've never heard of such a thing—have you?

Now that you mention it, no.

Thinking about it, the honour made little sense—unless the reception wasn't aimed at me, but at the people with the power to amend the *University Act*. This was a showing of diversity, I realized. I was playing a role in a minor production. I was merely the guest of honour, made king for a day, lifted up so all may see, not me, or my academic achievement, but what I stood for: another regional group, represented. I was Jimmy from the Bahamas. I wasn't being exalted. I was being exploited. It's because I'm Black, isn't it.

I tried to hide my feelings. Dr. Best was too perceptive.

Oh shit, she said, I ruined it, I'm sorry! Listen, this stuff looks great on you, and so does a diploma from a full-fledged university. She put a hand on my shoulder. Come on, Harrison, I'll buy you a beer.

But I didn't drink, and my parents were there, so I stayed, denying my own abuse, as always, to score a small win with my family. I went back for more melon, shaking hands with several VIPs along the way, and I soaked up every minute of my parents' simple pride, ignoring that it rested on their devastating blindness.

I wore my graduation cap to dinner at the White Spot.

Here's something to go with that, my mother said, placing a gift bag on the table. Inside was a brand-new, blue aloha shirt from the Patagonia in Whistler. The print was more mature, but it destroyed me, nonetheless.

This one has more of a college vibe, she said. I hope it's the right size. You've gained a little weight.

I'd come this far. Why say a thing? I tried it on in silence. It didn't fit or suit me in the slightest. Even after my transformation, she still saw the same little boy, and now I was wearing his clown suit all over again. I wanted to walk into the sea.

The spirit of rebellion raged all night. In the morning, I decided it was time to call Lynn Braidwood.

• • •

The golden nameplate on the door read: BURDEN BEARERS INTERNATIONAL. The *T* was a miniature cross.

I couldn't see inside—the glass was frosted—and I thought for a moment that the address I'd scribbled in pen on my palm might be wrong. So I turned away, roaming the zigzagging hall in confusion, past a therapist, a dentist, and a hearing clinic, all of which were listed on the second-floor directory. The Hope Adoption agency was not.

I had one foot in the stairwell when the door behind me opened.

Over here, Harry! Lynn Braidwood shouted, waving. The lady was a little teapot, short and stout, with a striking resemblance to

Officer Frost, the Sunday school teacher from Gateway. They had the same silver hair, thin and short in supply, showing scalp, the same pale complexion, the same eggy frame. The two women could have been sisters. She ushered me in and I thought of her lookalike, leading the little boy, James, to his doom.

The plaque confused me, I said, hanging my coat on the back of the door.

I've been meaning to change that, she said, grimacing playfully. We used to be Burden Bearers, back when you were born. But we've been Hope for nearly twenty years now.

It's definitely a better name, I said.

I agree. You're not a burden. Make yourself at home.

The office was set up like a living room, with multiple floral-print sofas arranged around an oval table. A dozen white women sat there, sipping coffee out of Styrofoam cups. Each one of them evoked, for me, my mother, and I thought of how close I had come to just leaving.

I'm so glad you chose to stop by, Lynn Braidwood said. I'm just finishing up with my group. I meet every week with some of the mothers I've worked with, women who took in Black babies—like you! I hope you don't mind, Harry. I told them you were coming today. They're very excited to meet you and, if you're comfortable with it, they have some questions.

It felt like an ambush. Lynn Braidwood had invited me to come for 1:30, but according to a schedule I spotted on the wall, her group met every Thursday afternoon from one to two. It was hardly a coincidence that everyone was here; she meant for me to crash her little party.

I was the guest of honour all over again.

I wanted to explode. I didn't come for show and tell. But Lynn Braidwood had information I needed, and my mother's phone number besides. Anything I said would make it back home before I did. I had no choice but to put up a good performance.

I'm fine with that, I told her, smiling, lying through my teeth, and I know we go way back, but please, try to call me Harrison.

She nodded, stepping aside, as the twelve disciples rose to meet me, wide-eyed, overeager, and the questions started coming, fast and furious. Are you happy? Do you feel loved? Do you feel like your birth mother made the right decision? Do you feel like *we* made the right decision to adopt? What's it like being Black with white parents? They crowded me, awaiting my response, desperate to be told that all was well within my soul.

It wasn't, though—especially surrounded by these women. I saw at once their need to solve their children, to decode them. I saw that not a one knew how to bridge the gap of race that kept them from connecting with their kids, that had them flailing at a stranger, seeking clues and validation. They couldn't see beyond the skin; they couldn't make it cease to matter; they couldn't close the ever-growing distance it created. Neither could they shake the sense that, somewhere, they'd gone wrong—that something seemed to undercut the love they claimed to have for their adopted sons and daughters.

It was clear that these people were completely ill-equipped to raise Black babies. They seemed to think that I could fix it for them. I was reminded of that movie, *The Truman Show*, where the character played by Jim Carrey discovers that his world has been constructed to entrap him, to exploit him in his ignorance, and that his reality is false and designed, above all else, to keep him from seeing himself as a product, consumed by the masses without his consent.

I was so upset, I nearly spoke my mind.

What the hell are you doing here? I almost said. Why lean on me when you could ask your own children? What stands in your way? What are you afraid to talk about? If Blackness so confounds you, just admit it. Let them know that you are lost. You think you can continue to avoid a touchy subject? You think your child believes that you are colour blind? Oh please. Your silence shouts the truth and drowns you out. The world is already teaching us all sorts of things about race and racism. If you haven't learned the language, you are losing, you have failed.

You enshrine our inferiority. Even now, your feelings take priority over mine. You allow us to be mocked. We wake up every morning and the sky itself is looking down, disgusted. We look up to you; you look down at your feet. Don't look down, you cowards, look closer, come closer. Tell me I am worthy of love every day, or in your silence you have said I am unworthy. You leave me to be beaten senseless by a world that hates me, and you raise me as though I should hate myself too. It is a vile way to treat a child you were given.

But I could never say these things to my own mother, let alone twelve of her. I wanted every one of them to like me. I knew that would happen if I sought to reassure them.

Of course I'm happy, I began, and more than that, I'm grateful—for the opportunities I've been given, for being rescued from darkness and placed on the path that God has prepared for me. I received nothing but love from my adopted family, and all the advantages they could afford. My education has been paid in full. I start graduate school in the fall. I'm the boy who made good. Look at me go: diploma in hand, a bright future ahead. The world is my oyster. I'm thriving.

I saw their eyes brighten. Relief washed over the whole group. One by one, they praised me for my eloquence and thanked me for my willingness to speak so candidly. They all left with smiles on their faces, and again I felt like a clown—a classier clown, mind you, like a stand-up comedian or something. I stood by the sofa, ashamed, as the room emptied out.

Satisfied, Lynn Braidwood led me into her office.

Now there are two ways we can do this, she said. There's the hard way, where you go through the government and submit some paperwork, and that paperwork is sent to your birth parents, and then it's sent to me, the intermediary, to give to you, and we go back and forth for months or years until everything is hunky-dory. It takes forever.

Oh, I said.

Or we can do it the easy way: I give you their names, and you can probably find them on Facebook.

Let's do that, I said.

Excellent, Lynn Braidwood said. Then you can have this now.

She handed me a document. BIRTH FAMILY HISTORY, it said, underlined. Scanning the sheet, I stopped at the second subheading—Racial and Ethnic Origins.

Mother was born in Ghana, Africa and is of Negroid racial background and Afrikkan nationality. The birth father is a Caucasian who's parents were born in the Ukraine and are of German national origin.

Maybe I'll read this later, I said. Their names aren't on it anywhere, and that's really all I'm after today.

Right, she said. Your birth father's name is Cory Klein. He lives in Langley. And your birth mother, Tee, lives in Seattle, last I checked. She bounces around, though. I never quite know where she is.

What's her full name?

Hold on, it's a real mouthful, Lynn Braidwood said, rifling through her papers. Ah, here we go. Her name is Trinika Arthur-Asamoah.

My heart sank. It was the Blackest name I'd ever heard. Again, I wished I hadn't come. I thought of Prophet K; I thought of Courage; I thought of the girl that I saw, sometimes, at Trinity. I hid from these people, consumed by self-hatred, afraid they would see my discomfort with Blackness. How could I let my own birth mother see it? How could I account for the limits of my language, or my lack of experience with life outside of whiteness? She would be dismayed to find I was not much of a Black man at all.

I logged on to Facebook that night, and I searched for my birth mother, hoping to hit a dead end. I entered two letters—the *T* and the *R*—and the rest filled in for me. The internet already knew there was something between us.

I sent her a friend request and a short message:

Hi Trinika, it's Harrison. By all accounts, I'm your son! It's taken me a long time to get to the point where I'm ready to meet you, but I think I'm there now, so here I am. At your earliest convenience, I'd love to reconnect and go from there.

Three days passed before my request was accepted. I checked for a new message and saw the chat bubble beside Trinika's name. She was writing something. I waited, but the icon disappeared, and I was relieved to have to wait a little longer. Why rush?

I clicked around, scanning my birth mother's Friends list, and that's when I located Cory. That was easy: Add Friend.

I copied and pasted the very same message.

He messaged me back right away.

I am very happy that you finally made contact with me.

You are right. You are my son. And although we have never met, we have never stopped thinking about you, and how life is for you. I know that you may have a lot of questions, which I would be happy to answer, but know this: You were given up for adoption purely out of love and, to date, it is the hardest thing I ever did. I think that when you hear the circumstances you will understand.

In my youthful careless days, when I decided to ink up my back, your name was the first thing that was permanently placed on my body. You since changed your name. Thanks for that. Now I need to have another baby and name him Jordan, just so the tattoo has some significance. (Joke.)

Your brothers and sisters know all about you and have been patiently waiting for you to come see them. When people ask me how many kids I have, I will occasionally say four. Tarana, my seven-year-old, is always there to correct me by saying: You forgot Jordan again, Dad. You have five kids.

We would love to have you over for a bbq anytime. We are available as early as tomorrow night.

Wait, I thought, did he just call me Jordan?

I reread the message. My birth father used the name twice. But it wasn't my name. Jordan is the guy I used to work with at the House of James. *My* name, I seethed, in my rearranged bedroom, is Harrison.

The following night, at his house, I tried to tell him.

9

HE'S BACK NOW

(or The Boy Who Loved His Captors)

The front door was open.

My birth father's house was on a quiet residential street in Langley, just off the road that I followed to Trinity. Coming up the walk to meet the man, it struck me that I'd been there once before, when I was lost: I made a three-point turn in his driveway, en route to somewhere else.

Maybe he saw me, I thought. Maybe he knew who I was, even then.

There were children playing, loudly. Squiggly, cartoon noise lines seemed to issue out from just inside, and peeking in, I espied my half-siblings, four of them, all Black, going bonkers, screaming at the top of their lungs as they leapt from the couch to cushions strewn about the living room.

The floor, it seemed, was lava.

I rang the bell. The children stood up straight and froze, staring like little deer, and the place fell silent, save for the sound of my heartbeat accelerating.

A white man emerged from the kitchen.

Cory had blond hair and blue eyes, but still, the resemblance was striking. Much about the man appeared familiar. He was stocky and short, with a wry, winning smile that I knew right away had been handed down. He had my nose. His wide-legged, pony-rider stride was inherited too, I suspected, as he headed right for me, a little too fast for my liking. The hallway was tilted against me.

How do you do, sir? I said, reaching out in an effort to slow the man down with a handshake.

He knocked my lance away and won the joust.

Son! Cory shouted, overly familiar, I felt, as he yanked me inside with a big, hearty laugh. He hugged me and I shrank away, not used to being touched.

Whoa, I said.

Welcome home, Jordan, he said, at my ear.

Happy to finally meet you, I said while extricating myself, stepping back into the doorway, and smiling to distract from my discomfort. Please, call me Harrison.

Sorry, I named you Jordan, after the basketball player, you're welcome. So I've just always known you as Jordan. He shrugged, matching my smile to the tooth, like a shape-shifter.

I haven't, I said.

I guess I'll get used to it! His arm became a vaudeville hook; he brought me inside by the crook of his elbow and shut the door behind me. Come and meet your brothers and sisters!

The little ones were lined up behind him. They stood in the hallway from smallest to tallest—to my mind, the same kid four times, like a growth chart. I imagined myself at the end of the line. Did I want that?

It's nice to meet you Jordan, the foursome said, in unison. It sounded rehearsed and, for a moment, it seemed they might break into song, like the seven Von Trapp kids all saying goodnight. Instead, they took turns introducing themselves, each one presenting a construction-paper card: Welcome Home! written in crayon, with silly self-portraits inside—a fun way to help me remember them all.

Trevin, the youngest, had twists in his hair. Troy and Terrell had voluminous afros. Tarana, the oldest, had braids. Who was styling their hair? It couldn't be Cory.

And this, you guys, is Jordan, Cory said, taking my trench coat and shoes to the closet.

We moved to the living room.

Watch out! Trevin shouted. He was shirtless. There's lava!

Oh no! I leapt atop a cushion shaped like Iowa, shouting Hot! Hot! Hot!, and followed a trail of throw pillows to the bare couch, where it was safe.

You'll fit in perfectly here, Cory said, surveying his now-complete set from an armchair. All five of you are the same kind of mixed: half-Black and half-white, from me.

That seemed, from my perspective, very specific. My first assumption was that Cory went on to have four more children with Trinika. But when I asked him, he said: Who's Trinika?

I've been led to believe she's my birth mother, I answered.

Oh, you mean *Tee*. No, no, no—these three have a different mom and this one, he said, pointing to the shirtless boy, has another.

Three Black women? I said, stunned. I looked at Cory, scanned the couch, conscious of the children's inner lives, and struggled to conjure a follow-up question that wouldn't echo in their minds forever. Where did you meet them?

Through friends and stuff, Cory said, smirking. I have a heart for Africa.

Clearly, I said—although others could call it a fetish, I thought. Not me, not with all these kids around. But it struck me that one white man does not sire five children by three Black women without a real sense of purpose.

Surrounded by these children sitting before their white father, the absence of the Black mother was suddenly striking. Did he swallow these women whole? Where did they go?

I asked the last question aloud.

Who knows, he said, shrugging. They left. It's a lot, you know, raising four Black kids. But I love it. Women say being a single parent is hard. I haven't found that. It's easy if you love your family. That's what I want people to know. I've actually been pitching a reality series to the networks. That's what I do. I'm a craftsman by trade. I work on those home makeover shows, behind the scenes, so the host takes all the credit for my labour, but lately I've been thinking of a show about *my* life: *Vanilla Dad, Chocolate Children*. I don't have any takers right now, but imagine what they'd say if *you* were onboard! *The four he raised alone, and the one that came home.* It's a great story! Bravo would order a pilot for sure.

It's your story, I said, smiling, I think I'll pass. But I get it. It must be a madhouse. I'm one of four myself.

This seemed to confuse Cory. But then he remembered that I lived a life without him.

Oh right, your adoptive family! He leaned forward. You know, giving you up was one of the hardest things I ever did. It was for the best, though. If you love something, you have to set it free, isn't that what they say? Every night since, I've prayed that I made the right call, and look at you, with your nice, new car out front, I definitely did! So what were your folks like?

They still exist, I said. What *are* they like? Well, my mom has never quite known how to deal with me, I guess. She can be hard to talk to. Or maybe it's me. Although, honestly, I don't know that she's ever quite accepted that I'm Black.

She sounds a lot like Grandma, said Tarana, the oldest, as she straddled the armrest beside me. Leaning over, she added: I think she might be a little racist.

I don't know about *that*, but that's her problem, Cory said, referring to his mother. Grandma can think what she wants. We don't see colour here, do we, kids?

No! Four Black children responded, as one.

Cory continued: If I'd known that I was sending my son to live with someone like my mom, I would have picked another family. If I knew before today, I'd have snatched you the heck out of there.

Was it your choice to make? The placement, I mean. What's the story?

It was *our* choice, he said, me and Tee. We were just too young, and my mom was so against us. I met Tee in junior high. I was sixteen and she was fifteen, I think? We had a unique relationship, but we were very much in love. She was a track star, and I played a bunch of sports: basketball, baseball, soccer. Tee had been told at a young age that she would never get pregnant due to a medical condition, so I'm sure you can understand the shock we felt when we found out about you. And then our families found out, and life became difficult. Tee was sent to a special school for teenage mothers, and I was sent away to a boarding school in the Prairies. But I wanted to raise you, so I got myself kicked out. My mom threatened to disown me, and she refused to acknowledge you or your mother at all. Tee was in foster care, so she had no real support either, and I had soccer . . . it felt like there was no other option.

I remember the day we went to sign the adoption papers. Tee and I just broke down, and we talked about how we would never be able to live with our decision. Never. And not a day goes by that I don't think about you, Jordan. Your birthday is always an especially difficult day.

Cory's countenance fell. He was clearly in need of a cuddle. The children attended to Cory at once, the youngest three climbing up into his lap, making faces. His laughter was bittersweet.

It should have been touching, heartwarming, but in that moment, instead of seeing family love in action, I began to see my

birth father as a broken man, traumatized, trapped in a racial path-
ology, recreating the particular circumstances of my conception,
over and over, collecting half-Black children in a bid to fill the hole
created by my absence. He lost me, I thought, so he made four
more of me. I thought of the toll this must take on his children,
my brothers and sisters, collateral damage, born to a man making
Jordans obsessively, filling his storehouse with breakable figures. I
blamed myself for what I imagined were incomplete lives with a
father obsessed by a brother who haunted the house. And all of it
traced back to me. It was my fault.

Or maybe I was just so cynical by then that anyone who claimed
to love me triggered my intrusive thoughts. Spit, Cory said, clapping
with one hand, upturned.

Trevin leaned over. *Pleh.* A loonie, all drenched in saliva, fell out
of his mouth.

Disgusting, Cory said, stuffing the sticky gold coin in his pocket.
Why don't you go put a top on, pal?

Trevin dove behind the armchair. He emerged seconds later,
sporting a Habitat for Humanity T-shirt.

We build homes in Africa, Cory explained, which reminds me:
you don't have storage space for twenty twin mattresses, by any chance?

No, sir.

Forget I asked! You know, I still carry a photo of you in my wallet. It's from when you were two or three, I think.

He drew it out, and there I was, still a happy baby, facing forward in somebody's lap. You couldn't tell whose, but it wasn't my
mother—the hand at the bottom was clearly a Black woman's hand.
It could only have been Esther Stratford, the adopted daughter of my
pastor at Stone Rolled Away. I wondered how the photo had come
into Cory's possession.

Are you hungry? he asked, interrupting my thoughts. Because
Rosie is making spaghetti.

So we moved to the kitchen, where a Filipina housekeeper was laying the table for six.

It's ready, Rosie said, removing her apron. I'm done for the day. Very nice to finally meet you, Harrison. She left through the living room, skipping from cushion to cushion, avoiding the lava before landing in her slip-ons by the door.

Just before we sat down, the door to the basement swung wide, and an interracial couple, a Black woman and her white partner, eased their way into the kitchen.

Hey, Cory, the Black woman said. We're making spaghetti but we don't have any tomato sauce, so we were wondering—oh wow, is this your *estranged son*? We forgot that was tonight.

It sure is, Cory said, beaming with pride. This is Jordan, the one I told you about. Funny thing: we're having spaghetti too. I'm sure he wouldn't mind if you joined us.

The more, the merrier, and most people call me Harrison, I said, ignoring their obvious ruse. These people had no intention of making spaghetti. They just wanted to come up and meet me. It's not every day that a lost boy comes home.

Kids, Cory announced before we dug in, Jordan's been gone a long time, but he's back now. If you have any questions for him, go ahead, now's the time, you can ask him whatever you want.

The table fell silent. Nobody knew what to say after that. We sat there a moment, watching the heat emanate from our plates. Anyone? Cory encouraged, waiting for one of his children to step up and ask me an excellent question. But the children had no clue what they didn't know. In lieu of spaghetti, they swallowed their tongues.

Tarana broke the silence. Dad, it's my birthday, she said.

After a pause, Cory replied: Oh my God, Tarana, I'm so sorry, I forgot.

I assumed he must be joking. If he was, Tarana didn't find it funny. It's fine, she said, flashing a flimsy smile.

That's okay, Tarana, *we* remembered, said the woman from the basement. She went to Cory's freezer, retrieving a massive Dairy Queen ice cream cake. The theme was the Cat in the Hat.

We spent the rest of the evening celebrating Tarana, Who Was Turning Eight.

But it was my fault that her birthday was an afterthought. All her life, she had been living in my shadow, the oldest, but not really, her father's first of four attempts to try his luck again. Then one day, I walked through the door, and suddenly, there was no room on the sofa. She sat on the armrest, demoted, displaced, just sat there, her birthday forgotten, as her father confessed, breaking down, that he could never forget about mine. I thought of the trauma I brought to her doorstep, and I left there ashamed at my role in her life.

What could I do for her? How could I help any of them? I had come to help myself and even this had proven fruitless. I had nothing to offer these kids—nowhere to take them, and nothing to say. I was a terrible role model anyhow: at best, they'd grow up to develop bad Blackness. They would learn to smile and nod instead of speaking for themselves. They would imitate me to their doom. Cory's kids were better off without me in their lives.

I never went back. I saw too much that troubled me—too many Black kids just like me, trapped in the same kind of life, unexamined, unseen by the eyes looking down on them daily. I was finding my way, all on my own; I didn't need to know about the copies. I didn't want their lives to be my problem.

So I decided not to see them anymore.

In the Echo, I distanced myself from the day. Twenty twin mattresses? Reality shows? Michael Jordan? I wrote the whole thing off as a farce, laughing hysterically, thinking aloud: How does a man miss the cake in his freezer?

• • •

I went home.

The place was sitting empty. I was glad. Visiting Cory felt like being unfaithful, and I crept into the house with guilty eyes. What a relief to have no one to face.

The main Mooneys—my parents, Mike and Tom—were summering just east of 100 Mile, the northern BC community so remote that it was named for its distance from somewhere that mattered. Just past the village of the Canim Lake Band, where the pavement stopped but the road went on forever, there was a ghost town: some fifty lakefront houses, sitting empty—a mining community wiped from the map, abandoned when asbestos lost its value in construction.

A Realtor bought the whole place for a penny. He sold a bunch of plots to folks attending Stone Rolled Away. My father bought the foreman's house: a piggy-pink mansion at the edge of the forest, three bedrooms upstairs, another downstairs, and a basement bar with a ten-foot billiard table.

A regular pool table would have been better: this one was too big for the room, and nobody knew the first thing about snooker. But there was no getting it out of there. The custom-built house was constructed around it.

Mike and Tom and my parents were practically living there now, renovating furiously, knocking out walls, repainting the structure a less tacky green. The Captain imagined a second family home, not just for his retirement but for his children and grandchildren to use at their leisure. Between school and Sport Chek, I didn't have the time to raise a hammer, however, so I missed something. Visiting for two weeks over my twentieth birthday, stepping on everyone's toes in the daytime and struggling to make conversation with anyone, then sleeping by myself downstairs in a bedroom as frigid as being outside on the lake, I felt like a guest in another bird's nest.

So I left a day early to watch movies with Isaac.

• • •

They went off again. My mother left a note with three commandments:

1. Water my plants.
2. Call me every night when you get home.
3. NO GIRLS.

The last one was circled.

Eventually, I called her to contest a couple rules. All of the house-plants were fake, for one thing. I used to dust them. Where were the real ones?

The kitchen windowsill, my mother said. You've never noticed them?

Not really, I said.

The second rule was basically a curfew.

No it isn't, my mother said.

How late can I call without waking you up?

I usually go to bed around midnight, she said. Anything later and I'll start to worry. What if you're hurt or dead?

Mom, if I'm dead, then I can't call anyway, I said. And that's your problem, not mine, I'm dead, I have no problems. Again: what you're describing is a midnight curfew.

No, it isn't, she said.

I moved on. The third rule was the real sticking point anyhow. If they were never here, then I could never bring my college girlfriend home. Where were we supposed to go when everything but Boston Pizza closed at 10 p.m.?

Go to her house, my mother said.

In Maple Ridge? Christina's doing summer classes down the road, and she lives a half hour away, I said. We can't come up the hill? So I have to follow her home and basically turn right around to call you for no reason?

You don't need to be spending hours at her house anyway. If you have time for that, you have time to help us paint.

The cottage is a six-hour drive, I said.

I don't care, my mother said. No girls. Not without somebody there.

Mom, if I was going to have sex, I'd have had it by now. I'm through with you policing my penis, I said. It's not up to you to protect my virginity.

I just don't want you to do something you'll regret, she said.

Next, she would bring up Trinika's mistake. That's where she always took it. I interrupted her as she began.

Mom, I don't want to talk about this. It's my business where I go, what I do, and when I come home, I said.

Not when you live in my house, she said. Call me by midnight or call me to say you'll be late. Nothing good happens after midnight anyhow.

Conversations continue, I said.

Call me by midnight, she said. Are you home for the evening?

Yes, I said, furious.

What did you get up to tonight?

I hung out with Isaac, I lied.

Is Isaac a Muslim? She asked, out of nowhere.

Not really, I said. He's coming around to Christianity.

Isaac and I were having very spirited debates these days. His father was a Muslim, but his mother was a Christian. He stood somewhere between the two faiths, noticing the similarities, commenting on the differences, and never committing to one or the other. Often, he just laughed at my devotion to a dogma based on parable and poetry, weaponized by evil men, from his perspective. But I held my ground: these are the lies told by Satan.

Isaac had tired of his homestay arrangement. He wanted to get an apartment with me. But I was bound to remain where I was.

I invited him to church, I said. He's thinking about it.

And my mother said: Hmm.

I'm not going to defend my relationships to you, I said, getting defensive. And I'm not calling every single night. I'm twenty-one in a month. I have a bachelor's degree. I'm starting grad school in the fall. You can't control me.

Do you still want us to pay your tuition?

Of course, I said, losing another debate.

Then keep it in your pants and call your mother, she said.

I hung up, irate, and the phone rang again. I was just about to really let my mother have it when my girlfriend said: I'm home.

Christina was back after ten days in Mexico. Her sister got married in Mazatlán. I'd been invited—her parents would pay for my flight and my stay at the posh, all-inclusive resort—but, of course, my mother wouldn't let me go. A room by the beach with my girlfriend just wasn't appropriate.

That's a honeymoon, she had said, nixing the idea.

I explained that Christina and I were committed to waiting. She was newly Saved and a born-again virgin when we met in Dr. Best's communications class two years ago, so purity was paramount to her.

It didn't matter. Neither did her whiteness count for much. My mother still didn't approve, and she didn't trust the girl to keep me virtuous. So Christina went to Mexico without me.

But now she was back unexpectedly early. The timing was perfect. I had so much to say about adoption, and Cory and the kids, and, having already made my curfew call, nobody would ever know. I turned around and drove to Maple Ridge.

Christina and I talked for hours, mostly about Mexico: her sister's dress, the flowers, sand, the all-time greatest guacamole. I mentioned Cory in passing but I didn't have my thoughts in order. The topic changed again before I had a chance to think. We fell asleep in her bedroom, beneath the same blanket, on opposite sides of the top sheet—a good Christian couple.

The phone rang at Christina's place, a little after seven in the morning. Incredibly, the caller asked for me.

I'm at home. Where are you? the Captain demanded. I'd forgotten he was flying back from Montreal that morning.

You obviously know where I am, I said, sighing.

You spent the night at Christina's house, he said, and he sounded upset.

On the couch, I lied. Dad, you woke up her whole house.

Come home *now*, he ordered. Get your ass back here. You're in big trouble, my boy.

I raced right home, to wonder why I had to. I arrived as the Captain was leaving for 100 Mile. We passed each other, shouting from our vehicles, like strangers who collided on the road.

Your mother is very upset, he said. You lied to her.

I didn't lie! I answered him, competing with the sound of roaring engines. I wasn't planning to go back out! But then Christina got back from Mexico early, and I was excited to talk to her about something!

Tell it to Mom, he responded.

She's not going to believe me, I whimpered.

Tough boots, said my father, abandoning me.

I called the cottage right away to grovel, prepared to confess that I visited Cory. The phone just rang and rang. I spent the morning fighting a stomach ache, pacing, too anxious to do much but wait by the phone. In search of distractions, I logged on to Facebook.

Trinika's response was there, waiting for me. She gave me her email, her number, and this:

My beautiful baby boy,
*   You are so grown. I always knew you would make your way.*
I am so proud of you. What a rush of emotions. I have so much
to say.
*   Thank God for Facebook. I am a firm believer that He*
knows what He is doing and He does keep His promises.

Harrison, patience is not one of my virtues but I have loved you since I first laid eyes on you. Sounds cheesy but true, and I have had all the patience for you. I have been believing and praying. I will tell you a little secret: I have been reading your blogs and that has been sustaining me for the last two years.

You definitely exist. Today I exist too.

Who had time for *this* right now?

I reacted to the message as if it would self-destruct in seconds. I clicked away. I fled the room. I covered my head with my hands. My birth mother seemed to abound with love for me, if you could believe it, and she said so much that I'd been longing for a lifetime to hear from my parents. I was ashamed to be affected by her words, and I could not afford to have more secrets—not with my mother so angry with me and my master's about to begin. So I dismissed Trinika, for the moment.

Instead, I wasted the whole afternoon calling 100 Mile, obsessively. The Captain finally answered when he got there, after dark. He told me that my mother was too mad at me to talk.

I knew that she was listening in, however, so I said: I'm supposed to call her every night. Or are we not doing that anymore?

My mother emerged as a voice in the shadows. Hello, she spoke, over dead air.

Mom, I slept on the couch, I insisted.

Sure you did, Harry, she answered. Goodbye.

We did not speak again for several weeks.

My mother came home eventually, but she never came back to me. She moved through the house like a gust through the valley—a presence without any presence, or warmth.

• • •

261

The silent treatment lasted the remainder of the summer.

Mired in shame and disbelief, I spent the season desperate for a simple look of love. I tried everything to reconnect with my mother. I kept to her curfew while she was away: I'm back, I announced every night, to the answering machine. When she was at home, I would sit with her down in the kitchen, watching CBN and Fox News programming with her, never speaking up in my defence.

I waited for her; I waited on her. I wasted weeks striving, in vain, for forgiveness.

Marvelling daily at coldness a wiser man might call an ice age, I started to fear for the future. I counted on my mother's contributions. A week before September, with my first tuition payment coming due, she held my whole world in her hands, and she was angry.

I hadn't planned to work much in the fall. The graduate course load at Trinity was heavy, they told me. Part-time hours were strongly recommended. I applied to two secular universities, both of which were more esteemed and cheaper, but neither accepted me, even with the highest GPA among Communications minors. Trinity's grad school, on the other hand, was too new and too costly to be in demand. The Master of Arts in Interdisciplinary Humanities program—a recently launched combination of philosophy, English, and history—needed bodies.

I had one to give them, as ever. But suddenly, I didn't know if I had any money.

With time running out and the walls closing in, I challenged my mother directly.

Mom, this has to stop, I demanded one afternoon, sitting down in the kitchen. The summer's almost over.

She harrumphed and looked down at her newspaper, scowling. We were worlds apart by then. Cut off emotionally, I couldn't seem to find her in her eyes. She wasn't there.

Yeah, I get it, you're still not speaking to me, I said. It's very mature. But classes start up again soon. I can't just twist in the wind. I still live here, in case you forgot. Are you guys still planning to support me?

Harrumphing again, she looked up—not at me, but at some Black man she didn't know—and as her lovelessness broke my heart, she smirked: Why don't you go and talk to your father about that?

I knew what she meant from a lifetime of spankings: the painful part had been outsourced to the Captain. Fury and fear formed a ball in my stomach. I ran to him, hoping I had it all wrong. He stood in the driveway, pressure-washing an old boat.

Feast your eyes on my new fishing vessel, Harry, he said.

I pressed him: Dad, are you still planning to pay for my college? That's what we talked about before. The first tuition payment is coming up quick.

My father couldn't even look at me. He stood up, his back to me, blasting the boat as he spoke, knowing full well that I couldn't hear him.

I missed that, I told him. Put down the nozzle and *look at me*.

Harry, he said, turning halfway around, I don't think we're going to be paying for your school anymore.

Why *not*? I demanded.

No money, he said. Your college fund is tapped out, my man.

I lost it. Dad, what the hell! You could have told me that sooner. I would have spent the summer saving. I would have worked a second job or borrowed money from the bank. I would have made a plan. I'm out of time now. Where do I go? *What* am I supposed to do?

Tough boots, he said. You should have thought of that before.

Before *what*? What unforgivable sin have I committed?

You lied to your mother, the Captain said. You made a fool of her.

So now you avenge her, is that it? You do her dirty work, as usual. Do you really think this is a reasonable way to treat your own son?

And my father said nothing, which was his confession.

I had to get out of that house.

Isaac was shocked when I told him what happened. He packed while I ranted and raved, and he made it official by telling his billets he planned to move out by the end of the month. We spent the day apartment-hunting, setting our sights on a two-bedroom suite down the street from my church, where the vacancy sign was a permanent fixture.

The elderly superintendent, a white man, explained that the space had been empty for months. The previous tenant, an unmarried woman, moved out after finding a man in her bed. Word got around, so the ground-floor apartment sat vacant, for fear of the creep coming back. To make matters worse, a homeless man camped in the alley outside with his dog, living on scraps from Mr. Sub. He frightened the tenants but they couldn't make him go away. Walking by the window, half-undressed, he ate a sandwich. We met eyes. He offered a neighbourly wave.

But you guys wouldn't have to worry about intruders, the landlord laughed. You're the ones we're *really* all afraid of, isn't that right?

Oh yes, Isaac said, sarcastically. Harrison here is a regular villain. That's why I'm moving in with him. Keep your enemies close.

He's joking, I said quickly.

The landlord laughed again. You boys seem nice enough, he said. He handed us the forms, insisting everything was standard.

It wasn't, though: I'd never seen a rental application in my life, so I didn't know that asking for a headshot was uncommon. Isaac used his passport photo; I went with one that depicted me, smiling—the picture I used for my student ID—and added a line where the form asked for more information, explaining my ties to the church down the block. When everything appeared in order, I took the package home and faxed it from my father's office.

As soon as it went through, I told my parents I was leaving.

Is that so, my mother said, coldly. When do you think you'll be out?

Next week, I said. First of the month.

Good luck with that, she scoffed. Apartment-hunting is hard. It takes longer than that. And people might be a little wary about renting to *you*. Since it's your first place.

I already found a two-bedroom with Isaac, I said.

Unconvinced, my mother asked: Does Isaac have any furniture?

I don't think so, but we don't need much, I told her. I've got my bed, and my bookshelf and dresser. That's enough to start out with.

No you don't, my mother said. The stuff in your bedroom belongs to us.

What are you talking about? You bought it for me, I said.

I bought it for *your room*, she said. If you're leaving, Tom will probably move back in there, and he's not sleeping on the floor.

You'd prefer that *I* sleep on the floor, I said.

Buy an air mattress, she said. There's a sale at Canadian Tire. Here's a flyer.

And I can have it—as a gift? Thanks for thinking of me, Mom, you're the best, I muttered, hiding my sorrow behind it and storming upstairs for the very last time.

The call from the management company came the next morning. I assumed that they were looking for my father, who was listed as a character reference, but the woman asked for me.

I said: You got me. Expecting good news, prematurely atingle, I rose to my tiptoes and waited.

It's bad news, I'm afraid to say, she started. Your bid for the suite on Marshall Road has been rejected.

And why is that? I asked her, landing flat-footed.

I don't know, she said. But we do appreciate your interest.

No, you don't, or you'd be renting to us, I said through gritted teeth. This apartment has been sitting empty for months because a woman was assaulted in the bedroom, and you'd rather keep losing money than rent to us? You didn't call our references. You didn't have the time. Which means that *this* decision was based on nothing more than our names, and our faces. You took one look at us and said no. So I'd just like to know if our application was rejected because I'm Black, or because my roommate is Arab.

Excuse me? The woman sounded rattled—or perhaps it was simply the sound of her pearls being clutched.

Or was it the lethal combination of both of us? Is two dark-skinned men one too many? Because if either of us can live there with a white person, we can find someone and flip a coin for the second bedroom. Or maybe you think that we're lovers.

I clenched my fists and huffed and puffed, all full of piss and fire.

Ma'am. Clearly, this decision is based on bigotry, and I would simply like to know: Which kind?

She sputtered a moment and put me on hold. Ten minutes later, a man joined the call.

Harrison, I have some good news, he said, sounding managerial. We've finished reviewing your application, just now, and you've been approved for a six-month lease. Congratulations.

Laughing to myself like only I survived the plane crash, I unfurled my fists, and I watched as the blood flushed my fingers. Some of it seeped out from little cuts along my palms—crescents, where my fingernails had broken through the skin.

• • •

I don't know what I expected.

On Saturdays, the Captain often woke up early, jet-lagged, and he made himself a heaping plate of fried rice for breakfast. If you missed it, you were out of luck. If the smell of bacon woke you and you caught him by the wok, he would double the portions, for sharing. Then we would watch baseball together all morning.

But when I woke up to move out, no one was awake, and there was nothing in the air to stir my senses—no inviting aroma, no crowd sounds or crack of the bat, no movement—no acknowledgement of any kind, except for a handwritten note from my mother.

Taped to the front door, it read: *Leave your key.*

Left to fend for myself like the last soul, unraptured, a nightmare I'd never forgotten come true, I gorged on a big box of Cinnamon Toast Crunch, sobbing softly into soggy, sugar cereal. Then I packed up the Echo, which didn't take long, and I loitered downstairs in denial.

Certainly someone had something to say after twenty-one years. Was I nothing to them?

Nobody slept in this late. Incredulous, I wandered upstairs, floating through the hallway like the ghost of a boy who got lost in the walls, keen to spook a family member sneaking to the bathroom—someone to confront, or hug, or tell me I'd be missed.

No such luck. No one came; no one said boo. The trio of white bedroom doors remained closed.

This was something more than silent treatment. I was being excommunicated, likely on my mother's orders. My father, Mike, and Tom were just following instructions. I imagined the men in their beds, lying perfectly still, beneath blankets, in wait, hoping, praying I'd just go away. I could only forgive them. There was no defying my mother, not ever, and if the cost had been unclear before, they hid from me now, understanding.

I blamed myself. I had fought for this. I brandished independence like a sharpened sword. I should have known my mother would not hesitate to gore me with it—Lord, I should have known, I should have known, I should have known.

I shut the only open door—my bedroom—just for symmetry.

Outside on the front steps of the place where I once stayed, I stood between pillars, like Samson, and I thought about bringing the whole temple down, proclaiming liberty to the captives. But then

I remembered: I wasn't that strong, and I couldn't go out this way anyhow. I had to leave the key behind and still lock up, by magic. So I left through the garage, smashing the button at the top of the stairs, and escaping through the falling door like Indiana Jones.

Dusting myself off, I fired up the Echo and drove to my new home, alone, feeling nothing.

• • •

Mothers teach love and survival, said the warrior poet, Audre Lorde. But mine taught me how to survive without love. Abandoned by two mothers by the age of twenty-one, I scorned them both and told myself I never needed either.

I don't need anyone.

In the solitary confinement of my new master bedroom, a carpeted box in a carpenter's beige, I said it until I was sure I believed it, proclaiming my ambivalence aloud to kill the silence, content to be unworthy of a love I couldn't keep.

I suppose you could say I was free. But I didn't feel very free. Does the runt of the litter feel free when rejected as offspring, and eaten? Free like a victim of filial cannibalism. Free like the Black man who crosses a slave state that hates him for winning his freedom. This is a cruel kind of liberty, if you can call it that: the personal freedom of orphans and outcasts, the homeless, the loveless, the lost. Nobody wants to be this free—it's death. It's hell, as described by the Bible and by Officer Frost, where you can see your family, but they can't see you.

I squirmed as a baby, my mother told me more than once. I fought to get away, she said. I struggled. But when she put me on the floor, I cried and screamed until she scooped me up. The fidgeting started all over. The only way you wanted to be held was sitting at the edge of my knees, facing away, she would say, always adding: So

I thought you didn't like me.

Of course I liked her. She said she was my mother. I believed her, so I loved her. I wanted to be held, but not so tightly. That was all.

The unknown world is a terrifying place. The devil you know is a luxury, often, when faced with the option of no one you know. This is how you get a Black white supremacist. I know these men, for I was one of these men: the ones who feel safer among those who hate them than all by themselves in the world. The world hates them too, and they know it. But if it's all the same to you—and in my experience, while the flavours change, the core components stay the same, like ice cream—then dare I say it's better to be lynched by friends and family.

I suppose this is why I hung around for so long.

This was my tendency, after all, for I was my birth father's son. The reunion with Cory was a disaster, but the context had been valuable: the man lived in thrall to his mother and spent his days fighting to earn her respect, I imagined, repeating the same feckless patterns, again and again, blind to who she really was. This sort of behaviour came naturally to me, in other words, and that's before it was nurtured for decades. My whole identity had been crafted as a response to my mother, just as Blackness is carved out of white expectations. We either reject the white gaze or accept it; either way, it remains the foundation. Greater is she that is in me, than me that is in the world. But now the ground beneath my feet was gone, and I was falling—out of what and into what, I couldn't really say. How now shall I live? I prayed to God, who didn't answer.

Who else could I be but who I'd been?

This is the essential question. *If we do not define ourselves for ourselves*, the warrior poet said, *we will be defined by others—for their use and to our detriment.*

But I wouldn't know that for several more weeks.

• • •

My freedom set me back ten thousand dollars. With no other choice, having so little time, I took out a large line of credit to cover my classes at Trinity. The money went fast. I was surprised by how soon I ran through it—how quickly freedom descends into debt—and I was annoyed to have to spend so much on a course that didn't interest me.

History? No thanks, I'm full.

If Trinity allowed it, I'd have registered for strictly English classes. Fiction was gripping; the other stuff struck me as tedious. But the graduate program was interdisciplinary. You must wade into all three streams at least once, I was ordered. So, I registered for Philosophy 600: Heidegger and Hegel, where I learned why the jug exists—no other idea holds water—and after turning my nose up at History 600: Historiography, which sounded, to me, like word salad, and History of Christianity II, having seen enough already, I settled on History 592—Sugar, Slaves, Silver: Atlantic History.

At least it won't be boring, I told myself. Perhaps there will be some discussion of Ghana.

On the first day of classes, I arrived apathetic and empty as ever, expecting to learn about pirates. But into the hole in my heart flowed a history hidden from me for nefarious purposes, filling me up to the brim, like a jug, bringing everything ever internalized back to the surface.

The professor, Dr. Robynne Healey, opened with a thought-provoking question: How do you know what you know, and who told you?

Speaking to a class of mostly undergrads, except for me and an older woman, Rochelle, who looked just like my mother from the back and blocked my view, Dr. Healey challenged us to abandon the perspectives we were raised with.

Easy, I thought. They abandoned me first.

Most of you were brought up with a Eurocentric worldview—a way of seeing the world that elevates white voices and erases all competing, coinciding ways of seeing, Dr. Healey said. The European narrative is narrow, and designed, as James Baldwin put it, to reassure us that no crime was committed. To make it all appear okay. The colonizers ascribed no agency to the people they oppressed, no history disrupted, no humanity considered. This allowed them to commodify these cultures over time, and later to silence survivors and whitewash the violence inflicted against them. Many modern-day historians commit this same malpractice. Until we shift our approach, we'll never understand who we are, or how we got here.

I sat up straight to see beyond Rochelle.

When you take a step back, beyond national borders and constructed categories—race is a big one—suddenly it's not a narrative that begins when the Europeans first landed in Africa or the so-called New World, as though everyone who lived there already was just sitting around, waiting for something. In this course, Dr. Healey said, our main character is the Atlantic Ocean, a soup of shifting currents, completely indifferent to the colonists' agenda. What happens when we take a topographic view? We are afforded space to turn the history over and look at it from manifold perspectives. What happens is we get a glimpse of other kinds of stories.

What happens, I would learn, is that the awful truth is brought to light, at last.

When you are born, you open your eyes, and you take the baton and you run. That's how I was brought up, and it's madness. For if you look back far enough, and frankly, not that far, you'll see that the baton comes from the crime scene, and you're an accomplice, as well as the victim. The blood on your hands might as well be your own.

The first slaves, I was shocked to learn, were actually Indigenous. Captured by conquistadors and transported south to the sugarcane fields of Brazil, most succumbed to heatstroke, new diseases, and despair within a year. But soon the settlers found a better source of unpaid labour: West African slaves could live up to four years, on average. They were simply superior products, the slavers decided, replacing the workforce with African peoples and making space by murdering the ones who had lived there before.

So it is that chattel slavery and Indigenous genocide are intertwined and must be resisted in tandem. These genocidal projects are ongoing, all across the continent. Our fight is their fight—we're brothers and sisters. We mustn't forget: we are one and the same.

Where were we? Brazil.

Four hundred years of sheer horror ensued, as some twelve million Africans were trafficked across the Atlantic. Men, women, and children kidnapped from their homeland to be brutalized and branded, families torn apart, separated into strangers, bound by shackles, frog-marched onto stinking ships, the reek of death detectable from five miles off the coast. Bodies on bodies, stacked like non-perishables, crammed onto vessels packed tightly or loosely, depending on the captain, who sailed around the coast, collecting fifteen slaves here, maybe twenty slaves there, gambling on how much inhumanity his human freight could bear. On the gruelling, months-long trip across the Middle Passage, miscalculations were corrected by tossing the dead overboard, some 15 per cent of the cargo, on average, and sometimes 100 per cent, if the slaves were insured, thrown to the sharks swimming after the ships, where the red meat of man seemed to fall from the sky, Black lives as manna from heaven, abundant, delectable, free for the taking—wave after wave of humanity, wasted. For every slave who crossed the sea, another one to five did not survive the wars of capture, and the slow devaluation over trails of sun-bleached bones from the savannah to the shore, to somewhere else. Twelve million is the low end. Upward of sixty million souls cry out for justice, most of whom were counted as collateral damage, having never really counted in the first place.

But the ocean holds onto this history. No one is lost, where the seas are concerned. They're simply lost to us, and what do we know? The bodies of our ancestors are piled up along the seabed, water levels rising, transforming the whole earth. Nothing has been the same since.

In Dr. Healey's class, I came to see that racism did not beget the transatlantic slave trade. Quite the opposite, in fact. Divisions of race were necessary not only to justify these horrors, but to silence the fear that this could happen to anyone. Whiteness exempted the slavers, empowered them, offered a licence to kill whomsoever they wanted, and the Bible seemed to speak in their support, if read correctly. Consider Blackness a curse, which was easy when you saw how the people were treated, and one was left to wonder where the curse had first begun.

Noah's son, Ham, had been cursed. Must be him.

To hear the Ham doctrine again in this context was almost as shocking as when I first heard it. At Gateway, they said it was true, and my mother was still being influenced by it. But Dr. Healey said it was an obvious lie, weaponized in defence of chattel slavery.

She added that the Christian church no longer taught it.

They taught it at *my* church, I said, and I must have sounded livid. The classroom fell silent, and I was embarrassed not only by my outburst, but for spending my whole life uncertain about something so hateful and nakedly false.

Twenty years before I was born, Dr. King called it a blasphemy. Two hundred years before I was born, this false teaching was condemned by the former slave Ottobah Cugoano, a Fante boy kidnapped from Ghana at thirteen and later rechristened John Stuart. As a free man, he went by both names, claiming both identities at once. It hadn't occurred to me that you could do that. Nobody told me that I could be more than one person.

I wasn't supposed to find out.

White people, Cugoano explained, *have in general endeavoured to keep the Black people in total ignorance as much as they can.*

What are they afraid of? What they owe us: a lifetime of service, unmaking the world. But I was not supposed to know that. Neither had I known that I was raised on lies, centuries old. But this is the way of the world, even now. Whiteness is still being taught far and wide. Abolition has made many gains, but the movement has yet to breach the limits of the white imagination, which was handed down to me and kept me blind. The slave trade has been partly abolished, but the systems designed to reduce me to nothing and sell me off for parts remain in practice, and so do their justifications. Yet we wonder how white mothers could make slaves of their Black sons when the summer heat becomes too much to bear.

It's simple, though: they're as brainwashed as anyone, mindlessly minding their homes in a slave state. We give them Black children to raise, as if they're flowers in a vase, and perhaps that's what they think of us. It's certainly what they expect us to think of ourselves.

Well, think again. Lovely as they look inside your living room, the flowers are dying.

• • •

One Sunday after church, more than a month after I moved out, my mother broke her silence. She came by the apartment, uninvited, with a present: a plastic shower curtain in a gaudy leopard print.

I took it as a kind of veiled insult.

I might have hung it up, not long before. But we already had Isaac's *Scarface* curtain, and that would have to suffice. I was no longer willing to let my mother colour my life—not when she couldn't give a gift without making it weird.

The distance between us was striking. I kept her at arm's length

274

until she left. Better informed now, I saw that we'd run the whole gamut—a forced relocation, some blackface, some slavery, emancipation, and eventual enshrinement as a second-class citizen. I began to see my mother as American history come to life, and my childhood as a metaphor for centuries of suffering.

The woman was utterly dizzied by whiteness, just as my white fathers were—just as I had been. And as I wondered how it took me, a Black man, so long to see the world for what it really was when all the signs had been there, for the first time in my life, I put the blame on someone else.

It was you, mother. I learned it from watching you.

As soon as she was gone, I threw the curtain in the trash.

I had to be outraged. The facts were outrageous—the trauma of all that was wrought, and the cancer it gave to the culture, malignant as ever, its violent systems still metastasizing so relentlessly that every living soul is sick, and every set of hands is slick with someone else's blood.

And this blood is my blood. I saw that, finally.

Nine slave routes in Ghana alone. Sixty slave markets all along the Gold Coast. Every footstep follows in the footprints of the captured in the land where my family was born. No one is untouched. Nothing has changed but the means of extraction. It's pathological now. I still lost my mother, and I wasn't even there. I was gold from the Gold Coast, wasting away in some white west coast mansion, way the heck out in the Bible Belt. I severed my ties with this past long ago. But the past was not through with me. Jolted from apathy, I returned to a vision I had as a child, the one with the young boy who floated away, and saw not the grim coast, but the Gold Coast, and not a bunch of savages screaming at my escape, but a community calling *Come home.*

Emerging from my boyhood fear, I saw my mother's nightmare coming true: her terror of a future in which I learned of my past and expanded beyond her, looking back in judgment at the truth of who she was, confirming her worst fears about herself. I saw myself, the boy who loved his captors, sitting dumbly, simply, pining over people whose oppression he'd escaped.

So I wised up.

Don't tell me that I can't go back. I'll go back even further. Turns out there's a motherlode of mothers in the motherland, including mine. Don't tell me that I can't go home. Homecoming, like becoming, is an act of constant movement. You can always go home, so long as home is yours to redefine.

Loss remakes you, Saidiya Hartman once wrote. *To lose your mother was to forget your past.* This is not some abstraction, or poetic licence, my dear friends; it happened to me. Losing my mother for the second time, I finally forgot the recent past, and from the ashes of my condemnation, I rose again, remade, revived, remembering I came from someone else.

Late one night, punch-drunk on history, I dialled Trinika's number.

She answered, trembling audibly: Hello?

It's Harrison, I said, and in my voice I heard a boy I thought was dead.

Trinika inhaled three times sharply, and before she could respond, she started crying.

She wept for what seemed like a lifetime.

10

THE BOY WHO SAW
WHAT WASN'T THERE

Trinika began to suspect she'd been stolen a year after landing in Canada.

That night on the phone, I began to suspect the same thing. My birth mother lived in Seattle now, in the ghetto, she said, where she fled after giving me up for adoption. She was born in Sekondi, a Ghanaian city along what was once the Gold Coast. She grew up in a little house, surrounded by family—her mother, her grandparents, a brother and sisters, her cousins, her clan, her foundation. They were Fante fisherpeople who spent their days trolling the deep-water harbour, where European merchants once erected duelling slave castles, a gunshot apart, on twin hillsides: Fort George, for the Brits had a king by the name, and Fort Orange, for the Dutch have a favourite colour.

A war in 1690 brought the British fort to ruin and left the Dutch a tidy trade monopoly. The Hollanders insisted they were not the instigators, but somehow, all the English goods were transferred to their fortress while the city by the sea was still on fire. Sekondi, once a wealthy Fante town, did not recover. The European settlers saw to that: they worked to keep the people underfoot, and underground, while the Ashanti Kingdom inland, where the tropical diseases held the colonists at bay, amassed its power. The hierarchy created to preserve the booming trade of human lives in Ghana still endures today.

Fort Orange is still standing as well. The castle—where confounded human beings were once consigned for months to dungeons black as blindness, sitting, suffocating in the filth of fellow strangers, until ships arrived to take them through the Door of No Return and out to sea—is a lighthouse now. The fishermen use it to find their way home.

But the lighthouse only works for boats. Trinika took a plane.

At five years old, the little one was sent to see her father, a man she barely knew. He was a brilliant aerodynamics engineer, wealthy and worldly, with homes in three cities, who felt his firstborn daughter was above a Fante upbringing. Certain she was better than a fisherman, just as he was, he sent a friend to whisk her off to Accra, out of nowhere.

I remember shadows, Trinika told me. One minute I was there. Then I'm at the airport. The next thing I know, we're on a plane, and I've never been on a plane, so that's when the panic set in.

She boarded the flight with a boy introduced as her brother.

I knew my only brother, so I knew that was a lie, Trinika said. But I realized that bold-faced lies were going to become a big part of my life—clear lies, where you know it's a lie, but the people around you say otherwise.

Lies are only lies when you are free to disbelieve them. The girl had little choice. So where's the lie?

She strapped herself in. She'd been given a middle seat. Trinika was sandwiched between the strange boy and an even stranger boy, with see-through skin and orange hair, the first white boy she'd ever seen up close. He gazed at her through hungry eyes she'd never seen be blue. Unnerved by how he seemed to stare and how it made her feel, Trinika spent the flight afraid of him, and fearful there were more of him where she was going. The food was frightening too. The in-flight meal, spaghetti, had the look of worms or bloody guts. Repulsed at what these people said was food, she pushed the tray aside. The little redhead ate her meal without so much as asking.

It was freaky, she said. He was like a little demon.

Deplaning in Toronto, in a snowstorm, under-bundled, Trinika stood and shivered with her brother by the gate.

All that she remembers of her first day in Canada, and every day thereafter, is the cold.

They moved to Vancouver, not far from the airport where her father worked. But the man wasn't around much, and Trinika's new mother grew resentful of the daughter dumped on her. Her punishments, Trinika told me, pausing for effect, could be severe. She was rarely slow to wrath.

My parents used to spank me all the time, I said, commiserating.

Trinika gasped. They spanked you?

Spare the rod, spoil the child, I said, chuckling.

But really, it's the rod that spoils the child. A body accustomed to violence is always in danger.

I'm sorry, she said. That's not right. I'm so sorry.

It's fine, I responded, I got your big butt.

I'm sorry for that too, she said, and together we laughed at our threshold for pain.

So a little more cushion turned out to be useful, I said. The hair, on the other hand . . . do you know what's worse than a paddle? *A nit comb*.

You had lice too?! Did they shave your head?

I wouldn't let them.

I didn't have a choice, Trinika said. My teacher cut a huge chunk off before I even knew what she was doing. It never grew back the same way.

This is, of course, an old wives' tale. No haircut alone can alter the way that hair grows—except for in the mind from which it sprouts. Where once Trinika's hair was a shrine to maternal love and care, it now became a metaphor for loss: the loss of family, bodily autonomy, sense of safety, sense of place, the loss of the self as it breaks from a body in trouble. She didn't even see a little girl when it was over. The creature in the mirror was a boy she did not know—déjà vu—and this is when she knew she'd been abducted.

I still don't know how to take care of my hair, I admitted.

Shea butter, Trinika said, matter-of-factly. And never let white people touch it. They think it's just hair.

All hair is dead—that's what I was told, I said.

Not when it's *yours*.

The larger world would soon remind Trinika of her gender. At ten years old, fearful of both her father and her brother, she called a 1-800 number that was advertised on TV while she sat at home, alone. A social worker came to retrieve her at once. Off she went, again, into the shadows. Trinika was left at a group home in Richmond—the infamous Golovin house.

The place had the look of a paradise. But nothing that does ever is.

John and Betty Golovin had a trampoline, a pool, and toys enough for all the children in their care. But they did not offer safety: the man of the house was a kid-toucher. Trinika was never intended to stay there, but shortly after dropping her off, the social worker went on maternity leave. So the girl lived with the Golovins for three awful years.

A doctor who examined Trinika during this ordeal told her she couldn't have children. It was meant to assure her, securing her silence. Instead, it destroyed her. With no history and no future, Trinika had nothing to lose. So she told.

The popular group home was closed.

Three other victims came forward. Mr. Golovin was brought to court on six separate offences. But the man was a pillar of the Richmond community—a former fire chief, who had fostered some 150 children. His accusers, in comparison, were no one. Trinika had no family and no ties to the community, which reflected poorly on her, as did her vindictive decision to tell on the man. With no one to stand for her goodness, the defence was free to blame her for her badness. The BC Supreme Court justice who tried the case, without a jury, ruled that she was the unfortunate product of a depraved background. The abuser was swiftly acquitted.

It was in all the papers, Trinika said, laughing. They said I was a bad Black girl. By the end, I believed them.

Another person might have been surprised to hear her chuckle. But I understood completely, for I too have learned to share my stories as if the person starring in them doesn't matter much at all. Trapped as we are in the valley of whiteness, the secret is knowing your audience. With enough experience, one begins to see oneself, on purpose or otherwise, through other eyes, indifferent, standing off a ways, reacting to the violence like the victim isn't you.

It helps to stay away from those who might remind you who are—those who might destroy the myth of singularity, just by sharing similar experiences. Speaking to other Black people after living apart for a lifetime, the strangest things are often revealed as systemic. It's deeply disheartening. Even the freedom derived from self-blame seems to fade: it's never been you, it's the Blackness, as always; you're trapped in a system that hates you, surprise. But nobody wants to return to their body; they just want to fly around, seemingly free. So it is that Black folks in white spaces often stand alone, afraid to stand together lest they see their lives in context, or at all. Better to remain lost than to find yourself imprisoned, and in pain.

Trinika didn't even know her age. At fourteen, she was fifteen, having lost a year in Accra. Whatever chicanery brought her to Canada left her with false information. But what did it matter? Birthdays are for those who were there when it happened. Trinika spent the rest of her childhood in Fraser Valley group homes—abuses abounding, her head shaved by strangers again and again—before finding a home with a white family living in White Rock. They gave her a birthday at random. She took it like Paddington Bear takes the name of the station where someone was kind to him. Her sweet sixteen came eighteen months ahead of when it should have.

That's kind of cute, I said.

It meant more to them than to me, she responded.

Tee met Cory at Richmond High. She was precisely his type. He was a popular jock with a sports car, accustomed to getting his way. So when he asked for an audacious sixteenth birthday gift—his girlfriend's virginity—she gave what she imagined was already gone, and together they created what she thought she could never have.

And life became difficult, I said aloud, recalling how Cory had once put it.

I named you Jordan Nathanael. You were my gift from God, she said. I wanted to keep you.

I knew that from Cory, but I hadn't expected to hear it from her. I held the phone upside down, fighting back tears, blinking and squinting to keep them from falling.

We wanted to raise you, she said. But his mother was mortified. She sent Cory away to this boarding school in the Prairies, hoping to change his mind. I think it was called Briercrest?

Bridalquest! I shouted.

Saskatchewan's Briercrest Christian Academy was known for its marriage material. Girls outnumbered boys there three to one, it was said. It was perfect for righteous young men seeking wives, and for God-fearing families who wanted their children to fall for the right kind of people. New couples were created every day, and save-the-date announcements came so early and so often that, at Trinity, the students called it Bridalquest. Anyone who goes there gets engaged, they said, and everyone who transferred here from Briercrest is married.

But others called Trinity Bridalquest West. Teenage engagements were common on campus, and all of us knew two or three kids whose parents had sent them to find a good wife, or good husband. My family had tried it, to rid them of Ashley; my birth father's family, it turned out, employed the same trick in their bid to get rid of Trinika.

While he was away, Trinika said, his mother wrote this really nasty letter. She said I was a slut, and Cory was never coming back. Her letters were just brutal. She really hated me. She accused me of trying to trap him. But I'd been speaking with Lynn Braidwood and she was really kind. She took me out for dinner at this mansion in Vancouver. She promised that if you were placed in a good Christian home, you'd have a much better life than I did.

Debatable, I said.

We had five days in the hospital together, Trinika said. I kept on asking to see my baby. I remember the ward nurses arguing in the hallway, afraid that too much time with you would make me change my mind about the adoption. So each time they brought you in, the women would hover, and they'd take you back out after five or ten minutes.

You'd hate for a baby to bond with its mother, I muttered.

We bonded anyway, Trinika said. I called you the Frog-Man. You had the biggest eyes. Like you could see everything clearly already.

Turns out I needed glasses, I said, I couldn't see a thing.

I left you with a couple of stuffies, she said. Do you still have them?

I have the bunny, I told her. The unicorn . . . I've only seen it once. My mom put it away until I was older, for safekeeping, and I never got it back.

Of course you didn't, she scoffed. That's so typical. I picked that one out special for you. Maybe she could tell. It's a wonder she didn't bury it in the backyard.

She mostly buried scripture with her friends, I said. But wait—if you wanted to stay in my life, then why didn't you push for an open adoption?

I did, Trinika said. And originally, it *was* open. I saw you a few more times that first year. But after your birthday, your mom cut me off.

What do you mean, she cut you off?

She closed the adoption.

Closed it? I stood up on my bed, my head spinning, suddenly defensive on my mother's behalf. How did she close it? No, she didn't.

I got another letter, Trinika said. Your mom explained that the family was moving to Fiji or something, so it wouldn't make sense to see me anymore. That's what I was told, and legally you belonged to her, so there was nothing I could do but go away.

We did go to Fiji. That's where the elephant statues were from. But still, I wasn't ready to accept what she was saying. I crawled back into bed, sitting speechless, convincing myself that this woman was trying to manipulate me. But who else could I ask about her claims? Certainly not my mother. We were barely speaking now, and we'd never speak again.

Many open adoptions are closed retroactively. Once the birth mother becomes inconvenient, she's easy enough to dismiss. Her rights have been completely signed away.

But I didn't know that then.

The accusation addled me, disrupting our chemistry, creating an audible distance between us. I wanted to think that Trinika was lying; the context of my life changed if she wasn't. No longer sure of what to say or what to do, I only listened to Trinika breathing in and breathing out, the shallowness of every breath a disconcerting sound. I couldn't handle any more tears, and my growing agitation was apparent from my silence.

I'm sorry, she said.

Everything had been taken from Trinika. They took her history, and then they took her future. She spent her life a stranger, seeking shelter. No one helped her. They helped themselves to her. First her body, then her baby. Whatever she could not protect was theirs before she knew it.

But at some point, I thought, sneering, siding against her, you have to take responsibility for your actions.

It's not your fault, I lied to her.

Trinika said: The last time I saw your face was in a photo Lynn gave me. It must have been around your second birthday. You were still my little Frog-Man, with your big, huge eyes, and I was encouraged, because a Black woman was holding you.

I know that photo, I said. Cory showed it to me. He keeps it in his wallet.

She paused for a moment, laughing quietly to herself. I thought she was crying again. That bozo, she finally said. What a goof. He told *me* that he lost it.

That night, the Scary Man found me again. A banging at the front door woke me up inside a nightmare. Certain that Isaac had locked himself out, I went to the hallway to check. Instead, I saw the homeless guy who camped beside the Mr. Sub. He waved as he walked by the window. I waved back, and returned to bed. Then I heard the same pounding, so I woke up again, but this time, the hallway was different. Now it was the hallway of the house on Glenn Mountain. As soon as I stepped out and saw the white doors, the Scary Man burst from the Big Room, constricting me, dragging me off to the darkness. He wanted to take me to hell, I just knew it. I fought him as Harrison, squirming and flailing, desperate to show I was stronger than before. But the Scary Man's hood was reflective, and the mirror-mask revealed that I was not only back in my childhood home, but back in my childhood—still just a boy. Help! I cried out, retrogressing, terrified to live my life all over, and I woke up thrashing, weeping in a stranger's bed, forgetting I was grown, and that the bed belonged to me.

• • •

I hobbled down to Stone Rolled Away on Sunday, dragging my anguish and anger behind me like iron balls, chained to my ankles. I knew of nowhere else to go but church. My mother wouldn't have me, and my other mother couldn't, I decided, she was lying, so I'd better keep my distance. Only the Lord could clear up my confusion; only His Spirit could soothe me. In shambles, exhausted by dreams I kept having, I sat before the altar, demanding to see Him, and waited, intense and impatient, prepared to throw hands.

It's now or never, Lord.

The Schumachers arrived to start the service. They opened with a classic, based on Psalm 121: *I lift my eyes up to the mountains. Where does my help come from?*

The answer was swirling about us that Sunday. I could feel it. The presence of the Lord was in the building. Certain He was here for me, having heard my cries, I rose up to meet Him immediately. Everyone else seemed to follow my lead. The music swelled, a chorus came, and Stone Rolled Away erupted as the Spirit issued forth like living water from the stone.

God was in control of everything. That's what they had told me. Only by His grace had I been whisked away to safety. He knew me in Trinika's womb and moved me to another life, the one that I was meant to live. He rescued me from darkness. He chose me for a purpose that was yet to be revealed.

But now, I had been tempted to believe in something else, in something awful: that my mother was a thief; that I was a victim of the same sort of passive abduction that took Trinika out of Africa; that justice demanded I cleave unto her, defying God's will, and my family besides.

The devil was trying to trick me.

This is how he operates. He takes the truth and twists it. The enemy sought to draw me from the path with his deceptions, compelling counterarguments that made it seem like up was down. Satan tempted Jesus in the wilderness the same way; he hadn't changed his tactics in a thousand years. Trinika was summoned to confound me, to mislead me. Consciously, or moved by the Jezebel spirit, she enticed me with the things I wanted most of all: a context for my life, a sense of self, a love that seemed to come without conditions. These were false promises, rooted in false needs. The only love that mattered in the end was the love of God. She wanted me all to herself, when I didn't belong to her. I was a child of God.

But if He loved me so much, then where was He now, when I needed Him most? Was He waiting for me to have nothing, like Job? I was already broke. The spring semester took what little money I still had; I put enough aside to pay for rent and books and gas, but nothing was left over to buy food. Lately, I ate what my roommate threw out, or my girlfriend provided to keep me from starving. Once, in desperation, I stopped by the Sikh temple, a known demonic hotspot, and accepted the free lunch. It made me so ashamed I called the Captain afterward, begging for five hundred dollars. I promised to pay it all back in the summer.

He said he would give it some thought.

Bankrupt in one sense, I could not afford to be morally bankrupt as well. The enemy would like nothing more than to see me descend into Blackness, I thought, to run to Trinika, go down to the ghetto, and find myself trapped or imprisoned in no time.

I will not be persuaded, I swore to myself. I rebuke this false narrative in the name of Jesus.

Trust in the Lord with all your heart, and lean not on your own understanding, the worship leader said, quoting Proverbs. That's what God is telling us this morning: lift up your voices, press into his presence.

He launched into an old hymn, an unlikely song choice that could only have come from divine inspiration. We sang the first verse and the music dropped out, and we went through the chorus, again and again, a cappella:

Then sings my soul, my Saviour God, to Thee
How great Thou art, how great Thou art

As a seven-year-old boy, I encountered an angel. Looking back, I remembered my great need to see it. It seemed to me now that the need was far greater. The angel in the tent, the rock upon which I had built my church, was a fading memory, and my faith was fading along with it. God had been absent thereafter, I felt—unless, perhaps, I wasn't straining hard enough to see Him.

A cacophony of tongues went up, a rarity at Stone Rolled Away. It had to be a sign. This was the moment. I knew that if I did not press in, I would miss my encounter with God. So I lifted my hands and my voice, in a language I'd spoken since childhood but never for a moment understood.

Shattah talimama, shattolio talimama, shattah.

Something was happening. I trembled and staggered. The Spirit was moving within me. I was backsliding into ecstatic belief. My fingertips tingled, and my prayers became more urgent as I fought to keep my balance in the presence of the Lord. Praise God, praise His holy name, I cried out to the heavens. *Shattah talimama, shattolio talimama, shattolio talimama, mama, mama, mama, mama.*

And suddenly, I started crying for no reason.

The rains fell down and the floods came up, and I was swept away. I lost control completely, whipping back and forth and, finally, slain by the Spirit, I fainted, expecting to land in the arms of an usher.

But no one was standing behind me. My back hit the edge of an old wooden armrest, breaking it off, and I crumpled into a heap, writhing in pain, then denying the damage, and praising the Almighty God like he let me down easy.

When the service got out, I was stopped at the door by my brother. Tom had been told to invite me to brunch. I rejoiced in my soul, believing that this was a brand-new beginning. The Lord had been working on my mother's heart too. My prayers had been answered. Revival had come to the Mooneys at last.

The Sunday brunch buffet was like a miracle to me. I stood before the banqueting table and filled my plate with macaroni salad, meat, and tater tots until it seemed to sag. I sat with my family, stuffing my face, and relished their company, laughing at old jokes, remembering all of the good times we shared.

But when the cheque came, I reminded them I could not pay, and my mother looked at Mike as if she had just been proven right.

What's going on? I asked.

Oh nothing, she said. It's just, when I was your age, I didn't need to come running to mommy and daddy for money.

I didn't know how to respond, so I didn't. She paid for the meal and I thanked her.

In the Aerostar, I blamed myself for coming along in my armour-lessness. I knew this woman by now. I knew that you had to be strong, and I'd never been weaker. My biggest mistake had been thinking she wanted to see me, when all that she wanted, I thought, was to see herself, standing above me, victorious.

I decided not to ever ask these people for another fucking thing. If I am starving and you don't want to feed me, you want me to die; and I would rather die, hungry and all by myself, than owe my life to a cold-blooded killer.

I went back to not needing anyone.

• • •

On Tuesday, the first day of the fall/winter term, I fired up the Echo, returning to Trinity, feeling remarkably empty. I hadn't eaten anything since Sunday, but hunger was just a small part of the problem, and easily solved if you're clever. Before class, I scavenged a day's worth of food from the school cafeteria, where the campus community used their meal cards as if the balance was imaginary. By exam week, when reality struck and the hunger set in, students with money left over were treated like royalty. But it was still January, so the freshmen left plenty to eat by the garbage.

Stuffing my backpack with half-eaten bagels, I looked around nervously, feeling unusually seen. But nobody stopped me or offered to buy me breakfast.

The morning began with American Literature. I didn't expect to learn anything new. I'd taken it as an undergrad at UCFV, and I signed up for the graduate course in a bid to cut down on my overall reading load. Sure enough, most of the works were the same: *Moby Dick*, *The Great Gatsby*, *The Sun Also Rises*—the Black book this time was *Beloved*. (What was it last time? *Uncle Tom's Cabin*, and it was an optional book, so I skipped it.) But master's level students were assigned a bunch of extra works, by authors that I didn't know, and all of them were Black: Zora Neale Hurston, Langston Hughes, Ralph Ellison, James Baldwin.

It strikes me now that I might never have discovered these cardinal writers if I hadn't paid extra to upgrade to Premium English. These were the voices I needed the most, and all of my life they were deemed inessential, exactly as I was, just something to chew on, additional reading you don't have to look at to pass. Instead, a general education consists primarily of what white people believe is important, which is a way of rigging the world, and an education undermined completely.

White people have no idea what's important.

I started with the shortest work. *The Fire Next Time* was just a couple of essays. My afternoon free, I went down to the library basement and set up in a corner carrel, beneath a light that flickered, to see what the James Baldwin book was about.

The book, I discovered, was all about me.

The first part was a letter to his nephew, who was fifteen. He warned the boy to not believe what the white world said about him. *I tell you this because I love you*, he wrote, *and please don't you ever forget it.* Touched by the sentence, I thought of myself at fifteen, in my clown suit, aching to be loved and led away from limitation, and what I would have given for a message from an uncle who was wise enough to know what I was in for.

But this was the first time, apart from pleasantries with Prophet K a decade earlier, that I had ever heard a Black man speak to me. In my heart, in my need, I became the receiver, rehoming myself, hearing family.

I am writing this letter to you, he said to the boy who was me now, *to try to tell you something about how to handle them, for most of them do not yet really know that you exist.*

Hearing him speak of existence, I paused. How had he known about that? Either James Baldwin's been reading my blog or the feeling is more universal, I thought, and that's when I started to trust what he'd written, thereafter to *know* that this man spoke the truth.

Out with it, then.

You were born where you were born and faced the future that you faced because you were Black and for no other reason, he said.

And I groaned at the pivotal fact of my life, as it echoed a joke I'd been telling since Bible camp—it's because I'm Black, isn't it?—a joke that now felt as relentlessly cruel as I found it relentlessly true.

Surely it must be more complicated. Lives are complex. We are not all the same. This man doesn't know *me*, I bristled, disagreeing desperately—his life has been nothing like mine. He grew up in Harlem, in the ghetto, in poverty. I grew up in Abbotsford, medium-wealthy.

But then I read on, and I started to see that our lives were exactly alike.

Baldwin, like me, was a child of the church, and his faith was a product of similar fears. Raised by a hand raised against him, he tried to behave, and he strove to do right by the Lord. But as the boy came of age, he began to see the world for what it was, and like Trinika on the plane, or me, whichever way I wandered, he was scared. Detecting his resemblance to the wretched of the earth, and nothing but destruction down the road, he fled to the temple in search of the promised salvation. He worshipped as hard as he could, and he worked himself up into some kind of state. Soon, the Holy Spirit seemed to stir within his heart, with an intensity that had to be beyond him, for he did not know the depth of his own soul, or his despair, or his abiding power, and when he stood up, exhausted, supposedly edified, the magic was gone, and he saw that encountering God left him weaker than ever.

Well gosh, I thought. That happened to me two days ago.

We arrived at the same point from opposite paths. Young Baldwin was terrified by the men who were like him, for fear of becoming like them: lost, and unable to say what it was that oppressed them. What frightened me most, out in Abbotsford, was the absence of anyone like me. There were other Black children (but somehow we spoke different languages), nary a Black man, and very few Black women, either, and certainly none who suggested a future I wanted. Esther and Trinika and even Ashley, who was Black to the world and Blacker beside me, were all victims of theft and erasure, poured out like purses and sent away, shaken. One minute, they were holding me; the next, they were banished to borderlands. From any perspective but whiteness—the loss of perspective—it's terribly clear that white society, and every white community, disdains not only Black people but all racialized people, and is designed to keep too many from accumulating anywhere, except for little sections, set aside for us to die. I was hanging on, but any fool could see that one mistake will have you cropped from the picture. They'll cut you off so violently, you'll leave an arm behind.

And not just metaphysically—don't kid yourself—but physically. It happens *for real*. I am proof. My birth father is sitting on the evidence.

This is what young Baldwin was afraid of: this common condition, all but prophesied on every avenue, in every place, which must be resisted to live more abundantly. Many are fighting internally only, for going to war with the world seems impossible. The most effective way to oppress a people, after all, is to confine them to a solitary existence. What is one person, pitched against infinity? Nothing to worry about.

But a man with a mirror is infinity plus one.

Thus, the barrier between the world and me began to crumble. There was no love in the church whatsoever. I knew it, and I knew I'd always known it. The faith was a mask for self-hatred and misanthropy, a means of manufacturing virtue while denying the horrors we wrought, in God's name, against me and my analogues—everyone ever encountered by whiteness. No wonder I clung to the cloak for so long. I needed to believe that I was bought by the blood, or I would see that the blood was my own. How blindly I followed along, and when the fires of hell seemed to rise up anyway, how quickly I marshalled the forces of God. But what was the power I called upon, really? Only my need to believe it was not simply white power.

James Baldwin was the first to disabuse me. He grabbed me by the temples and he gave it to me straight: *God is white.*

I groaned again and thought about the so-called good book. Good to whom? Certainly not me. The Bible was a weapon, fashioned against me, and so was my sense of reality. A raft of irrational people had written my history, and even rewritten my memories, casting themselves in a flattering light. Under their spell, I had misperceived everything. I was brainwashed, not anointed, and I never had a vision, and I never saw an angel. I was just a boy whose vision was so clouded that he saw what wasn't there.

Uncle James said it best: *If the concept of God has any validity or any use, it can only be to make us larger, freer, and more loving. If God cannot do this, then it is time we got rid of Him.*

So I did.

Belief is what powers the world, and the only transformative power that it offers. All that we see with our natural eyes is imagined, at first, and made manifest thusly, while all that we choose not to see disappears. Once, I believed some ridiculous things; in my faith, every lie became true. Up was down. But I had never quite believed, ecstatic and desperate, that I could be free.

So I let myself go, and was saved.

• • •

I tried to explain.

At the end of the semester, I went back to my mother's house. I thought that she should hear from me, in person, that I planned to meet Trinika. She deserved to know my reasons.

We would speak as two adults, and she would have to hear me out.

But I was kidding myself. In truth, I went in search of validation, out of habit, and I was willing to debase myself, as necessary. I would share my revelation, sharing blame for every trauma. The blindness afflicted us both, after all, so how could she know? Even I didn't know. I was just as much at fault, I was prepared to concede in order to spare her from shame and self-pity, and to spare myself from how she might lash out if she felt cornered. I didn't want to fight. I wanted to heal. I thought that I could make her understand where I was coming from, for I had come from her, and she had known me all my life, and I would always be her son, and I would always chase her love. I wanted to show her how badly I needed to do this, and leave with permission.

Maybe she'll finally see me this time, I thought, pulling up in the Echo. Maybe she'll give back the unicorn, saying: Godspeed, I'll love you wherever you go.

The front door was locked. So I knocked. My mother answered, but only just barely, peering out through a sliver, as though I was dangerous.

Hi Harry, she said, looking back at somebody. What are you doing here? I wasn't expecting you.

I thought I'd drop by, I said. Sorry, is this a bad time?

And my mother said: Yes. I have company.

I can't come inside? I asked, dumbstruck.

Not today. Call ahead next time and we can make arrangements.

Who are you hiding in there? I demanded, attempting to see through the crack.

Oh, it's only Mrs. Gazette. We're just catching up.

Are you getting the band back together? I asked with a smirk.

She stared at me blankly.

The Prayer Warriors, I said. All you need now is Tilda Eubanks or Yvette Rempel.

It's funny, I just talked to Yvette, my mother said. Do you remember Mr. Rempel? He's a carpenter. He'll be redoing the kitchen this summer. I'm thinking French doors. What do you think?

Sounds great. But Mom, I said, unwilling to muster the courage to come back again, I didn't drop by to talk baseboards and mouldings. I wanted you to know that I'm meeting my birth mother.

She nodded, losing interest in the conversation.

I scrambled to say something meaningful. I told her I loved her, and nothing would change that, and no one could ever come between us. I swore that her place in my heart was secure, and explained that I did not intend to recast her. I downplayed my need to make contact, insisting the woman meant nothing to me, that it was just a way to satisfy my curiosity. I babbled about Blackness, what it meant, after all, and the ways that we'd misunderstood it. I promised: This isn't goodbye.

Happy to hear it. You've always had questions, good luck getting answers, my mother said, shutting the door.

I went away knowing I'd failed to communicate.

The next day, a message arrived in my inbox. My mother, who never used email, had more on her mind. This is how it started:

Dear Harry,

It was a pleasant surprise to hear from you yesterday and get a visit. We don't hear from you often or see you.

I'm so sorry that I was not the Mom you wanted or needed. You have often said you don't feel a part of the family. I am sorry you feel that way. I do not feel that way at all. That I don't does not change how you feel, and I'm so sorry that I have failed you so badly that I have somehow missed it.

My mother said she thought that we had fun. She said she did her best to give me everything I needed. She told me that I mattered, that she loved me, that I played a major role in who we once were as a family. She said that she'd been giving me my space these days, since I seemed so uncomfortable around her, and I didn't have to visit if I really didn't want to. She insisted that her message wasn't meant to be a guilt trip. This is how it ended:

I don't need or want a response to this. I just wanted to free you up so you don't feel obligated. I hope you find the happiness and acceptance you deserve.

I didn't quite know how to take it.

She'd written so much that I wanted to hear. She said she was sorry. She swore that she cared. She poured out her heart and I saw the despair and confusion I'd caused her by being her son. I cried for a while, full of shame and self-pity, not only my own but my mother's now, too, the very emotions I'd gone to the mountain to blunt with a thorough discussion.

But my mother wouldn't see me. She didn't want to see me. She wanted to carry on blindly and blame me, to send me away as if my heart was defective and nothing she did could convince me to love her the way she liked best and go back to being her version of me.

She couldn't even call me by my name in her apology.

She spoke of embarrassment. Hardly, I thought. More like gratuitous humiliation. Even now, she sent me to my big reunion just destroyed.

I'd come by the house, hat in hand, for her blessing. Instead, she was letting me go. She spoke of me in the past tense, like I died and didn't know it. My mother would rather start over without me than share me with somebody else, and I mourned for her, knowing how awful it was to lose someone you tried to hold on to.

• • •

I dropped out of graduate school, though I'm only admitting it to myself now. My thesis is pending. But the woman I meant to impress had departed.

So had her on-campus counterpart.

Rochelle, the older woman I befriended in the slavery class, reached her limit one night when the lesson hit too close to home.

The topic that evening was slave holds along the Gold Coast. The largest, at Elmina Castle, just east of Sekondi, sent thirty thousand souls to sea each year. But this was no single-use fortress. Elmina was a marketplace, a general store, where the merchants could load up on everything. You grab a few spices, a few sacks of this and of that, and a few human beings, freshly caught. Slavers made selections through a crack in the wall, where they squinted at bodies, afraid to engage with their own inhumanity.

The castle had a chapel too, and this is where Rochelle began to squirm. The conditions in the dungeon were positively subhuman, and the cries of the captured were monstrous. On the Sabbath, God-fearing folk went to church, and they worshipped as loud as they could in an effort to drown out the weeping and wailing they heard from the basement, interminably. The cries of the Saved and enslaved intermixed, depravity smoothly incorporated, every single Sunday at Elmina was the Day of Pentecost. The saints go marching in to be delivered from the truth about themselves, and the slaves go marching out.

Historically, our professor explained, the cross has been a harbinger of death and destruction for all but the people who preached it.

Rochelle was not ready to hear this. She had spent the last decade in Indonesia, converting non-believers, planting churches. She hadn't expected a Christian institution to undermine the practice of evangelism; she hadn't expected to learn that the children of God were the authors of hell.

It was snowing that night. We walked back to our cars, which were parked side by side. She was crying. Rochelle didn't want to waste gas, but I could see that she needed to talk, so we cranked up the heat in the Echo.

She didn't really talk to me. She only talked aloud. Her tears were projectiles; they landed on me. Where do I go? she cried out, to the Lord. Where do you want me, God? Where do I go? And when the snow outside began to pile up, so that we could no longer tell the roadway from the ditch, she wiped her tears away and said: I don't believe it.

You can't just not believe it, I responded.

I was wrong. I never saw Rochelle again. I asked around. Apparently, she'd gone back to her post in Indonesia. Faced with the facts, she rebuked them at once, and returned to a life of not knowing. This was her luxury, and white privilege writ large: the right to live by faith and not by sight. Your victims do not have this option. We know who you are, for we see what you do. Your beliefs are a blindfold. We stare at you, wide-eyed, in horror.

You know this. You try not to know, but you know. Enough about white guilt. It's shame that consumes you, and wherever there is shame, there is denial, and denial becomes delusion in the moment that discomfort is alleviated.

White people are deeply delusional. They don't even know what it means to be white, to be Black, to be mixed, to be anything, really. They don't know they made it all up, just to steal. They have forgotten on purpose—subconscious, in one sense, but consciously buried there not long ago. Nowadays, they simply know it's better to be white than not to be, and they know this from looking around, and it makes them afraid, because whiteness is not all that firm.

The rest of us live in your fantasyland, fully fictionalized, fighting every moment to exist in full and, somehow, keep it real. It's impossible: whiteness asks the racialized to move very slowly, with plenty of notice and no real intent. Any guff is an automatic disqualification, and if you touch the sides while extracting what you need to be a person, a little buzzer sounds and then you're gone.

Lily-white spaces are borne of these acts of erasure. Where are the Black faces? All disappeared. For more than two decades, I never even knew another Black man. There were few around to know. There is no benign explanation for that, and I'm through with deluding myself.

My mother may appear to be especially myopic, but don't kid yourself. She represents the vast majority. *Mutual recognition of racism*, the great writer and theorist bell hooks said, *is the only stand-point that makes possible an encounter between races that is not based on denial and fantasy.*

Yet still we give Black children to white parents, who play with their colour like preschoolers finger-painting, smearing things around without an ounce of inner vision, touching everything with wet, sticky hands. They say they will love you as their own. But soon you come to learn the love they have for their own is powered by their hatred of you.

It takes a toll on everyone.

The burden of having a Black son destroyed my poor mother. It complicated her reality. It gnarled the edges of her sensibility. It created the conditions for this book. She had no idea what she was getting into, or what she was already in, and her worldview was not built to withstand the pressure of daily regard from Black eyes. For a time, she could battle them back. She could force me to look away, overpower me, or put out my eyes and describe what I should have been seeing.

Once she could not, we stopped seeing each other.

Well, look at me now. If my mother was paying attention, she'd have known she was raising a storyteller—and then, perhaps, the story would be different. You cannot simply collide with a human life and send it away into silence, defeated.

I thought we had fun, my mother had written.

But I don't recall having much fun at all. Only unbearable pain, same as you—the child follows in the condition of its mother. So I'm sorry, dear mother, but I've written this memoir to save us. You believe that these structures are built to support you. You tell yourself you're living at the top of the pyramid. Get real. A pyramid is nothing but a tomb, triangulated. Don't run away from me. Stand where I'm standing, and let us look together at the world that buried both of us.

• • •

I met Trinika at Bean Around the World, in downtown Vancouver. Craving something sweet, I ordered chai. Sitting down, first to arrive, I wondered how I'd know that it was her. We hadn't arranged to wear brooches or hats.

Then I remembered: it's easy. She'll be Black.

But she entered, and I saw myself, only older, still uncertain, still encumbered by the thought that I did not belong in any place I wandered, and I could barely believe I'd been anxious about recognition. She sat down, jittery, and I saw my exact face, and both of us burst into laughter at the utterly uncanny doppelgängers sitting before us, staring from across the tiny table, with a fondness we could never quite find in the mirror.

I wanted to look at Trinika forever. You can tell when the eyes that regard you are in love with you. I knew it the moment she walked in the door.

I brought you a few things, she said, reaching into her purse and pulling out a small tub of goop.

Shea butter, she said. Use it when you get out of the shower. Work it into your hair while it's wet.

How much is too much?

No such thing, she said, digging back into the bag. Oh, and there's this.

It was a plastic unicorn skeleton, posed at a trot, with its right leg raised, triumphantly, under an empty rib cage. The unpainted dollar-store toy had a skull that could swivel the whole way around.

I found your unicorn, Trinika said. He's not as soft as he was. He's weirder now, and a little gaunt, after so long in the dungeon. Don't forget to feed him this time.

We laughed again, like two old friends, our bond still unbroken after twenty-odd years.

Trinika's shame was triggered first. We both had it. Hers was just stronger.

I'm sorry if that joke was in poor taste, she said, lowering her head. And I'm sorry for your life. I'm sorry. Please don't hate me, Harrison. I'm so sorry.

Trinika, I get it, I said, ashamed to be the mess that she regretted all her life, the life-wrecking error that triggered such shame in Trinika by being born, then stolen, then away for so long.

But she saw that and said: You don't have to be ashamed. I knew you'd find your way.

Neither do you, I said. You did what you had to, and here we are now.

She cracked a smile that cracked my outer shell. In my heart, I climbed into her lap, and I said: Tell me again about how I was born.

She started to talk about Cory.

No, no, no, I interrupted her. I don't want to know what Cory was doing while you were pregnant. What were *you* doing?

Getting huge, she said. I got expelled from high school because the other kids weren't allowed to see me pregnant. So I was taken to a home for teen moms.

The Maywood Home for Unwed Mothers was just across the bridge from Richmond, in the Vancouver suburb of Marpole. It was run by the Salvation Army, whose motto, women and children first, appears to allude to the lives they'll be ruining. The place had been in business since 1906 and would not close until the turn of the century. The setting was an old Victorian mansion surrounded by thick laurel hedges. From the street, it looked spiffy, but once past the trees, you arrived at an ugly little building with beige walls and brown linoleum floors, and twenty other women ashamed to have been secreted away.

Maywood came up in the news quite a bit while Trinika was there. The Salvation Army had plans to open a drug treatment home right next door. This was a major concern to the neighbours, who called up their media contacts to create a controversy, claiming they feared for the mothers. They were fine with the teenage girls, coerced into adoptions behind the bushes, but addicts were a bridge too far: they would fill up the sidewalks, disturbing the peace, and they might even menace the unwed, besides.

Few really knew what went on there. A *Vancouver Sun* report published that summer called the house a place of refuge. But Anne Petrie, who shared her own experience in *Gone to an Aunt's*, called it a big baby farm, and a prison.

I really felt like I was in jail, Petrie wrote. *It was the feeling of not being free.*

This feeling was more universal. Some thirteen thousand women were processed at Maywood, and roughly ten thousand surrendered their children. In 2005, a woman named Cassandra Armishaw, who was at Maywood on the day that I was born, became the lead plaintiff in a class-action lawsuit against the province of British Columbia. Armishaw alleged that her baby was taken from her against her will.

A social worker had testified in court that Armishaw did not eat nutritious food and thought other people were possessed by spirits. This demonstrated parental unfitness. So the baby was given to someone much more like my mother.

The women at Maywood were told they were sinners, Trinika recalled, and that sin was the thing growing larger inside them. It was sin that kicked them in the ribs at all hours, sin that sickened them, and the road to salvation was simple: a private adoption.

Luckily, these babies were in high demand elsewhere, especially in rich white women's houses. Another 1980s *Sun* story quotes a social worker blithely describing a relative shortage of healthy, white babies put up for adoption. As a result, Vorna Butler explained, couples had become more aggressive in their search for parenthood.

Money can buy almost anything. But some things are bought with great difficulty.

Transactions at Maywood, the victims allege, were born of a rigorous brainwashing, beginning the moment you got there. Just like the bathhouse in *Spirited Away*, your name was taken from you at the front door. No allusions could be made to the young women's former lives. No pining for boyfriends or calling for freedom, no asserting one's rights or identity, and therefore, no last names.

So Trinika Arthur-Asamoah became Tee, losing two names and a half, and a great deal beyond. From that day on, everyone she spoke to, every piece of mail that came for her, made one thing pretty clear: there is only one way out of the mess you've created, and it's without that baby—hand it over. The burden bearers soon arrived, on cue, preaching salvation, and adoption became a kind of performative self-negation—a sentence imposed by a hypnotized mind.

By agreeing, Anne Petrie explained in her book, *unwed mothers were signalling our understanding of the moral order, and our wish to follow it. Having clearly flouted the rules once, we were relieved to be doing something that was so obviously right.*

But Trinika believed she was bad to the bone. In her hopelessness, soul beyond saving, she shrugged at the all-out assault on her worth. What else is new? She might as well keep the damn baby, and raise it with Cory, she had reasoned.

She almost succeeded.

I was waiting on both of you, she explained. Cory made all sorts of promises. But in the end, he gave in to the pressure, and left me with nothing instead.

But you didn't want to leave me, said Trinika. You liked it right where you were. You turned to the side and you held on for dear life. You were a breech baby; did you know that? You'd have stayed in there sideways forever.

Sure sounds like me, I scoffed.

They didn't notice right away, and when they did, they didn't tell me anything, she said. I laboured for a whole day, and then, out of nowhere, I felt a prick. I guess the doctor decided on a C-section. But nobody thought to inform me. I woke up and you were gone. They cut you out while I was sleeping.

Some things just keep happening. The methods change, the victims stay the same. Time was, you could sell a Black baby right out from his mother's arms. These days, you have to trigger self-surrender, to trap her in oblivion and take the child before she regains consciousness. It was for the best, you say; she was unwed and pregnant, which is proof of her irresponsibility; we haven't stolen anything, we have only intervened on behalf of the infant. You're deluding yourselves. But such is the power imbalance between us that the white imagination overrides the Black reality, and so it is that white families can abduct Black babies, senselessly, and come away believing they did right by their children.

You call it a kindness. I'd call it kidnapping. What system of help separates a child from his mother? A system with no love for either. Adoption should be a last resort. It is an unthinking transplant. We do open-heart surgery with our eyes closed, pumping the patient with anti-rejection drugs, hoping the host can be fooled.

But the victim remains, threatening your innocence, attesting to the truth of what's been done to us both, for the hole in her heart matches mine, interlocking, and this is why the mothers disappear. Racialization is useful here, and you can racialize anyone, really. The white world is constantly moving the goalposts. Blackness expands and constricts like it's breathing, when really, it's whiteness that breathes down our necks.

In the end, the choice was Trinika's to make, but the options were curated by the Burden Bearers. Lynn Braidwood provided three folders with three different families, and asked her to make a selection. Trinika picked the rich white couple with another son, adopted. She was told that they had Black family too. Esther Stratford, the arm in the photo used later to keep up appearances, was not really family, of course—not even among those at Stone Rolled Away who would claim that she was. In this particular instance, she was little more than Jimmy from the Bahamas. But Trinika believed them, and the lie became true.

A piece of me went with you and I never got it back, she said.

In that moment, I finally realized that God didn't choose my family—Trinika did, as a desperate teenage girl, believing that the baby in the basket would be carried down the river to the whirlpool where she waited. She knew what I would go through, for she had waded through it first. She knew that I would never quite believe that I belonged, and she believed—or else, by then, she knew—that I could not be whole until I found her.

She was never far away. But we were worlds apart, and mine was designed to acclimatize me to her absence, to keep me aligned with my captors. How could I ever hear Trinika crying out to me? This world has been intimately shaped by systems that silence our voices.

Erasure means you never have to see what you have done. The consequences of your actions are simply not there. Rendered invisible, you can go on believing whatever you like, so you wander around in white spaces like little voids, wringing the life from your teabags, never even wondering why everything is gone.

But the victims are not gone. This very afternoon, they're at a downtown cafe, corroborating one another's stories. Sipping chai, they wreck the world, for the primary threat to this system is the vanished beginning to find each other, revisiting the past, and thereby revising the present.

They say life begins at conception. But the mother is born with her children already inside of her. Her life is inscribed in their being. Life begins, half-begun, and to insist otherwise is to cut me in half. King Solomon once offered to settle a dispute this way. It was the woman who said go ahead, carve him up, that was proven a thief and a liar.

When you adopt me, you adopt my history, and if you refuse, I will never be yours. You cannot take the boy, rejecting Blackness. The damage has been done. Necrosis fills the wound. The boy emerges even Blacker.

Freed from the white gaze, our lives are quite obvious. Watch yourself from overhead: the truth rings out. You'll see the lengths you go to avoid us, even if it means a refusal to intervene in our murders, to advocate for the mattering of our lives. Your inaction leaves you thoroughly discredited.

People will say we've made progress. Have we, really? What does it matter if we are more polite, if we do it in code now, if we speak our hatred in tongues? If we have only modified the slave system, I wonder by what metric we call it progress. Progress for whom? What are we walking away from, and what does the world where we're going even look like?

You are not exempt. You are a victim of white supremacy too, whoever you are, whatever your colour, whoever has raised you. This is your story as much as it's mine. Your history lies in wait for you, to be brought back to life, to defend your existence, to give you a reason, a life that's worth living. Don't just decolonize your mindset, or decentre whiteness—destroy it at once. Rebuke it in the name of something greater than your God. True love has nothing to do with this nonsense. Whiteness has taken everything from you, and now it serves to keep you from the truth about yourself. You have no idea what you've lost.

I know because I grew up in your house, and I escaped.

Harrison, said Trinika, as we went our separate ways, you should know that you descend from the first king of the Ashanti Kingdom. You come from noble blood. You're royalty.

I come from you, I told her, and I started towards the Echo.

Fumbling for my keys, I heard her calling out to me again. Looking back, I saw Trinika sprinting after me.

This is so embarrassing, she told me, out of breath, but I think my car's been towed.

It never ends, I said. Come on. Let's get it back.

We drove to the towing yard, laughing so hard that I teared up and had to pull over. We parked, and I paid the steep impoundment fee myself, for my birth mother admitted that she didn't have the money. I passed the carbon paper receipt to Trinika and, smiling, I said: Here's a little something for your troubles.

I was going to pay for your coffee, she answered, ashamed. I didn't want you to think I was some deadbeat. But now you know: I'm broke, man. I just moved back to Richmond and I don't have a job yet. The car isn't even insured. I drove the speed limit all the way here. I was so nervous. I'm sorry, I'm sorry.

Not me, I said, climbing into her Honda. I'm pretty broke too. But one day, we'll be rich. I'll write a whole book and I'll end it right here.

And I did.

We pulled up to the public exit. The red light before us went green. The massive, metal wall was rolled away, and the setting sun came pouring in from over East Vancouver. Blinded by the light, I lowered the passenger mirror, and the eyes looking down were my true mother's eyes, and the face was my true mother's face, and for the first time in my life, I saw that I was beautiful.

SELECTED BIBLIOGRAPHY

Als, Hilton. "Toni Morrison and the Ghosts in the House." *The New Yorker*, October 19, 2003. https://www.newyorker.com/magazine /2003/10/27/ghosts-in-the-house.

Baldwin, James. "My Dungeon Shook: Letter to My Nephew on the One Hundredth Anniversary of the Emancipation." *The Fire Next Time*. New York: Vintage, 1992.

Cugoano, Quobna Ottobah. *Thoughts and Sentiments on the Evil of Slavery*. New York: Penguin Classics, 1999. Originally published in Great Britain in 1787 as *Thoughts and Sentiments on the Evil and Wicked Traffic of the Slavery and Commerce of the Human Species*.

Fanon, Frantz. *Black Skin, White Masks*. Translated by Richard Philcox. New York: Grove Press, 2008.

Hartman, Saidiya. *Lose Your Mother: A Journey along the Atlantic Slave Route*. New York: Farrar, Straus and Giroux, 2008.

hooks, bell. *Black Looks: Race and Representation*. Boston: South End Press, 1992.

Lorde, Audre. *Sister Outsider: Essays and Speeches*. Foreword by Cheryl Clarke. Berkeley, CA: Crossing Press, 2007. Essay originally published in *The Black Scholar*, vol. 9, no. 7 (1978).

Petrie, Anne. *Gone to an Aunt's*. Toronto: McClelland and Stewart, 2013.

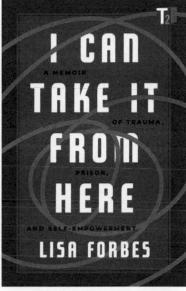

Steerforth Press
Truth to Power Books

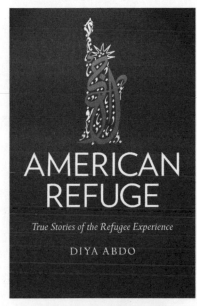

AMERICAN
REFUGE

True Stories of the Refugee Experience

DIYA ABDO

HOW FREE SPEECH
SAVED DEMOCRACY

*The Untold History
of How the
First Amendment
Became an Essential
Tool for Securing
Liberty and
Social Justice*

Christopher M. Finan
Executive Director of the National Coalition Against Censorship
FOREWORD BY RANDALL KENNEDY

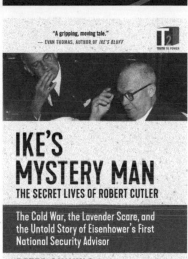

"A gripping, moving tale."
— EVAN THOMAS, AUTHOR OF *IKE'S BLUFF*

IKE'S
MYSTERY MAN
THE SECRET LIVES OF ROBERT CUTLER

The Cold War, the Lavender Scare, and
the Untold Story of Eisenhower's First
National Security Advisor

PETER SHINKLE

FOREWORD BY
CHARLES KAISER

Steerforth Press
Truth to Power Books

TRUTH
TO
POWER

THE WOMAN WHO INSPIRED
AN AFRICAN #METOO MOVEMENT

TOUFAH

Toufah
Jallow
with Kim Pittaway

T2P BOOKS // TRUTHFUL NARRATIVES = BETTER UNDERSTANDING

"Hope finds a prominent presence in what so many think is a hopeless, endless conflict."
— KIRKUS

FRIENDLY FIRE
A MEMOIR

How Israel Became Its Own Worst
Enemy and the Hope for Its Future

AMI AYALON

WITH
ANTHONY DAVID

INTRODUCTION BY
DENNIS ROSS

"A book that is both a history and a sports classic." — DETROIT FREE PRESS
"One of the most compelling sports biographies [ever]. A must-read."
— (starred review) BOOKLIST

HARD DRIVING
THE WENDELL SCOTT STORY

The American Odyssey of
NASCAR's First Black Driver

BRIAN DONOVAN

FOREWORD BY
JOE POSNANSKI

T2P BOOKS // TRUTHFUL NARRATIVES = BETTER UNDERSTANDING

"[A] nuanced, open-minded, de-politicized discussion of our post-#MeToo world."
— REFINERY29

HAD IT COMING

Rape Culture Meets #MeToo:
Now What?

ROBYN DOOLITTLE

"A must read for nonhistorians seeking a firm grasp of accurate American history."
— *KIRKUS REVIEWS*

A TRUE HISTORY OF THE UNITED STATES

Indigenous Genocide, Racialized Slavery, Hyper-Capitalism, Militarist Imperialism, and Other Overlooked Aspects of American Exceptionalism

DANIEL A. SJURSEN

T2P BOOKS // TRUTHFUL NARRATIVES = BETTER UNDERSTANDING

"This moving and sprightly book is filled with backstories from America's struggle for religious freedom that I'll bet you have never heard before . . . a brilliant scholar's telling insights on the right way for church, state, and society to interact."
— E.J. DIONNE JR., AUTHOR OF *SOUL RED AND WHY THE RIGHT WENT WRONG*

SOLEMN REVERENCE

THE SEPARATION OF CHURCH AND STATE IN AMERICAN LIFE

RANDALL BALMER

T2P BOOKS // TRUTHFUL NARRATIVES = BETTER UNDERSTANDING

"Margaret Kimberley gives us an intellectual gem of prophetic fire about all the US presidents and their deep roots in the vicious legacy of white supremacy and predatory capitalism. Such truths seem more than most Americans can bear, though we ignore her words at our own peril!"
— CORNEL WEST, AUTHOR OF *RACE MATTERS*

PREJUDENTIAL

BLACK AMERICA AND THE PRESIDENTS

MARGARET KIMBERLEY

T2P BOOKS // TRUTHFUL NARRATIVES = BETTER UNDERSTANDING

"Investigative journalism at its relentless and compassionate best." — *KIRKUS REVIEWS*
"Methamphetamine was a huge part of this case . . . A horrible murder driven by drugs."
— PROSECUTOR CAL RERUCHA
"A gripping read." — *PEOPLE MAGAZINE*

THE BOOK OF MATT

THE REAL STORY OF THE MURDER OF MATTHEW SHEPARD

STEPHEN JIMENEZ

NEW INTRODUCTION BY
ANDREW SULLIVAN

Steerforth Press
Truth to Power Books

"This short, powerful book should be required reading for anyone who has ever wondered what it's like to be an ordinary citizen living in a war zone." — *PUBLISHERS WEEKLY*

WHEN THE BULBUL STOPPED SINGING

LIFE IN PALESTINE DURING AN ISRAELI SIEGE

RAJA SHEHADEH

NEW INTRODUCTION BY
COLUM McCANN

One of three books people "should read to understand what happened in Vietnam." — *THE MARINE CORPS GAZETTE*

WAR OF NUMBERS

AN INTELLIGENCE MEMOIR OF THE VIETNAM WAR'S UNCOUNTED ENEMY

SAM ADAMS

FOREWORD BY
COL. DAVID HACKWORTH

NEW INTRODUCTION BY
JOHN PRADOS